SHVETASHVATARA UPANISHAD

Swami Tejomayananda

Central Chinmaya Mission Trust

First Edition – October 2011 to July 2024 – 9,100 copies
Reprint – September 2025 – 2,500 copies

Published by:
Chinmaya Prakashan
The Publications Division of
Central Chinmaya Mission Trust
Sandeepany Sadhanalaya
Saki Vihar Road, Powai, Mumbai 400072, India
Tel.: +91-22-2803 4900
Email: ccmtpublications@chinmayamission.com
Website: www.chinmayamission.com

Distribution Centre in the USA:
Chinmaya Publications West
560 Bridgetown Pike
Feasterville, PA 19053-7240, USA
Tel.: (215) 396-0390, Fax: (215) 396-9710
Email: publications@chinmayamission.org
Website: www.chinmayapublications.com

Designed by: Chinmaya Kalpanam, Mumbai

Printed by: Usha Multigraphs Pvt. Ltd., Mumbai

ISBN: 978-81-7597-528-6

Publisher's Note

Param Pūjya Gurudev, Swami Chinmayananda wrote commentaries and gave discourses on the major Upaniṣads in English thus bringing this ancient, yet timeless knowledge before a worldwide audience. The Chinmaya Mission continues this great tradition with commentaries, translations and discourses on many major and minor Upaniṣads and other scriptures in many more languages, including French.

Pūjya Guruji, Swami Tejomayananda, the Head of the Chinmaya Mission gave discourses on *Śvetāśvatara-upaniṣad* in his inimitable style at Piercy, USA for the Dharma Sevak Course in 2009. We are happy to publish this priceless knowledge as a commentary on *Śvetāśvatara-upaniṣad*. This invaluable contribution towards the spread of spiritual knowledge was possible because of various people.

The talks were transcribed, edited and proofread by Pami Wig (Delhi), Tulsipriya Goyal (Faridabad), Shibani Khorana (Delhi), Gayatri Balasubramanian (Coimbatore), Brni. Darshika Chaitanya (Thrissur) and Chinmaya Prakashanam. The serialisation of these talks by Smt. Parvathy Raman in Tapovan Prasad also helped. The book is beautifully designed by the Chinmaya Kalpanam team. We thank them all for their Guru Sevā and invoke God's blessings and Param Pūjya Gurudev's grace on them.

May this light of knowledge lighten the burden of saṁsāra and enlighten us – **tamaso mā jyotirgamaya.**

Central Chinmaya Mission Trust
Mumbai - 400 072

Transliteration and Pronunciation Guide

In this book, Devanagari characters are transliterated according to the scheme adopted by the International Congress of Orientalists at Athens in 1912. In it one fixed pronunciation value is given to each letter; f, q, w, x and z are not called to use. An audio recording of this guide is available at http://chinmayamission.com/scriptures.php. According to this scheme:

Devanagari	Translit-eration	Sounds Like	Devanagari	Translit-eration	Sounds Like
अ	a	son	ढ्	ḍh	adhesive*
आ	ā	father	ण्	ṇ	under*
इ	i	different	त्	t	tabla
ई	ī	feel	थ्	th	thumb
उ	u	full	द्	d	this
ऊ	ū	boot	ध्	dh	Gandhi
ऋ	ṛ	rhythm*	न्	n	nose
ॠ	ṝ	**	प्	p	pen
ऌ	ḷ	**	फ्	ph	phantom*
ए	e	evade	ब्	b	boil
ऐ	ai	delight	भ्	bh	abhor
ओ	o	core	म्	m	mind
औ	au	now	य्	y	yes
क्	k	calm	र्	r	right
ख्	kh	khan	ल्	l	love
ग्	g	gate	व्	v	very
घ्	gh	ghost	श्	ś	shut
ङ्	ṅ	ankle*	ष	ṣ	sugar
च्	c	chuckle	स्	s	simple
छ्	ch	witch*	ह्	h	happy
ज्	j	justice	ं	ṁ	improvise
झ्	jh	Jhansi	ः	ḥ	**
ञ्	ñ	banyan	क्ष्	kṣ	action
ट्	ṭ	tank	त्र्	tr	three*
ठ्	ṭh	**	ज्ञ्	jñ	gnosis
ड्	ḍ	dog	ऽ	'	a silent 'a'

* These letters don't have an exact English equivalent. An approximation is given here.
** These sounds cannot be approximated in English words.

Introduction

Veda means knowledge – knowledge of the truths that governs the universe. As texts, they were compiled by Bhagavān Veda Vyāsa into four volumes, namely *Ṛg Veda, Yajur Veda, Sāma Veda* and *Atharva Veda*. They are the very foundation of Hindu philosophy and are considered the highest authority and the supreme means of knowledge in determining the nature of Dharma and the nature of the absolute Reality – Brahman.

Each Veda has three sections – karma-kāṇḍa, upāsanā-kāṇḍa and jñāna-kāṇḍa. Karma-kāṇḍa is the ritualistic portion whose practice is meant to purify the mind of its impurities (mala) like attachments, dislikes, anger and so forth. It also contains rituals to fulfill our special and other worldly desires like knowledge of rituals for one desiring a son (putra kāmeṣṭi yajña), even though incapable of bearing one or means to attain a specific heaven (svarga kāmeṣṭi yajña).

Upāsanā-kāṇḍa contains mantras, means of worship and meditations which are primarily meant for removing the distractions of the mind (vikṣepa) and rendering it single pointed. They also promise attainment of extraordinary powers (siddhis) and various heavenly bodies and heavenly worlds (lokas).

Jñāna-kāṇḍa contains Self-knowledge which removes the ignorance (ajñāna-āvaraṇa) of our own true nature/Self/Truth. It is this ignorance of our infinite nature (avidyā) that gives rise to all our desires (kāma) to become full and complete. They in turn engage us in various actions (karma) which result in the experience of joy and sorrow. We often feel that joy comes and goes, but sorrow seems to remain all the time. Total fulfilment and peace can therefore arise only by the removal of the basic ignorance behind all desires, actions, joys and sorrows.

Jñāna-kāṇḍa is also called Upaniṣad. The word Upaniṣad therefore means Self-knowledge (upaniṣad śabdena brahma-vidyā ucyate). An object can be known by different people by different names, but its knowledge remains the same. For example, a book is known as a book, even if it is called 'pustakam', 'copaḍī' and 'livre' in Sanskrit, Gujarātī and in French respectively. Again, knowledge takes place through a specific means of knowledge (pramāṇa). For example, the colour of an object is perceived only by the eyes and not the ears. Self-knowledge is the means that removes ignorance of the Self and therefore Upaniṣad is the means for knowledge of the Self/Truth. Self-knowledge is one and therefore Upaniṣad is also one. However the knowledge of the Upaniṣads was revealed as various texts, hence these texts are also called Upaniṣads.

Someone asked a saint, "How many Upaniṣads will I need to study to know the Truth?" He asked back, "How many mirrors do you need to see your face?" One is enough. You may look into many mirrors, but what you need is just one. Similarly the study of just one Upaniṣad is enough to know the Truth/Self. However we do love to look at ourselves in every reflecting surface and admire ourselves. In the same way we can enjoy looking at the Self through different Upaniṣads as each has its own special beauty and reveals some aspect of the Truth elaborately. So it is good to study different Upaniṣads.

As texts, the Upaniṣads are found mostly in the end part of the Vedas and therefore its knowledge is called Vedānta (veda + anta). Some consider that there are 108 Upaniṣads. Amongst them, ten are well-known as major Upaniṣads as Ādi Śaṅkarācārya has written commentaries on them. If we study them well, the others can be understood easily. They are *Īśāvāsya Upaniṣad, Kenopaniṣad, Kaṭhopaniśad, Praśnopaniṣad, Muṇḍakopaniṣad, Māṇḍūkya Upaniṣad, Aitareya Upaniṣad, Taittirīya Upaniṣad, Chāndogya Upaniṣad* and *Bṛhadāraṇyaka Upaniṣad*. They are referred to as Daśopaniṣads – the ten Upaniṣads.

Some say that Ādi Śaṅkarācārya has also written a commentary on *Śvetāśvatara Upaniṣad* and therefore consider it also as a major Upaniṣad. However the language and the style of the commentary available do not seem to be that of Ādi Śaṅkarācārya. Perhaps a later Śaṅkarācārya[1] of a particular pīṭha might have written the commentary. Also, Śrī Ānanda Giri has written explanatory notes (ṭīkā) on all the commentaries of Ādi Śaṅkarācārya like the Upaniṣads, *Brahma Sūtras* and *Bhagavad Gītā*. He has not written notes on *Śvetāśvatara Upaniṣad*, which is another indication that the commentary available on the *Śvetāśvatara Upaniṣad* is not written by Ādi Śaṅkarācārya. This however does not detract from its merit and its study surely helps us in understanding the Upaniṣad better.

[1] After Śaṅkarācārya established the four (pīṭhas) posts or places of Dharma in the north (Badarinath), south (Śṛṅgerī), east (Puri) and west (Dwarka) of India, all those who adorn those seats or posts of knowledge are called Śaṅkarācāryas.

Śvetāśvatara Upaniṣad is part of the *Yajur Veda*. It has six chapters and 112 mantras. All Upaniṣads are dialogues between the teacher and his disciples. The last chapter of this Upaniṣad mentions that sage Śvetāśvatara is the teacher in this Upaniṣad and he taught some highly qualified disciples. Nothing more is known about the background of this Upaniṣad. Śvetāśvatara does not appear to be the name of the sage, but a title given to him. Śveta means white or pure and aśva is a horse which symbolises our senses[1]. Śvetāśvatara means one endowed with pure senses.

We may wonder how the senses can be pure or impure. The mind that entertains likes and dislikes for sense objects is called impure. For example, one may love chocolates and dislike greens. Like unbroken and untamed horses, the mind driven by likes and dislikes is uncontrolled, whereas like the well disciplined horses, the controlled senses and mind make life's journey comfortable and joyous. The point being made is that Sage Śvetāśvatara was a wise man who had full control over his senses and mind.

The speciality of this Upaniṣad is that many of its mantras are found in the Saṁhitā portion of the Vedas where their meaning is related to the performance of rituals. It also contains many mantras of other Upaniṣads. Also, *Brahma Sūtras* composed by Bhagavān Veda Vyāsa to reveal the true meaning of the Vedas, comments on many of the mantras of this Upaniṣad. All in all, it is an elevating and beautiful Upaniṣad.

[1] indriyāṇi hayān āhuḥ – *Kaṭhopaniṣad* 1.3.4

Peace Invocation

Traditionally we begin the study of an Upaniṣad with the chanting of a peace invocation by both the Guru and the disciples.

ॐ सह नाववतु । सह नौ भुनक्तु । सह वीर्यं करवावहै ।
तेजस्वि नावधीतमस्तु । मा विद्विषावहै ॥
ॐ शान्तिः शान्तिः शान्तिः ॥

om saha nāvavatu, saha nau bhunaktu, saha vīryaṁ karavāvahai,
tejasvi nāvadhītamastu, mā vidviṣāvahai.
om śāntiḥ śāntiḥ śāntiḥ.

ॐ – Om; सह नौ – us both; अवतु – may (He) protect; सह नौ – us both; भुनक्तु – may (He) cause us to enjoy; सह वीर्यं करवावहै – may (we) put forth effort; तेजस्वि – being brilliant; नौ अधीतम् अस्तु – may our study be; मा विद्विषावहै – may (we) never misunderstand each other; शान्तिः – peace; शान्तिः – peace; शान्तिः – peace

Om! May He protect us both (the Guru and disciple). May we both enjoy (the knowledge). May we both put forth effort (towards that). May our study be brilliant. May we never misunderstand each other. May peace be. May peace be. May peace be.

Om: It is the universal name of God/Truth and is therefore an auspicious sound that is chanted to invoke auspiciousness and the blessings of God. Remembrance of God/Truth makes all undertakings blessed and successful. The Guru and the disciples together chant the peace invocation, understanding well that in the happiness of others lies our own happiness. The prayers of the Vedas were always chanted for peace and happiness for all.

The prayer: They together pray – May God/Truth protect us (avatu) and nourish us (bhunaktu) just like a mother protects the child from harm and nourishes it with food. May we remain healthy for the learning process to be successful. May He also protect our knowledge and nourish it with deeper understanding. May the Guru enjoy teaching and the disciple enjoy learning. May the study never become tedious and boring. A clock in the classroom had the words below it – 'This clock will never be stolen as the students keep a constant watch over it.' May we enjoy the process of learning and also its results. In the case of Self-knowledge the result is supreme Bliss. May we both revel in the supreme Bliss. For such a great reward, both the Guru and the disciples have to put forth effort. May we study with patience and perseverance.

tejasvi nau adhītam astu – May what we learn be bright and brilliant: May it serve us in moments of need and may we remember it in meeting situations in life. Bright knowledge is that which is translated into action. It should shine forth and not get overpowered by desires, greed and the like. The knowledge should be bright enough to totally remove the darkness of ignorance.

mā vidviṣāvahai – May we not dislike each other: May the Guru and disciple never misunderstand each other or entertain negative feelings for each other. May the learning happen in an environment of mutual love and respect.

śāntiḥ śāntiḥ śāntiḥ – Let there be peace: Let there be no obstacles from the unknown or known sources, the unseen or seen sources or from within. Let there be peace in the world, the external surrounding and in our own mind.

Chapter 1

Once upon a time in a hermitage (āśrama), there was a group discussion amongst seekers of Truth. The topic of discussion was the ultimate cause of the world.

हरिः ॐ ॥ ब्रह्मवादिनो वदन्ति -
किं कारणं ब्रह्म कुतः स्म जाता जीवाम केन क्व च सम्प्रतिष्ठाः ।
अधिष्ठिताः केन सुखेतरेषु वर्तामहे ब्रह्मविदो व्यवस्थाम् ॥ १ ॥

hariḥ om. brahmavādino vadanti -
kiṁ kāraṇaṁ brahma kutaḥ sma jātā jīvāma kena kva ca sampratiṣṭhāḥ,
adhiṣṭhitāḥ kena sukhetareṣu vartāmahe brahmavido vyavasthām. (1)

हरिः ॐ – Hari Om; ब्रह्मवादिनः – those (spiritual seekers) who discuss about the Reality; वदन्ति – ask; किम् – what (is); कारणम् – the ultimate cause (of this world); ब्रह्म – the Reality/ Brahman; कुतः – from where; जाता स्म – have we come; जीवाम – do we live; ken – by what; क्व – where; च – and; सम्प्रतिष्ठाः – do we exist or rest (after death); अधिष्ठिताः – governed; केन – by whom; सुख-इतरेषु – regarding happiness and its opposite (sorrow); वर्तामहे – follow; ब्रह्मविदः – O knowers of the Reality; व्यवस्थाम् – the law or rule

1. Those (spiritual seekers) who discuss about the Reality ask, "What is the ultimate cause (of this world)? Is it Reality/Brahman? Where have we come from? How do we live? Where do we exist or go after death? O knowers of the Reality! Under whose governance do we follow the rule regarding joy and sorrow?"

hariḥ om: In Chinmaya Mission we greet each other with the words 'Hari Om'. People often ask us what it means. 'Om' is the nameless, formless, attributeless Reality/Truth. 'Hari' is the same Reality/Truth with form and attributes often referred to as God/Īśvara. Hari also means one who removes our ignorance, bondage and sorrows. Through the worship of Hari/God with form we are able to realise Om the Reality/Truth which is formless as He removes our ignorance. 'Hari Om' sounds like 'hurry home' which indicates that we should hurry back to our original abode – Om – the Self/Truth within.

The seekers of Truth ask (brahmavādinaḥ vadanti brahmavidaḥ): Questions regarding worldly matters can be answered by the worldly wise and those regarding spiritual matters should be addressed to the spiritually wise. Here the students came to the Guru seeking knowledge of Truth.

Discussion regarding Dharma (dharma vicāra) – duties, values, right conduct, merit and sin and the like help us to determine how to lead a good life. Discussion about the Truth (brahma vicāra) helps us to determine and realise our true nature.

Is Brahman/Reality, the ultimate cause of the world? (kiṁ kāraṇaṁ brahma): Though the question appears simple, there are many questions that are inherent in it. Is the Reality (Brahman) the cause of the entire world? If so, is It the material cause or the sentient cause or both? What is Its nature? If the cause is something other than the Reality, then what is it and what is its nature? Is the ultimate cause of creation one or many?

Where have we come from? (kutaḥ sma jātā): What existed before creation? Where is our origin? Did we exist or not before we came into our mother's womb?

How do we live? (jīvāma kena): What gives us life? Can it be air, water and food? But people die, even when these are available. Can what gives us life and sustains it, be inert in nature? Can the combination of inert substances bring about the creation of life? Will science and technology enable us to create life in a laboratory? *Kaṭhopaniṣad* says that man does not live merely because of inhalation and exhalation (breathing), but by something else on which these two depend.[1]

Where do we go after death? (kva ca sampratiṣṭhitāḥ): What is our final place of rest? Have we come from dust and go back to dust? That may be the destination of our body, but what about the life that sustains it? Into what does the creation finally merge?

Under whose governance do we follow the rule regarding joy and sorrow? (adhiṣṭhitāḥ kena sukhetareṣu vartāmahe vyavasthām): What is the law that governs our joy and sorrow? What is the power that presides over our actions and their results, that makes us happy and unhappy? In any given country one has to abide by the laws of its constitution. Even the lawmakers are governed by those laws. But can man-made laws govern our very existence, our joys and sorrows or nature? Does something within us govern our joy and sorrow or is it an outside factor? Does that factor enjoy

[1] na prāṇena nāpānena martyo jīvati kaścana,
itareṇa tu jīvanti yasmin-etau-upāśritau. – *Kaṭhopaniṣad* 2.2.5

a greater place? (adhika sthāna = adhiṣṭhāna) or a longer existence (adhika sthiti = adhiṣṭhitā). Are we independent in creating or getting joy and sorrow? If so, we would never be unhappy and always be happy. Since we are not independent, then on what do we depend?

Generally people have ready answers to all such questions. We are born from the mother's womb, food sustains us, unto dust we return and we are governed by the laws of the land. They believe that to think further about such questions is a waste of time and that we should focus our attention on more important matters like our career and relationships.

Superficial answers may satisfy some; but seekers of Truth will enquire deeper and study and discuss, research and reflect, ask and persist till they find the Truth. Such are the students of this Upaniṣad.

Every effect must have a cause. Cause hunting is a natural preoccupation of man. Here spiritual seekers too like scientists look for the ultimate cause of the world. Like the sweetness in sugar candy, the nature of the cause is reflected in the effect. The students therefore thought that the Truth (Brahman) could not be the ultimate cause. How can the never changing Truth be the cause of this ever-changing world? How can the non-dual and absolute Truth cause all the multitude and finitude in this world? The students therefore started examining other possibilities.

कालः स्वभावो नियतिर्यदृच्छा भूतानि योनिः पुरुष इति चिन्त्या।
संयोग एषां नत्वात्मभावादात्माप्यनीशः सुखदुःखहेतोः॥ २॥

kālaḥ svabhāvo niyatir-yadṛcchā bhūtāni yoniḥ puruṣa iti cintyā,
saṁyoga eṣāṁ natvātmabhāvād-ātmāpyanīśaḥ sukhaduḥkha-hetoḥ. (2)

कालः – time; स्वभावः – inherent nature; नियतिः – the law (of karma); यदृच्छा – chance; भूतानि – the (five) elements; योनिः – the cause; पुरुषः – the intelligent being; इति – thus; चिन्त्या – need to be ascertained; संयोग – combination; एषाम् – of these; न – not; तु – but; आत्मभावात् – because of the existence of the individual self; आत्मा – the individual self; अपि – too; अनीशः – not independent; सुखदुःखहेतोः – being subject to joy and sorrow

2. Time, inherent nature, the law (of karma), chance, the (five) elements, intelligence – neither these nor a combination of these can be ascertained as the ultimate cause (of the world) because

of the existence of the individual self, but the individual self also cannot be the cause (of the world) being subject to joy and sorrow.

The various factors which can be considered to be the ultimate cause of the world are being debated upon. Each is being dismissed on the basis of 'ātmabhāva'. The combination of many causes is also not tenable as the ultimate cause because of 'ātmabhāva'.

The word 'ātmabhāva' has three meanings:

- The above mentioned factors cannot be the ultimate cause because of their 'identity or oneness with the world' (ātmabhāva). They are a part of the world.
- These factors come into being and are subject to change (ātmabhāva).
- There exists another factor the individual being or Self other than these factors (ātmabhāva). The relevance of this logic becomes clear as we proceed in our analysis.

The word 'yoni' can mean cause or energy. If we take it to mean the cause, then it links with each factor like kāla yoni, svabhāva yoni... Some consider it to mean energy; then it becomes one more factor like time or inherent nature. However since matter and energy are interconvertible, they are grouped together under matter (bhūtāni) by some people. Now we examine each factor.

Time (kāla) is not the ultimate cause: Time seems eternal since everything happens in time. The seed is sown at some time and sprouts in its own time. Some feel that they are going through bad times and hope that their problems will get solved when the right time comes. Time appears to cause and govern everything. However is it the sole cause or governing factor or one of the factors?

The awareness of the sequence of events (krama saṁvit) gives rise to the concept of time. Without events happening in space, time would not exist. Hence it is not independent. Also time is a part of creation, the cause of which is the subject of our enquiry.

Further, time also appears, changes and disappears. The experience of time is often subjective, is different in different time zones and measured differently. In the deep sleep state there is no concept of time at all. If time itself is created how can it be the cause of creation?

The third meaning of ātmabhāva which refers to existence of an entity which is aware of time is also applicable here. 'I' am aware of time. I exist before time and know the passage of time. So time being dependent, transient, finite and known cannot be the ultimate cause of the world.

Inherent nature (svabhāva) is not the ultimate cause: Svabhāva is the essential nature of a thing. It is the unique property of a thing that makes it what it is. Heat is the inherent nature of fire and the sun. Does not this inherent nature seem to create the object – make it what it is?

Svabhāva as the cause too stands refuted due to ātmabhāva. The object and its essential nature coexist and are inseparable. But by the theory of cause and effect the cause exists before the effect. On the other hand the inherent nature does not exist before the object and then create the object. Heat cannot exist apart from fire or before fire.

Also the properties of objects may change. Milk becomes yogurt which has very different properties. A changing cause cannot be an ultimate cause. Also the essential nature of an object is part of creation and the part cannot be the cause of the whole creation. The finite cannot cause the infinite.

Further we are aware of the properties of objects which means there is the pre-existence of another entity other than the object and its property. The ultimate cause must exist before everything and hence the inherent nature of objects cannot be the ultimate cause of the world.

Nature's laws (niyati) are not the ultimate cause: Nature's laws seem to govern everything in the world. Fire burns, a dog gives birth to a dog and so on. The results we get when the laws are broken also are governed by nature's laws like weather changes due to global warming caused by carbon emissions. But are they the ultimate cause?

Nature's laws come to manifest along with the objects governed by the laws, but they do not create them. For example, the law of gravity did not create the solar system which is governed by it. Being part of creation the law does not exist before creation. The laws are many and govern different objects in different circumstances. They are interdependent and not absolute. Further there must be a lawmaker who existed before the law and created the law as well as a law upholder who sees that it functions.

Niyati is also said to mean fate, destiny or luck. But fate is also governed by the law of cause and effect. A person who overeats and gets a stomach ache the day after may call it his fate or bad luck, but the doctor understands the symptoms of overeating and the wife predicts them. Thus nature's laws cannot be the ultimate cause of creation.

Creation cannot be caused by a mere accident (yadṛcchā): Events seem to happen quite suddenly and most predictions in the world go wrong. Many discoveries are made by accident and there seems no logic behind most things that happen in the world. Some scientists postulate an accidental Big Bang as the cause.

However it does not seem right to think that such a well-ordered world which runs by nature's laws could come into being by accident. Some may be too lazy to think deeply, so accept chance to be the cause. However we see that everything seems to be governed by the law of cause and effect. So creation cannot be causeless or mere chance cannot be the cause of anything, leave alone the ultimate cause of the world.

Matter (bhūtāni) and energy (yoni) cannot be the ultimate cause: The whole world is made up of energy and matter. Some scientists postulate primordial matter, fundamental elements or unifying energy as the cause of the world. However matter and energy are interchangeable and interdependent. Matter and energy are inseparable from the world, are a part of the world, are created, are ever changing and are known by us. They cannot therefore be the ultimate cause of the world.

Intellect (puruṣa) cannot be the ultimate cause: The mind-intellect instrument or thoughts seem to be the cause of all. The world exists in our thoughts, is sustained by them and merges back into them. All discoveries are made by the intellect and all joys and sorrows are experienced therein.

However thoughts are part of creation and cannot exist without objects of this world. They too come into existence, keep changing all the time, are inert and known by us. They are therefore not the cause of creation.

A combination (saṁyoga) of these factors cannot be the ultimate cause: Even if individually they may not be the cause, can inherent properties, nature's laws, matter and energy which together make up this world, be the cause of the world?

This does not seem logical as the cause precedes the effect. They have to have existed before creation for them to create together. Also an assemblage is always meant for something other than the various assembled parts (saṅghātasya parārthatvāt). For example, the car is assembled not for the sake of the engine which is a part of the car, but for a driver or owner, an entity other than the car. Factors like time, space, matter or energy are inert and combine to form the world which is experienced by a sentient entity apart from them. What comes together also disintegrates in time. A combination of many factors cannot be the one ultimate cause of the world.

The individual self (ātmā) cannot be the ultimate cause: The word ātmā here means the finite being (jīvātmā), the individual self, the entity which experiences this world, and not the pure Self (śuddha ātmā). Am I not the creator of my own world? Can I experience the universe if I the individual did not exist? Do I not create my own joys and sorrows?

The individual is born in the world, a part of this world, finite, helpless and powerless. We are compelled into actions which cause joys and sorrows. We are not independent in creating joys and sorrows. How can such a finite and powerless entity be the ultimate cause of this infinite world?

The students are confused. The Truth/Reality being changeless cannot be the cause of this ever changing world and the factors like time or matter being finite, created and changing also cannot be the cause. Since creation exists, it must have a cause. What can it be?

Every field of knowledge has its own way of knowing. A skill is mastered by practice and a poem is appreciated through language and emotions. Logical reasoning and intellectual discussion did not give the students the answer to the ultimate cause of the world. They then decided to meditate. In the seat of meditation they realised the infinite Truth/ Reality along with its inexplicable power.

ते ध्यानयोगानुगता अपश्यन् देवात्मशक्तिं स्वगुणैर्निगूढाम् ।
यः कारणानि निखिलानि तानि कालात्मयुक्तान्यधितिष्ठत्येकः ॥ ३ ॥

te dhyānayogānugatā apaśyan devātma-śaktiṁ svaguṇair-nigūḍhām,
yaḥ kāraṇāni nikhilāni tāni kālātmayuktānyadhitiṣṭhatyekaḥ. (3)

ते – they; ध्यानयोगानुगता – following the path of meditation; अपश्यन् – saw; देवात्मशक्तिम् – the power of the Lord; स्वगुणैः – by its own qualities; निगूढाम् – hidden; यः – who; कारणानि – causes; निखिलानि – all; तानि – those; कालात्मयुक्तानि – starting with time upto the individual self; अधितिष्ठति – presides (over); एकः – alone

3. Following the path of meditation, the students saw the power of the Lord, hidden by its own inherent qualities, the Lord who, alone presides over all the causes – from time to the individual self (discussed in the previous verse).

Path of Meditation (dhyāna-yoga): We need to work hard for material success. Similarly we have to put forth right efforts for spiritual gains. However the nature of efforts to know the infinite Truth is completely different. The Truth is realised by following the path of meditation. *Kaivalyopaniṣad* too says - 'Know the Truth through faith, devotion and following the path of meditation.'[1] In meditation we withdraw our attention from the world, the body, the prāṇas (life forces), the mind, intellect and ego – and just be. In that state of pure being, the Truth and its power is revealed spontaneously.

Bhāgavatam describes a similar incident. Despite writing the *Mahābhārata* and many *Purāṇas*, Bhagavān Veda Vyāsa was not feeling fulfilled. Sage Nārada asked him to write about the divine sports of the Lord. In order to be able to undertake this task, Bhagavān Veda Vyāsa meditated. In a state of deep absorption (samādhi), he saw the divine power of the Lord and how it creates the whole universe.

The divine power of God/Truth (devātma śakti): This phrase has rich layers of meaning. The students realised in meditation that there was a creative power behind all creation and its locus was the infinite Truth. The infinite Truth has an infinite potential to create. This inscrutable divine power is called māyā or prakṛti.

Thus the infinite Truth (Brahman) associated with māyā is the cause of the world. It therefore becomes both the material as well as the sentient cause of creation. The various factors like time, inherent nature, nature's laws, matter and energy are manifestations of māyā, or creations of māyā.

The relationship between God/Truth (Brahman) and His power (māyā): Indeed this relationship is difficult to

---

[1] śraddhā-bhakti-dhyāna-yogād-avaihi – *Kaivalyopaniṣad* 1.2

understand. It is said that the Truth is One without a second and attributeless. Then how can there be Truth (Brahman) and māyā, its power – power itself being an attribute? Also does māyā have a separate existence from God/Truth or is it one with the Truth?

Māyā cannot exist separate from Truth as Truth is of the nature of Existence. Anything other than Existence cannot exist. Then māyā must be one with the Truth. If so it becomes the Truth itself. Hence māyā cannot be said to be either separate or one with the Truth. Then maybe it does not exist at all. Since creation exists, its cause, the creative power also must exist and this power must exist in the infinite Truth alone. Hence this power is called inscrutable (anirvacanīya) and enjoys an indescribable relationship with the Truth. Tulasīdāsa expresses it beautifully as 'it can be said to be separate, yet not separate.'[1]

This relationship becomes clearer through an example. When we say 'my book' the book is separate from me and it has its own existence. But my power of hearing, smelling or speaking is not separate from me and cannot exist without me. I can remain without speaking, but my power to speak exists in me, and because of me.

Māyā is called devātma śakti as it belongs to God/ Truth and exists because of Him. In God/Truth this power lies dormant and expresses as creation. 'God/Truth is said to preside over and māyā creates the world.'[2]

---

[1] kahiyata bhinna na bhinna

[2] mayādhyakṣeṇa prakṛtiḥ sūyate sacarācaram – *Gītā* 9.10

From the standpoint of Truth (Brahman), māyā does not exist (yā mā sā māyā – that which does not exist is māyā). Hence māyā is not an attribute of the Truth/Brahman. Yet from the standpoint of the world it is said to be the divine power of God/Truth which exists in God/Truth and creates the world. It indeed is difficult to comprehend.

Hidden by its own qualities (svaguṇair-nigūḍhām): This infinite divine potential power of God/Truth remains hidden by its own expression which also veils the Truth/Brahman, like the sun being hidden due to its own effulgence. Māyā has the qualities of knowledge (sattva), activity (rajas) and inertia (tamas). Māyā creates the five elements – space, air, fire, water and earth with their special qualities of sound, touch, colour, form, taste and smell. This variety in the world is due to the permutation and combination of the three qualities and the five elements with their special qualities. Creation indeed hides both – the power of māyā and the Truth. We experience this fascinating creation and not the power and Truth behind it.

This elusive power can only be known along with the Truth through meditation and so the students meditated further.

In their meditation the students envisioned the Truth/ Brahman as a wheel – cakra. Various aspects of creation are included in this metaphor of the wheel.

तमेकनेमिं त्रिवृतं षोडशान्तं शतार्धारं विंशतिप्रत्यराभिः ।
अष्टकैः षड्भिर्विश्वरूपैकपाशं त्रिमार्गभेदं द्विनिमित्तैकमोहम् ॥ ४ ॥

tamekanemiṁ trivṛtaṁ ṣoḍaśāntaṁ śatārdhāraṁ viṁśati-pratyarābhiḥ, aṣṭakaiḥ ṣaḍbhir-viśvarūpaikapāśaṁ trimārgabhedaṁ dvinimittaika-moham. (4)

तम् – Him; एकनेमिम् – having one rim; त्रिवृतम् – with three tyres; षोडशान्तम् – having sixteen extremities; शतार्धारम् – having fifty spokes; विंशतिप्रत्यराभिः – with twenty fasteners; षड्भिः अष्टकैः – with six sets of eight; विश्वरूपैकपाशम् – a belt or cord that is single, yet manifold; त्रिमार्गभेदम् – having three different paths; द्विनिमित्तैकमोहम् – with a single delusion that gives rise to duality

4. (They saw) Him (as a wheel) having one rim, three tyres, sixteen extremities, fifty spokes, twenty fasteners, six sets of eight strengthening it, a belt or cord that is single, yet manifold, driven along three different paths, and a single delusion (each revolution of the wheel) that gives rise to duality (merit and sin leading to happiness and sorrow).

The word adhīmaḥ, meaning 'we know' at the end of the next verse is the governing verb for this verse also. It indicates that this understanding of the Truth has arisen out of deep thinking and meditation.

The wheel of Truth (brahma cakram): The wheel of creation (saṁsāra-cakra) is understood to be the wheel of Truth (brahma-cakra) after meditation, as the Truth alone appears as this creation. It is the substratum of this creation and is all-inclusive.

Everything in creation is cyclic like the wheel that rotates as it moves forward. Days follow nights, Monday morning blues come each week as do seasons, years and yugas. Galaxies rotate and creations dissolve to re-emerge – all superimposed on the changeless Truth/Brahman. 'Like seasonal crops man too dies to be born again and again.'[1]

The rim (eka nemi): The wheel exists within the rim which alone leaves an impression on the ground as it rotates. The rim symbolises the inscrutable divine infinite potential power of God/Truth which stores the impression of each creation and manifests as this world. It is also referred to as māyā, prakṛti, chāyā, pradhāna, avyakta, avyākṛta or avidyā in different contexts.

The three tyres (trivṛta): The wheels of big vehicles have three tyres, each tyer strengthening the wheel and facilitating its rotation. This huge wheel of Truth which includes the entire creation is triple tyred with the three qualities (guṇas) which constitute the divine power of God/Brahman. They are sattva (goodness and knowledge), rajas (activity) and tamas (inertia and ignorance). It can also be understood as the time (kāla), space (deśa) and causation (kāraṇa) which governs creation.

[1] sasyamiva martyaḥ pacyate sasyamiva ājāyate punaḥ – *Kaṭhopaniṣad* 1.6

The sixteen extremities (ṣoḍaśānta): The circular form of a wooden wheel of a chariot is made with several smaller pieces of wood; cut, shaped and fixed together. The wheel of Truth has sixteen such parts which give shape to this creation. They are the five elements (pañca bhūtāni – space, air, fire, water and earth), the five instruments through which we perceive the world (pañca jñānendriya – ability to hear sounds, to touch or feel sensations, see colour and form, taste and smell) the five instruments of action through which we respond to the world (pañca karmendriya – the ability to speak, grasp, move, procreate and excrete) and the mind which is the inner instrument which thinks, feels and co-ordinates the other instruments.

The fifty spokes (śatārdhārā): The spokes connect the hub to the rim of the wheel, maintaining its shape as they rotate. The wheel of Truth has fifty spokes. They are also described in *Kalpopaniṣad* of *Brahma Purāṇa*. They are:

1. **The five misconceptions (viparyaya):** It is strange but true that our misconceptions and false notions keep the world going. They can give us untold misery and are also described as hell or naraka. The five misconceptions are:
    a) **tama**: To mistake the not-Self to be the Self (anātmani ātma buddhi) i.e. to think that 'I am the body' which is made up of inert matter is the first misconception.
    b) **moha**: From the mistaken notion of the Self arises the fascination for the world of objects. Man gets attracted to and attached to the eight extraordinary powers (aṣṭa siddhis) like the ability to make oneself miniscule (aṇimā) or the power to make oneself very heavy (garimā). Man starts measuring himself

by these powers and gets deluded and enslaved by them. That is moha.

c) **mahāmoha**: Bigger delusion sets in when we think that the transient world as experienced is real (jagati satyatva buddhi) and get attached to the five worldly sense objects (sound, touch, color and form, taste and smell) and the same five objects, subtler and more pleasurable, which are experienced in heavenly realms.

d) **tamisra**: It is the gloom and anger that arises when despite efforts one is unable to get the aforementioned ten worldly and heavenly sense objects and the eight extraordinary powers. *Gītā* says that anger arises from frustrated desires (kāmāt krodho'bhijāyate). The more intense the desire the greater is the anger one feels.

e) **andha-tamisra:** It is the feeling of enrage, frustration, dejection and dissatisfaction when the pleasures and powers are lost before we feel fulfilled. The loss can be because the pleasures or powers are taken away or because of our own inability to enjoy them due to disease or death.

2. **The twenty-eight disabilities (aśakti):** Like our misconceptions, strangely it is our disabilities that keeps us engaged in worldly activity and keeps the world moving.

Eleven of our disabilities are related to the aforementioned eleven instruments – five instruments of perception, five instruments of actions and the inner instrument – the mind. For example, the eyes may be afflicted with cataract or blindness, with respect to speech one may be impaired with a stammer or dumbness or be mentally challenged.

Other nine types of disabilities are the discontentments (atuṣṭi) which are the opposites to the nine kinds of contentments mentioned hereafter. Added to them are the eight disabilities (asiddhi) corresponding to the inabilities to achieve the eight attainments enumerated later.

3. **The nine kinds of contentment (tuṣṭi):** Like the spokes of the wheel, the advantages and disadvantages, the abilities and disabilities, the understanding and misunderstandings in life keep ascending and descending as life moves on. The same things in life make us content at one time and leave us dissatisfied at other times. The same things fulfill someone and frustrate another. Some are satisfied by collecting things, some by renouncing them. The worldly person wants material, emotional or intellectual satisfaction and the spiritual person seeks spiritual satisfaction.

People may appear to be content, but the reasons behind that may be quite different. For instance, one person is satisfied in remaining in a certain post and refuses promotion because promotion may entail longer working hours and he wants to devote more time for his family, whilst another refuses promotion to avoid responsibility and yet another to avoid the transfer associated with the promotion. Tuṣṭi is categorised as mentioned below based on the reason for contentment.

i. **Nature (prakṛti jñāna):** Some develop the power to unravel the secrets of nature and revel in the wonders of the created world. Some are fascinated by the study of subjects like geology, physics or biochemistry and spend years in research and are thrilled by discoveries in these fields.

ii. **Material (upādāna):** Some are charmed by material things and derive satisfaction in possessing them. They are satisfied by the external or the gross. For instance, wearing the garb of a renunciate makes them feel a sense of achievement rather than striving for inner renunciation of weaknesses.

iii. **Time (kāla):** Some are convinced that the right time will bring everything in life including liberation. They are content in their belief that time will take care of all their needs and that they need not strive for anything.

iv. **Good fortune (bhāgya):** Some depend on fate, luck or destiny and thus remain satisfied with what they have or get. For them liberation is also like a lottery which the lucky person wins.

v. **Renunciation of objects and activity because acquisition of things is difficult (ārjana doṣa):** Some feel satisfied after working hard and getting things, whereas some feel, 'why not be satisfied now itself' and save oneself from putting all the effort for something one is not sure of getting.

vi. **Renouncing objects or activities because maintenance of acquired things is difficult (rakṣaṇa doṣa):** For instance, seeing the difficulty in maintaining relationships, some would rather not marry as they think, 'marriages may be made in heaven, but maintaining it will become my responsibility.'

vii. **Some people see the inherent flaw in all pleasures (viṣaya doṣa):** For instance, the possibility of disease resulting from enjoyment like in smoking cigarettes (bhoge roga bhayam). The very process of enjoyment depletes one's vitality, dullens the senses[1] and exhausts one's resources. Such people feel satisfied with whatever they have and refuse to strive for objects of pleasure.

viii. **saṅga doṣa:** There are those who remain content as they feel that the more one fulfills one's desires, the more one gets attached to the objects and the more the desires grow like adding fuel to fire. Since it is impossible to fulfill all our desires, it is better not to pursue them at all and remain content.

ix. **hiṁsā doṣa:** In every pleasure or acquisition there is a possibility of causing harm or injury to another and therefore some people desist from them and remain content. For example, some people do not burn firecrackers during Diwali celebrations as it may cause injury to other beings.

The nine kinds of disabilities mentioned earlier are the corresponding opposites of those nine kinds of contentment.

4. **The eight achievements (siddhis):** The siddhis mentioned here are different from the well-known extraordinary powers (aṣṭa siddhis) like aṇimā, garimā (ability to become very tiny, heavy) and so on. The siddhis referred to here

[1] sarvendriyāṇāṁ jarayanti tejaḥ – *Kaṭhopaniṣad.* 1.1.26

are in terms of acquisition of knowledge as knowledge is power. It empowers us and keeps this world moving. Depending on how the knowledge is acquired the siddhis are categorised as:

i. **ūha (Inborn):** Some are born with knowledge and talents acquired by them in previous lives.[1] Child prodigies display knowledge and abilities without having been taught. Hastāmalakācārya had Self-knowledge right from birth without being taught.

ii. **śabda (Listening):** Some have the ability to know the subject just by listening.[2] They may not even be very literate, but this does not hinder their learning quickly without the necessity of studying systematically. Toṭakācārya, one of the four main disciples of Ādi Śaṅkarācārya, even though not intellectually brilliant like many other disciples, acquired the knowledge of the Truth by mere listening, simple faith and grace of the Guru.

iii. **adhyayana (Study):** Knowledge gained through study and research. Some learn by their own study and some through constant revision (abhyāsa).

iv. **ādhidaivika duḥkha vighāta:** Knowledge gained through forbearance of afflictions due to phenomenal forces like earthquakes, floods etc.

v. **ādhibhautika duḥkha vighāta:** Knowledge arising out of cheerfully facing the challenges presented by the circumstances around us like criticism by others, loss of wealth and so on.

---

[1] upadeśa antareṇa janmāntara-saṁskāra-vaśāt prakṛtyādi viṣayaṁ jñānam udpadyate

[2] abhyāsam antareṇa śravaṇa mātrāt jñāna-prāptiḥ

vi. **ādhyātmika duḥkha vighāta:** Maturity and wisdom gained through patiently going through physical ailments or mental agitations.

vii. **suhṛt prāpti (well-wisher):** A mentor who guides us and is willing to teach out of good will or compassion is difficult to get. If we are fortunate, we gain knowledge from such people or through a well-wisher or friend.

viii. **dāna (fees):** Knowledge gained through a paid tutor or knowledge received when the teacher is pleased with your gift or service.[1] In present times gaining knowledge by paying fees is most common.

The twenty nails (viṁśati pratyarābhiḥ): The spokes are fastened to the hub and rim by nails and wedges and strengthened by counter spokes. There are twenty such fasteners in the wheel of Truth. The five sense organs of perception along with the five sense objects they perceive, and the five organs of action along with their corresponding objects, together form the twenty fasteners. They keep us well pinned to this world. For instance, the ability to see various colours through the eyes and hear various sounds with our ears keeps us glued to the world of television.

The six sets of eight factors (ṣaḍ aṣṭaka): Innumerable variety of gross and subtle objects and beings, thoughts and feelings constitute this wheel of Truth. Some of them are grouped into eight (aṣṭakas):

[1] ācārya-hita-vastu-pradānena jñāna-prāptiḥ

1. **Prakṛti-aṣṭaka:** The eight-fold prakṛti consists of the five elements (space, air, fire, water and earth), the mind, intellect and the ego.[1]

2. **Dhātu-aṣṭaka:** Dhātu is that which sustains the body. The physical body is composed of the outer skin (carma), the inner skin (tvak), blood (rakta), flesh (māṁsa), fat (medas), bones (asthi), marrow (majjā) and semen (vīrya or śukra).When the outer and inner skin (dermis and epidermis) are considered one, it is categorised as sapta dhātu – seven factors.

3. **Aṣṭa siddhi:** The eight supernatural powers are:
    a. **aṇimā:** The ability to become minuscule.
    b. **mahimā:** The ability to become huge like a mountain.
    c. **garimā:** The power to become very heavy.
    d. **laghimā:** The ability to become light as a feather.
    e. **prāpti:** The power to reach anywhere at will. For example, Sanat Kumāras could in an instant travel from heaven to earth. Prāpti is also understood as the power to see any world from where one is. For instance, sitting in the Sābarmatī Āśrama in Ahmadabad, a yogī was able to give the exact details of the secret place where the Britishers had detained Mahātmā Gandhi.
    f. **prākāmya:** The ability to assume any form at will. Hanumāna took on the form of a brāhmin when he first met Vibhīṣaṇa in Laṅkā.

[1] bhūmirāpo'nalo vāyuḥ khaṁ mano buddhireva ca,
ahaṅkāra itīyaṁ me bhinnā prakṛtir-aṣṭadhā. – *Gītā* 7.4

g. **īśitva:** The ability to command the forces of nature. The Bible mentions that Jesus stopped a storm.

h. **vaśitva:** The ability to control and influence people.

Hanumāna is said to have all these supernatural powers and he used them only to serve God and accomplish His work.

4. **bhāva-aṣṭaka:** The four virtues and the opposite states of the mind constitute the eight bhāvas. They are dharma (righteousness) and adharma (unrighteousness), jñāna (knowledge) and ajñāna (ignorance), vairāgya (dispassion) and avairāgya (lack of dispassion), aiśvarya (lordship or prosperity) and anaiśvarya (helplessness or poverty).

Everything in creation – the good, bad and the ugly are part of God/Truth. It is said that virtues appear on the front side of the body of God and the vices on His back. It means that when we go behind His back or ignore Him, we commit unrighteous acts, live in ignorance, become overindulgent, helpless and poor.

These eight can also be understood in a broader sense. For instance, poverty could mean a petty and miserly state of mind and not just the lack of wealth. One person showed his miserliness by offering a cheap plastic chair instead of a throne to the Lord even whilst doing mental worship!

5. **aṣṭa deva:** The eight kinds of celestial beings are Brahmā, Prajāpati, Devatās (like Indra, Varuṇa), gandharvas (celestial musicians), yakṣas (custodians of wealth like

Kubera), rākṣasas (demons), pitṛs (ancestors and manes) and piśācas (ghouls). Brahmā, Prajāpati and Devatās are predominantly sāttvika (noble). Yakṣa, gandharva and rākṣasas are predominantly rājasika (pleasure seeking) and paiśācas are tāmasika (ignoble) in nature.

6. **guṇa aṣṭaka:** The eight noble qualities are dayā (compassion), kṣamā (forgiveness), anasūyā (devoid of jealousy or fault-finding), śauca (purity), anāyāsa (effortlessness and vitality), akārpaṇya (generosity), aspṛhā (no craving for sense pleasures) and maṅgala (auspiciousness or goodness).

One cord (eka pāśa): Desire is the cord or the belt of the wheel of Truth that binds all in this world. Desires are many and varied (viśvarūpa). They can be sāttvika, rājasika or tāmasika. Everyone is driven by desires and even noble desires can prove binding.

The three paths (tri-marga-bheda): The wheel of Truth is driven over the three paths. Some follow the path of dharma (righteousness and noble deeds), some the path of adharma (unrighteousness and ignoble deeds) and yet others the pathless path of knowledge (jñāna). This last path frees man from the cycle of worldly existence (saṁsāra) and all bondages of the world.

The one cause of the two (dvinimitta-eka-moha): The reason why man is born again and again in this worldly cycle – sometimes going to higher realms because of good actions (puṇya) and sometimes to the lower realms due to sins (pāpa), is because of delusion (moha) – the identification with the body-mind-intellect. It also means that this delusion gives rise to the vision of duality due to which we see the world as different from us and create the distinctions of 'me and my' versus 'you and yours'.

Thus, through the metaphor of the wheel the entire creation is described – the unmanifest, subtle and the gross. *Gītā* says, 'Whatever things and beings, that are pure (sāttvika), active (rājasika) or inert (tāmasika), know them to proceed from Me; yet I am not in them, they are in Me.'[1]

[1] ye caiva sāttvikā bhāvā rājasās-tāmasāśca ye,
matta eveti tānviddhi na tvahaṁ teṣu te mayi. – *Gītā* 7.12

In the previous mantra the world was described as a wheel and now it is compared to a river.

पञ्चस्रोतोऽम्बुं पञ्चयोन्युग्रवक्रां पञ्चप्राणोर्मिं पञ्चबुद्ध्यादिमूलाम् ।
पञ्चावर्तां पञ्चदुःखौघवेगां पञ्चाशद्भेदां पञ्चपर्वामधीमः ॥ ५ ॥

pañca-sroto'mbuṁ pañca-yonyugravakrāṁ pañca-prāṇormiṁ pañca-buddhyādimūlām,
pañcāvartāṁ pañca-duḥkhaughavegāṁ pañcāśadbhedāṁ pañca-parvām-adhīmaḥ. (5)

पञ्चस्रोतोऽम्बुम् – containing waters of five streams; पञ्चयोन्युग्रवक्राम् – which has five powerful turnings due to five causes; पञ्चप्राणोर्मिम् – that has the five prāṇas as the waves; पञ्चबुद्ध्यादिमूलाम् – which has the mind, the basis of the fivefold perception, as the source; पञ्चावर्ताम् – which has five whirlpools; पञ्चदुःखौघवेगाम् – having the fivefold misery as the rapids; पञ्चाशद्भेदाम् – having fifty aspects; पञ्चपर्वाम् – which has five branches; अधीमः – (we) think of

5. We think of Him as a river that contains the waters of five streams, that has five major turnings due to five causes, that has the five prāṇas as the waves, the mind – the basis of the fivefold perception – as the source, and has five whirlpools, the fivefold misery as the rapids, fifty aspects and five branches.

The great river: The source of all rivers can be traced back to the oceanic waters and they again merge back into the ocean. Similarly the world emerges from and merges back in the Truth/Brahman, which is its very substratum. To enjoy a swim in the river we should be aware of its depth and the flow of current, otherwise there is danger of drowning. Rivers have tricky whirlpools and dangerous creatures. We are advised never to jump into unknown waters. So also in life – this world becomes calamitous for unthinking people who get caught up in it and suffer. However the wise ones derive great happiness from the same world.

The students meditated and saw the Truth/Brahman as a river. What appears to the ignorant as the river of worldly existence (saṁsāra nadī) is seen by the wise as the river of Truth (brahma nadī). The metaphor unfolds thus.

pañca-sroto'mbum: The waters of many streams come together to form the big rivers. The sense objects enter into us through the five sense organs of perception – ears, skin, eyes, tongue and nose.

pañca-yoni-ugra-vakrām: The world is made up of the subtle and gross five elements – space, air, fire, water and air (pañca yoni). When the sense organs of perception come in contact with the sense objects – both made up of the five elements – they gather force and become turbulent (ugra) and this takes us through many a twist and turns of life (vakra). Man can quite easily get swept away by the force of his senses into the world of pleasure and indulgence.

pañca-prāṇa-ūrmim: Ripples and waves are created as waters face obstacles and dash against the river banks. The five physiological functions – prāṇa (breathing), apāna (excretion), vyāna (circulation), udāna (reversal action) and samāna (digestion) are the waves formed in this worldly river.

pañca-buddhyādi-mūlām: What is the source of the five senses which are the streams that form this river? Indeed it is the mind, without the backing of which the senses cannot function. For instance, if the mind is distracted, even if the eyes are open and the car is right in front of us, one does not see it, and there is an accident. A preoccupied mind does not hear even when spoken to, loudly and clearly.

pañca-āvartām: As the streams of the senses flow downstream they get engaged with the whirlpools of the five sense objects – sounds, touch, colours and forms, tastes and smells. They are so tempting that one is easily drowned in them.

pañca-duḥkhaugha-vegām: The river has many rapids where the swift current can easily sweep us off. The five rapids of life are the sorrows associated with the five stages of life.

a. **asti:** The sorrow faced by the foetus living in the cramped conditions of the womb and totally at the mercy of the mother.
b. **jāyate:** The pain of birth is experienced by both the mother and the child.
c. **vardhate:** The pangs of growing. Each stage of growth – infancy, childhood, adolescence, youth and adulthood – has its own trials and travails.
d. **apakṣīyate:** The troubles of old age are very evident. Debility, senility, disease and other endless sorrows drag us through old age.
e. **vinaśyatī:** Man finally faces the sorrow of death.

pañcāśad-bhedām: The fifty factors could be understood as the same spoken of in the earlier mantra as the fifty spokes of the wheel. The *Yoga Śāstras* describe cakras which are the centres along which the kuṇḍalini śakti (psychic energy) travels to merge into the cakra on the top of the head called the sahasrāra. Each cakra is described as a lotus with certain number of petals. The mūlādhāra (4), svādhiṣṭhāna (6), nābhi cakra (10), anāhata (12), viśuddha (16) and ājñā cakra (2) together have 50 petals which represent various types of thoughts which prevail in the individual and the world.

pañca-parvām: Some rivers are seen to branch out. Some like the Brahmaputra branch out to form a delta region. The river of life has five such branches of avidyā (ignorance of the Self), asmitā (identification with the not-Self that gives rise to the notion of doership), rāga (liking towards that which is considered a source of joy), dveṣa (aversion towards that which appears to give sorrow) and abhiniveśa (fear of death).

Fascinating indeed is this river in which we find ourselves.

Now the Upaniṣad explains how we get caught up in this wheel of worldly existence and how we can get out of it.

सर्वाजीवे सर्वसंस्थे बृहन्ते अस्मिन्हंसो भ्राम्यते ब्रह्मचक्रे ।
पृथगात्मानं प्रेरितारं च मत्वा जुष्टस्ततस्तेनामृतत्वमेति ॥ ६ ॥

sarvājīve sarvasaṁsthe bṛhante asmin-haṁso bhrāmyate brahmacakre,
pṛthagātmānaṁ preritāraṁ ca matvā juṣṭas-tatas-tenāmṛtatvam-eti. (6)

सर्वाजीवे – that in which all beings live or exist; सर्वसंस्थे – which is the place of dissolution of all beings; अस्मिन् बृहन्ते ब्रह्मचक्रे – in this great wheel of Truth/Brahman; हंसः – the individual being; भ्राम्यते – wanders; पृथक् – separate; आत्मानम् – itself; प्रेरितारम् – the moving force or controller; च – and; मत्वा – considering; जुष्टः – blessed; ततः – then; तेन – by Him; अमृतत्वम् – immortality; एति – attains

6. The jīva (individual being), considering itself separate and different from the Lord who is the moving force, wanders in the wheel of Truth/Brahman, in which all beings live and rest. Blessed by Him and knowing itself to be one with the Lord, the jīva attains immortality.

Owing to the power of māyā, the Truth/Brahman appears as this entire universe. So the individuals, you and me, are also none other than the Truth. Being ignorant of our essential nature we revolve in this wheel of worldly existence.

Haṁsa: The word 'haṁsa' has many meanings. One who roams around is called haṁsa (hanti gacchati iti haṁsaḥ).

The sun is perceived to move from the eastern to the western horizon, so it is called haṁsa. The swan keeps moving its legs, assuming dancing postures and so is called haṁsa. It is said that the swan has the special ability to separate milk and water. Therefore one whose intellect can distinguish between the Self and the not-Self is also called haṁsa. Some orders of monks in Hindus are called haṁsa or paramahaṁsa. The wandering monk is also called paramahaṁsa parivrājaka. One who has realised 'I am (aham) that Truth (saḥ)' is also called paramahaṁsa. Here haṁsa means the jīvātmā, the finite individual as he keeps roaming in this world identifying with different bodies, becoming a human or an animal or a celestial being.

Bṛhante: The word Brahman/bṛhante comes from 'bṛhat', meaning the unconditional and unqualified 'big'. Hence bṛhante or Brahman means the infinite. The wheel of Brahman (brahma-cakra) is infinite. All living beings (sarvājīve) and inert objects exist and merge back in the infinite Truth (sarva-saṁsthe). Then why does the individual wander and suffer? It is because we the individuals think we are separate (pṛthak) from the infinite Truth/God who is the motivating force (preritāram) behind this entire universe. This thought of being separate and different makes us feel finite, helpless and at the mercy of the world. The individual also becomes the doer of actions and the enjoyer or sufferer of results.

The Path of Devotion advocates that we serve and worship God/Truth. The Lord being pleased by that showers His grace (tena īśvareṇa jīvaḥ juṣṭaḥ) and the individual attains immortality (amṛtatvam eti) as he becomes one with the Lord.

According to the Path of Knowledge when the individual realises his oneness with the infinite Truth (ahaṁ saḥ), he ceases to be the helpless and wandering finite being (haṁsa) and realises his immortal nature (amṛtatvam eti).

Thus the questions asked by the disciples in the first mantra are answered. The infinite Truth with its inscrutable divine power is the ultimate cause of this world. The infinite Truth alone appears as this creation due to this power and also governs it. We emerge from the Truth, are sustained by It, and go back to It. Till we realise our oneness with It, we roam about identifying with the body and living as finite individuals. When we worship God/Truth or realise our oneness, we attain immortality.

What is the cause of Liberation?

उद्गीतमेतत्परमं तु ब्रह्म तस्मिंस्त्रयं सुप्रतिष्ठाक्षरं च।
अत्रान्तरं ब्रह्मविदो विदित्वा लीना ब्रह्मणि तत्परा योनिमुक्ताः॥ ७॥

udgītametat-paramaṁ tu brahma tasmiṁs-trayaṁ supratiṣṭhākṣaraṁ ca, atrāntaraṁ brahmavido viditvā līnā brahmaṇi tatparā yoni-muktāḥ. (7)

उद्गीतम् – proclaimed; एतत् – this; तु – verily; परमं ब्रह्म – supreme Truth/Brahman; तस्मिन् – in it; त्रयम् – the triad; सुप्रतिष्ठा – exist; अक्षरम् – imperishable; च – and; अत्र – here; अन्तरम् – the inner essence; ब्रह्मविदः – the knowers of Truth/Brahman; विदित्वा – understanding; लीनाः – (they) get merged; ब्रह्मणि – in Brahman or Reality; तत्पराः – remaining absorbed in It; योनिमुक्ताः – (become) free from birth (liberated)

7. This is proclaimed to be verily the supreme Truth/Brahman. In it the triad exists. It is the firm support and is imperishable. The knowers of Truth/Brahman, understanding its inner essence and remaining absorbed in It, get merged in Truth/Brahman and become free from birth.

udgītam-etat paramaṁ tu brahma: The sages and the saints, all speak about the supreme Truth and its greatness. 'The Vedas (scriptures) declare the supremacy of Truth/Brahman.'[1]

tasmins-trayaṁ supratiṣṭhitā akṣaraṁ ca: The supreme Truth is the imperishable substratum of this perishable world of names and forms.

[1] sarve vedā yat padam āmananti – *Kaṭhopaniṣad.* 1.2.15

There are many triads – interrelated groups of three – seen in the world. At the individual level there is the experiencer-experienced object-experience (bhoktā-bhogya-bhoga), the knower-known-knowledge (pramātā-prameya-pramā), the waking-dream-deep sleep state (jāgrat-svapna-suṣupti), the waker-dreamer-deep sleeper (viśva-taijasa-prājña) and so on. At the totality level there is the Creator-Sustainer-Destroyer (Brahmā-Viṣṇu-Maheśa), the Total Gross-Total Subtle-Total Causal Being (Virāṭ-Hiraṇyagarbha-Īśvara), the three qualities of prakṛti (sattva-rajas-tamas) and so on. The Truth pervades (aśnute iti akṣaram), supports and illumines all these threefold factors of this world.

atra antaraṁ brahmavido viditvā: Even though the goldsmith creates different shapes, sizes and designs of gold ornaments, he buys the raw material and sells it for the price of the gold. The gold is neither created nor destroyed when the shapes change. Gold alone is the essence of the earring, nose ring or anklet.

'Every object has Existence, Consciousness, Bliss, name and form (with properties). The previous three are its changeless essence, the Truth/Brahman and the latter two belong to the changing world and are illusory.'[1]

We need not search for the Truth in the seventh heaven. It is available right here (atra) and now. Within the gross is present the subtle essence. The Truth is to be realised within (antara) as the very inner Self of the seeker.

[1] asti bhāti priyaṁ rūpaṁ nāma cetyaṁśa-pañcakam,
ādyatrayaṁ brahma-rūpaṁ jagadrūpaṁ tato dvayam. – *Dṛg Dṛśya Viveka* 20

līnā brahmaṇi tatparāḥ yonimuktāḥ: Those who consider the Truth as the supreme goal alone (tatparā), will constantly meditate on It with an alert and focussed mind (tatpara). They finally merge in the Truth and become liberated from the cycle of birth and death, never having to be reborn in the wombs of different species.

Terms like 'merging' and 'liberation' can be understood through daily life examples. When a person falls asleep and begins to dream, we can say that the waker 'merges' into the dreamer. When he wakes up we can say that he is 'liberated' from the dream world and the dream body he assumed. Normally, we speak of such experiences as 'I dreamt and I woke up' and not as 'merging' and 'liberation'. When one awakens from the nightmare, one is relieved to be free from the painful state of the dreamer and the horrific dream world one was facing. Imagine the relief of one who awakens to one's imperishable nature and realises that the world is unreal and that one will never be reborn in any womb!

What is the cause of bondage and what is the knowledge that liberates?

संयुक्तमेतत्क्षरमक्षरं च व्यक्ताव्यक्तं भरते विश्वमीशः ।
अनीशश्चात्मा बध्यते भोक्तृभावात् ज्ञात्वा देवं मुच्यते सर्वपाशैः ॥ ८ ॥

Saṁyuktametat-kṣaramakṣaraṁ ca vyaktāvyaktaṁ bharate viśvamīśaḥ,
anīśaścātmā badhyate bhoktṛbhāvāt-jñātvā devaṁ mucyate sarvapāśaiḥ. (8)

संयुक्तम् – combination; एतत् – this; क्षरम् – perishable; अक्षरम् – imperishable; च – and; व्यक्ताव्यक्तम् – the manifest and the unmanifest; भरते – nourishes; विश्वम् – universe; ईशः – the Lord; अनीशः – powerless; च – and; आत्मा – the individual being; बध्यते – bound; भोक्तृभावात् – due to the sense of being the enjoyer; ज्ञात्वा – having known; देवम् – the Lord; मुच्यते – freed; सर्वपाशैः – from all bondages

8. The Lord nourishes this universe, which consists of a combination of the perishable and the imperishable, the manifest and the unmanifest. As long as the jīva does not know the Lord, it is powerless and gets bound by the sense of being the enjoyer, but when it comes to know the Lord, it is freed from all bondages.

The perishable and the imperishable (kṣaram akṣaram): The Lord/God nourishes, sustains and protects the whole world. The world is called viśva as it moves in many ways (vividhaṁ śvayati). This changing world is a combination of the perishable (kṣara) and the relatively imperishable (akṣara). The body changes all the time – old cells die and new cells are continuously created. The individual however remains in this body for a lifetime. Both are sustained and nourished by God who is the absolute imperishable Truth.[1]

The manifest and the unmanifest (vyakta-avyaktam): The manifest world (vyakta) is made up of the gross and the subtle objects or matter. It is experienced by living beings through their gross and subtle bodies. Prakṛti, the infinite potential power of the Lord, is unmanifest (avyakta). It is the cause of the world and contains the individual vāsanās or causal body. The universe is a combination of the manifest and the unmanifest. The gross and subtle merge into the causal state to re-emerge again. However, the absolute unmanifest God/ Truth is beyond both, and is the nourisher of both, the gross and subtle, and the individual and total vāsanās.

Bondage: The individual Self (jīvātmā), even though sustained and nourished by God, feels helpless and powerless (anīśa). He even complains of being godforsaken and orphaned and with no Master to protect him. He gets bound by his compulsive desires to enjoy (bhoktṛ-bhāvāt) which pull him into actions and propel him into a vicious cycle of doing and enjoying.[2]

'The knowledge of pleasures enjoyed previously, the objects of pleasures and the notion of enjoyership

---

[1] kṣara sarvāṇi bhūtāni kūṭastho'kṣara ucyate.
uttamaḥ puruṣastvanyaḥ paramātmetyudāhṛtaḥ,
yo lokatrayamāviśya bibhartyavyaya īśvaraḥ. – *Gītā* 15.16,17

[2] kurvate karma bhogāya karma kartuṁ ca bhuñjate – *Pañcadaśī* 1.30

prompts man into action.'[1] The false notions of doership and enjoyership keep us bound (badhyate) and render us helpless (anīśaścātmā).

A man released the parrot he had kept caged, thinking that it deserved its freedom to fly wherever it wanted and be in nature with its own kind instead of the caged and artificial surroundings of a Mumbai flat. However after a couple of days, the parrot came right back. It had got used to the special food that it got in the home. He happily entered the cage and got itself locked. We are similarly bound by our sense of enjoyership (bhoktṛbhāvāt).

Liberation: When man realises that 'I am neither the doer of action nor the enjoyer of results' he gets liberated from finitude, compulsive desires, desire prompted actions and the joys and sorrows reaped thereof. This Realisation of God/Truth within, liberates him from all shackles. How does this happen?

The individual first must understand that he is not an orphan. It is the Lord that sustains and nourishes him. He starts worshipping the Lord and slowly his mind gets purified and experiences the Lord's grace in many ways. He approaches a Guru and learns, then reflects and contemplates and finally realises the Lord to be the all-illuminating Self (deva) within. He realises that it was the Lord alone who sustained him all along, even when he did not believe in the existence of God or when he ignored or rejected God.

[1] jñānaṁ jñeyaṁ parijñātā trividhā karmacodanā – *Gītā* 18.18

What is the difference and the oneness between the individual and God is explained hereafter.

ज्ञाज्ञौ द्वावजावीशनीशावजा ह्येका भोक्तृभोग्यार्थयुक्ता ।
अनन्तश्चात्मा विश्वरूपो ह्यकर्ता त्रयं यदा विन्दते ब्रह्ममेतत् ॥ ९ ॥

jñājñau dvāvajāvīśanīśāvajā hyekā bhoktṛ-bhogyārtha-yuktā,
anantaścātmā viśvarūpo hyakartā trayaṁ yadā vindate
brahmametat. (9)

ज्ञाज्ञौ – all-knowing and ignorant; द्वौ – the two; अजौ – (the two) unborn; ईशनीशौ – almighty and powerless; अजा – the birthless (māyā); हि – alone; एका – one; भोक्तृभोग्यार्थयुक्ता – which brings about the union between the enjoyer and the object of enjoyment; अनन्तः – infinite; च – and; आत्मा – the Self; विश्वरूपः – of the form of the whole universe; हि – indeed; अकर्ता – non-doer; त्रयम् – the three; यदा – when; विन्दते – knows; ब्रह्मम् – Brahman; एतत् – this

9. The two (Īśvara and jīva) are (respectively) all-knowing and ignorant, almighty and powerless; both are unborn. Prakṛti or māyā alone, unborn, brings about the union between the enjoyer and the object of enjoyment. The Self (Brahman) is infinite, of the form of the whole universe and indeed a non-doer. One becomes liberated when one knows the three (Īśvara, jīva and prakṛti) to be this Brahman.

The earlier mantra explained how we get bound because of the wrong notions of doership and enjoyership and how we are liberated when we realise God/Truth as our own true Self. The same thought is explained here, but in a different way.

I and God: I, the individual (jīva) is finite – with little knowledge (ajña) and little strength (alpaśaktimān), ignorant of my true nature (ajña) and helpless and dependent on the world (anīśa). God (Īśvara) on the other hand is infinite – omniscient (sarvajña) and omnipotent (sarvaśaktimān), ever united with His infinite nature (jña) and the Lord of all (īśa).

Being a part of God, the individual has His characteristics, but in little measure. He therefore desires to know more, increase his power and rule over others. He wishes others to listen to him and do his bidding. He acts like a mini lord over his mini world. However his knowledge is often forgotten or falsified, his mental and physical energy can get sapped away and he can get dethroned from his position of power and can even become enslaved by others whom he commanded. On the other hand God's knowledge, power or lordship never diminishes.

The individual wields one body in each birth which he considers his self (dehātmā) whereas God identifies with all bodies (sarvātmā). But both are unborn. Who indeed has witnessed one's own birth? We are only told by others about the birth in this body. And how can the part exist before the whole to see the birth of the whole/God? How can the individual exist before the Total/God? God does not have a date of birth (His incarnation in a particular form He assumes may be celebrated on a particular day!). The jīvātmā or individual, also does not have a date of birth. His entry and identification with a particular form or body is considered as the birth of his body. However the individual has been identifying with different bodies since beginningless time so he is indeed beginningless. Even though both are unborn, God knows that (jña), but the individual thinks he is born and dies (ajña).

The Divine Power: Prakṛti, the divine power of God ever residing in Him, is also beginningless. Presided over by the Lord, His divine power unites the individual with the results of his actions (kartā-karmaphala-yukta) and the enjoyer with the objects of enjoyment (bhoktṛ-bhogyārtha-yukta).

All is the One Truth: However, the Self (ātmā) or supreme Self (paramātmā) is infinite (ananta) in time and space and therefore eternal and all-pervading. Being of the form of the whole universe (viśvarūpa) it is infinite with respect to objects. Even though infinite it is neither the doer of actions (akartā) nor the enjoyer of results of action (abhoktā). When the individual (jīva) realises the essence of himself, God and His divine power, he understands them to be the one Truth (Brahman) alone. The differences are only relative, their oneness is absolute.

Bhagavān Ramaṇa Maharṣi says, 'All philosophies begin with the naming of the principles of the individual, the world and the Supreme. These three factors exist as long as the 'I' notion is there. They merge into one in the absence of the 'I' notion.'[1]

[1] ārabhyate jīva-jagat-parātma-tattvābhidhānena mataṁ samastam,
idaṁ trayaṁ yāvad-ahaṁ-matiḥ syāt sarvottamā-ahaṁ-mati-śūnya-niṣṭhā.
– *Saddarśanam* 4

All enquiry into the Truth begins with these triple factors. In fact it begins with me and the world. Then arises the question, 'Who created me and this world?' Thus starts the enquiry about God as the creator. When we think about their essence – their true nature – we realise that it is one infinite Truth alone. They all emerge from this infinite Truth alone.

There is another interpretation of the words jña and ajña. The individual being, is a conscious entity, the knower of his world (jña). The world of objects is the known and inert (ajña). The individual is the master of these objects and he owns or disowns them. The objects are owned and dependent. Prakṛti is the power that creates both the individual and the world and brings the individual in contact with the world of objects. However these three factors, the individual (jīva), the world (jagat) and the creative power (prakṛti) are in essence the one infinite Truth (Brahman) alone.

The difference and oneness between God/Truth and His divine power is further elaborated upon.

क्षरं प्रधानममृताक्षरं हरः क्षरात्मानावीशते देव एकः।
तस्याभिध्यानाद्योजनात्तत्त्वभावाद्-भूयश्चान्ते विश्वमायानिवृत्तिः ॥ १० ॥

kṣaraṁ pradhānam-amṛtākṣaraṁ haraḥ kṣarātmānāvīśate deva ekaḥ,
tasyābhidhyānād-yojanāt-tattvabhāvād-bhūyaścānte
viśvamāyānivṛttiḥ . (10)

क्षरम् – perishable; प्रधानम् – matter or prakṛti; अमृताक्षरम् – immortal and imperishable; हरः – the (supreme) God; क्ष रात्मानौ – over the perishable matter and the individual being; ईशते – rules; देवः – God; एकः – one; तस्य – His (essence); अभिध्यानात् – by meditating on; योजनात् – by uniting with; तत्त्वभावात् – by realising; भूयः – repeatedly; च – and; अन्ते – at the end; विश्वमायानिवृत्तिः – cessation of illusion in the form of the universe

10. Matter is perishable, but God/Truth is imperishable and immortal. He, the only God, rules over the perishable matter and the individual soul (jīvātmā). By repeatedly meditating on Him, by uniting with Him, and by realising His essence, at the end, all illusion (in the form of the universe) comes to an end.

The difference: God's divine power (prakṛti) is also referred to as pradhāna, especially in the Sāṅkhya philosophy. 'That in which everything is kept (at the time of dissolution and from which everything is brought out as creation)' is called pradhāna.[1] It alone manifests as this entire world of things and beings and is ever changing and perishing (kṣara). Everything is subject to constant change. Change can be viewed as a process of renewal or as ageing, as a beginning of the new or as the ending of the old, as constant birth or as perennial death.

God/Truth on the other hand is birthless, deathless (amṛta) and changeless (akṣara). Endowed with divine power (pradhāna), God/Truth is represented in the form of Śiva – the auspicious one. In this verse He is called Hara – the one who takes away all (harati). He takes away our ignorance, sorrow and attachments. He is also referred to as Deva – the self-evident Consciousness which illumines all. God/Truth is one (eka) – one without a second or non-dual. He cannot be divided into half or quarter, nor can He be added upon to become two or three. In the scriptures on Tantra, the sound syllable (bījākṣara) 'raṁ' which represents the water element is called amṛtākṣara – the immortal and imperishable. God/Truth rules over nature, the totality of matter (pradhāna) and also the entire creation of ever changing things and beings (jīvātmās) that emerge from the gross and subtle matter.

The oneness: The differences between the perishing things and beings and the immortal God/Truth are obvious and apparent. However their oneness is subtle and absolute. This essential oneness is realised by:

- **a.** abhidhyānāt – meditation: Facing the Truth and showing one's back to the realm of change (abhimukhena dhyānāt), seeing It in every form, in every place and at all times (abhito dhyānāt).

[1] pradhīyate adhīyate asmin iti pradhāna

b. yojanāt – union: Identifying with It as one's own Self.

c. tattva-bhāvāt – Realisation: Owning It as 'I am the immortal Truth' (ahaṁ brahmāsmi).

This practice of meditation has to be done again and again (bhūya) till the ego that creates all the differences ends (ante) and there is the total elimination of māyā.

The liberating Knowledge: Ramaṇa Maharṣi says, 'With the death of the ego the infinite Self shines forth in its pure pristine glory spontaneously in the heart.'[1]

The elimination of māyā (viśva-māyā-nivṛtti): This can be understood as the Total (viśva) elimination (nivṛtti) of illusion, or the illusion of this world created by ignorance (māyā).

In the Realisation of God/Truth the appearance of the world is not eliminated. We continue to perceive and transact in it, but without a sense of reality (satyatva buddhi) and duality and like in a movie, we watch this world, knowing that it is all an appearance.

With God-realisation the wrong notions of reality and duality come to an end (māyā nivṛtti), even though worldly existence and experience of the world continues. But with the fall of the body the worldly existence too comes to a total end – once and for all (viśva nivṛtti).

It is said that during the Mahābhārata war, Karṇa's fire-arrows (agni-astra) had burnt Arjuna's chariot. However

---

[1] ahami nāśabhājyahamahantayā, sphurati hṛtsvayaṁ paramapūrṇasat.
– *Upadeśa Sāraḥ* 20

Śrī Kṛṣṇa's presence kept the chariot in shape and Arjuna continued to fight using it. After the war, the moment Śrī Kṛṣṇa descended from the chariot, it turned to ashes. Similarly the fire of God-realisation burns away the ignorance, ego and duality. However the Man of Realisation continues to function through the body till the karmas (prārabdha) that maintains his body are exhausted.

The result of meditation and Realisation is now explained.

ज्ञात्वा देवं सर्वपाशापहानिः क्षीणैः क्लेशैर्जन्ममृत्युप्रहाणिः ।
तस्याभिध्यानात्तृतीयं देहभेदे विश्वैश्वर्यं केवल आप्तकामः ॥ ११ ॥

jñātvā devaṁ sarvapāśāpahāniḥ kṣīṇaiḥ kleśair-janmamṛtyu-prahāṇiḥ,
tasyābhidhyānāt-tṛtīyaṁ dehabhede viśvaiśvaryaṁ kevala
āptakāmaḥ. (11)

ज्ञात्वा – having known; देवम् – God; सर्वपाशापहानिः – the snapping of all bondages; क्षीणैः क्लेशैः – with the exhaustion of all sorrows; जन्ममृत्युप्रहाणिः – the destruction of (the cycle of) birth and death; तस्य – His (on Him); अभिध्यानात् – from meditation; तृतीयम् – third (state); देहभेदे – on destruction of (the identification with) the body; विश्वैश्वर्यम् – universal lordship; केवलः – the only one (absolute); आप्तकामः – one whose (all) desires are fulfilled (self fulfilled)

11. Having known God, all bondages are snapped, ignorance and sorrows are exhausted, and thereby the cycle of birth and death ends. By meditating on Him, one goes beyond the body and reaches the third state of universal lordship when all desires are fulfilled.

The liberating Knowledge: Bondage is notional. A bear that is born in captivity, gets used to living in a restricted area and even when it is released from its cage, it does not comprehend its freedom. It continues to move around in a limited area as it is still mentally caged.

We may say that we are free, but we all move around within our finite world of attachments and are limited by our thoughts. We may claim to be physically, economically or politically free, but we are bound by a hundred ropes of expectations (āśā-pāśa-śatair-baddhā), our likes, dislikes and prejudices and notions of right and wrong. All these arise due to ignorance or identification with the body. When these ropes of ignorance and wrong notions are cut off, we experience total freedom (niraṅkuśa svātantryam). This state is difficult even to imagine in our present state. It is experienced by knowing God/Truth as our own Self.

God-realisation puts an end to all pain, misery and sorrow (kleśa). It destroys all conflict and confusions. Wherever there is a clash (conflict) there is kleśa. It may be a clash of word or opinions, gross or subtle. Where there is an action, there is a reaction. Wherever there is change, there is a resistance to change.

A God-realised person has no clashes with anyone. He never argues, resists or opposes other's opinions.[1] What has he got to lose or gain by winning an argument? If someone insists that it is night in broad daylight, he accepts it – after all, somewhere it must be night-time!

Ignorance of the Self (avidyā) which gives rise to the identification with the not-Self and the notion of doership in action (ahaṅkāra), which gives results that we like or dislike (rāga and dveṣa) and fears (abhiniveṣa) are considered as the five kleśas in the *Yoga Śāstras*. God-

[1] vijānan-vidvān-bhavate nātivādī – *Muṇḍakopaniṣad* 3.1.4

realisation puts an end to all of them thus ending the cycle of birth and death.

Only when one fully comprehends that one is bound, does one seek to free oneself. Understanding that bondage is notional, we stop blaming others for our sorrow, or trying to find external solutions. We then put forth efforts to remove our wrong notions.

The scriptures advise us to meditate on God/Truth continuously (abhidhyāna). When we realise the Truth as our ownself, the identification with the body drops off (deha-bheda) and we reach the third state of Universal Lordship (tṛtīyaṁ viśvaiśvaryam). Generally, Realisation is said to be the fourth state (turīya) with reference to the three states of waking, dream and deep sleep. Considering the waking and dream as one, here Realisation is said to be the third state. It can also be interpreted differently. Awareness of the body is the first state, of the world – the second state and of God/ Truth – the third state. Ādi Śaṅkarācārya says, 'When the identification with the body ends and the supreme Self is realised, wherever the mind goes, we experience the state of absorption in the Truth alone.'[1]

All desires are fulfilled (āpta kāma) in the state of Realisation. Our desires are countless. If we try to fulfill them one by one, it will be impossible to do so. When one is fulfilled, the other pops up like a tissue in the pull out box. Since we want happiness alone through the fulfilment of

[1] dehābhimāne galite vijñāte paramātmani,
yatra yatra mano yāti tatra tatra samādhayaḥ. – *Dṛg Dṛśya Viveka* 30

desires, when we experience the infinite Bliss within, we are totally fulfilled. We then become the masters of the world, totally independent and free, instead of being enslaved by the world and begging for happiness from objects and beings. We seek nothing from the world and there is nothing more to be gained from the world.

This mantra is explained differently by Śaṅkarācārya. According to him the first line of the mantra describes the result of supreme Knowledge (jñāna) which is liberation whilst living (jīvan-mukti). The second line indicates krama-mukti – liberation in sequence. After the death of the body (deha-bheda), the seeker attains the result of the subtlest worship and meditation (upāsanā or dhyāna) which is the attainment of the highest realm of worldly existence (Brahma-loka). Thereafter through knowledge liberation is attained at the end of the cycle of creation. 'Worship and meditation on the Lord with attributes results in incomparable Lordship and unexcelled worldly joy (in Brahma-loka). Thereafter by giving up identification with the body through Self-realisation, one gains liberation.'[1]

In the Path of Knowledge, worship and meditation are means to purify the mind and become fit for liberation through Knowledge. In the path of worship (upāsanā) knowledge is a means which helps us to meditate on God and through meditation we attain the highest worldly Abode and enjoy great Lordship (viśva-aiśvaryam).

[1] dhyānāt aiśvaryam-atulam aiśvaryāt sukham-uttamam,
jñānena tat-parityajya videho muktim-āpnuyāt. – *Śiva-dharmottara*

What is the highest Knowledge one can attain?

एतज्ज्ञेयं नित्यमेवात्मसंस्थं नातः परं वेदितव्यं हि किञ्चित्।
भोक्ता भोग्यं प्रेरितारं च मत्वा सर्वं प्रोक्तं त्रिविधं ब्रह्ममेतत्॥ १२॥

etajjñeyaṁ nityamevātmasaṁsthaṁ nātaḥ paraṁ veditavyaṁ hi kiñcit, bhoktā bhogyaṁ preritāraṁ ca matvā sarvaṁ proktaṁ trividhaṁ brahmametat. (12)

एतत् – this; ज्ञेयम् – to be known; नित्यम् – ever; एव – alone; आत्मसंस्थम् – existing in one's own heart; न किञ्चित् – nothing whatsoever; अतः परम् – beyond this; वेदितव्यम् – to be known; हि – indeed; भोक्ता – the enjoyer; भोग्यम् – that which is enjoyed; प्रेरितारम् – the motivator; च – and; मत्वा – having understood; सर्वम् – all; प्रोक्तम् – are declared to be; त्रिविधम् – the three forms; ब्रह्मम् – Truth/Reality; एतत् – this

12. This Truth (Brahman) existing ever in the heart alone is to be known; indeed there is nothing whatsoever to be known beyond this. The enjoyer, that which is enjoyed, and the motivator are all declared to be three forms of the Truth (Brahman) alone.

'This' alone (etat eva): The pronoun 'this' indicates that God/Truth is not far away ('that'), but directly experienced within. God/Truth alone is realised as the Self, all else is experienced only as the not-Self.

Should alone be known (jñeyam eva): Some learn many arts, some master the sciences, yet others display various talents or skills. There is no end to what can be learnt. However knowing the knower – the Self in each of us is not an option as in the case of all other knowledges. It should be known by each and everyone (jñeyam eva), as God-realisation makes us fearless and immortal. 'I will tell you that knowledge which should be known, knowing which one attains immortality.'[1] Only when in the human life can we know God/Truth, hence It should be known. 'If this is not known there is a great loss.'[2]

Eternal alone (nityam eva): Everything in this world changes and so does its knowledge and understanding. New research falsifies old theories and even so-called facts change with time. For example, Cherrapunji in India at one time received the highest rainfall in the world and it now faces a water scarcity problem. God/Truth alone is eternal and so is God-realisation.

Within alone (ātmastham eva): God/Truth is all-pervading. But we do not have to go far to realise the Truth as It is seated within us as our own Self. The Self alone is the Truth. The Truth is always available as the Self (nitya ātmastham).

There is nothing greater to be known (nātaḥ paraṁ veditavyaṁ hi kiñcit): God/Truth/Self is infinite, eternal and all-pervading. There is nothing greater than the Truth or beyond the Truth. It is the ultimate that can be known. 'Knowing the Truth is ultimate Knowledge, knowing which all else becomes as good as known and nothing more is left to be known.'[3]

---

[1] jñeyaṁ yattat-pravakṣyāmi yajjñātvā-amṛtam-aśnute – *Gītā* 13.12

[2] na ced-iha-avedīt-mahatī vinaṣṭiḥ – *Kenopaniṣad* 2.5

[3] Yat-jñātvā na-iha bhūyo'nyat-jñātavyam-avaśiṣyate – *Gītā* 7.2

The disciple asks the Master, 'What is that knowing which everything becomes known?'[1] Often we waste time in knowing unimportant things. If only we devote some of our time in knowing the Truth, our life will be fulfilled. Bhagavān Śaṅkarācārya whilst commenting on *Gītā 7.23* writes that the efforts one puts forth remaining the same, the result of knowing the Truth is infinite and quest for material things yields finite and impermanent results. It is sad indeed that man does not understand this simple truth.

All this is the Truth (sarvam etat brahma): The world is always available for our experience and enjoyment. We may however not always get what we want to enjoy. Each of us finds enjoyment according to our individual nature expressed as our likes and dislikes. However all three – the experiencer (bhoktā), the experienced world (bhogyam) and the individual or total nature (prakṛti) are God/Truth alone. The Lord of the universe is the motivator (preritāram), the will and might behind the individuals and the world they experience. However in essence all are the Truth alone.

---

[1] kasminnu bhagavo vijñāte sarvam-idaṁ vijñātaṁ bhavati-iti.

– *Muṇḍakopaniṣad* 1.1.3

The following two verses explain beautifully the process of realising the Truth with the help of meditation on Omkāra.

वह्नेर्यथा योनिगतस्य मूर्तिर्न दृश्यते नैव च लिङ्गनाशः ।
स भूय एवेन्धनयोनिगृह्यस्तद्वोभयं वै प्रणवेन देहे ॥ १३ ॥

स्वदेहमरणिं कृत्वा प्रणवं चोत्तरारणिम् ।
ध्याननिर्मथनाभ्यासाद्देवं पश्येन्निगूढवत् ॥ १४ ॥

vahneryathā yonigatasya mūrtir-na dṛśyate naiva ca liṅganāśaḥ,
sa bhūya evendhanayonigṛhyas-tadvobhayaṁ vai praṇavena dehe. (13)

svadeham-araṇiṁ kṛtvā praṇavaṁ cottarāraṇiṁ,
dhyāna-nirmathanābhyāsāddevaṁ paśyen-nigūḍhavat. (14)

वह्नेः – of fire; यथा – just as; योनिगतस्य – when it lies (latent) in its source; मूर्तिः – form; न – not; दृश्यते – seen; न – not; एव – yet; च – and; लिङ्गनाशः – destruction of subtle form; सः – that (fire); भूयः – repeated; एव – same; इन्धनयोनिगृह्यः – manifested by the rubbing of its source; तद्वा – in the same way; उभयम् – (as in the case of) those two; वै – verily; प्रणवेन – through Oṁkāra; देहे – in the body

स्वदेहम् – one's own body; अरणिम् – the (lower) araṇi; कृत्वा – making; प्रणवम् – Om; च – and; उत्तरारणिम् – the upper araṇi; ध्याननिर्मथनाभ्यासात् – through the churning by the practice of meditation; देवम् – the Lord; पश्येत् – should see; निगूढवत् – seems to be hidden

13. Just as the form of fire is not seen when it is latent in its source, and yet its subtle form is not destroyed, and that same fire can be manifested by the repeated rubbing of its source, indeed in the same way, the Self can verily be realised in the body through the Oṁkāra.

14. Making one's own body the lower araṇi and Om the upper araṇi, through the churning by the practice of meditation, one should see the Lord who seems to be hidden.

Unmanifest to manifest: Just because something is not seen it does not mean it does not exist. Only the immature think that God does not exist because He is not perceived by the senses. Fire (vahni) is immanent in its source (yoni), a piece of wood. Even though wood is cold to touch and does not shine, the subtle form of fire is very much present in the wood. When two pieces of wood are repeatedly rubbed, the resultant friction manifests the fire. Even when the manifest fire is put off, its latent form is not destroyed (naiva liṅga nāśa) and can be manifested again through right efforts.

In the same way God/Truth is always present right within us even though we do not see Him. He can be directly realised by the regular practice of Om meditation. A sāttvika person may experience the joy of peace, one with devotion experiences the joy of all-encompassing love, but only by diligent practice can one abide in the bliss of our true nature. Śrī Haribābā asked the saint Acyutamuni, "May I realise the Truth by your Grace." The saint replied, "Do not be lazy. You will have to know the Truth by your own efforts as It lies within you. Meditate regularly." God/Truth is ever present in the body and is symbolised as 'Om' and therefore meditation can help us realise God/Truth (ubhayaṁ vai praṇavena dehe).

Om Meditation: The sacred fire used for the vaidika rituals was traditionally ignited by the churning of two wooden cups (araṇi) placed one over the other with the help of a rod connecting them. The churning of the rod with a rope created a friction between the cups which kindled the cotton and fuel kept within. The chanting of the mantras whilst churning the cups, purified the fire which was then used for performing the sacred rituals.

In meditation we must consider our body as the lower cup (svadeham araṇiṁ kṛtvā) and Om, the Lord/Truth as the upper cup (praṇavaṁ ca uttara araṇim). In meditation we repeatedly negate – 'I am not the gross body, I am not the subtle or the causal body. I am not the doer of actions, the individual finite self (jīva)' and assert – 'I am the supreme Truth.' This is symbolised in the pulling of each end of the rope towards us in turn whilst churning. This regular practice of negation and assertion (dhyāna nirmathana) results in the direct Realisation of God/Truth (devaṁ paśyet).

The meditation verse by Ādi Śaṅkarācārya has both these aspects. "I am not the mind, the intellect, the ego nor the memory thoughts. Nor am I the ears, the tongue, the nose nor the eyes. I am not the space, the earth, the fire nor the wind element. I am indeed Consciousness-Bliss. Auspiciousness am I. Auspiciousness am I."[1]

[1] mano buddhyahaṅkāra-cittāni nāhaṁ na ca śrotra-jihve na ca ghrāṇa-netre, na ca vyoma-bhūmir-na tejo na vāyuḥ cidānandarūpaḥ śivo'haṁ śivo'ham.
– *Nirvāṇa Ṣaṭkam* 1

We can also take the help of chanting of Om. As we chant we must listen to the sound, then become aware of the silence between two Om sounds and then consider the silence as the Silence beyond sounds and thoughts, as the infinite Truth/God, as one with our own Self. Such meditation is to be done intensely with alertness and total absorption.

The fire of Knowledge: The example of fire is most appropriate. In fire rituals fire carries all the offerings to the Lord. 'It leads us to the path of progress and prosperity.'[1] It always burns upwards or takes us higher. Following the daily fire ritual (agnihotra) brightens our day and enables us to lead a life of virtue. Fire is the presiding deity of speech. Invoking the subtle fire through the chanting of Om ensures a pure and bright mind. Meditating on God/Truth as Om manifests the fire of knowledge that removes the darkness of ignorance to illumine the Truth within.

[1] agne naya supathā rāye asmān – *Īśāvāsya Upaniṣad* 18

The principles explained in the previous two mantras are further emphasised through more examples in the following two mantras.

तिलेषु तैलं दधनीव सर्पिरापः स्रोतःस्वरणीषु चाग्निः ।
एवमात्मात्मनि गृह्यतेऽसौ सत्येनैनं तपसा योऽनुपश्यति ॥ १५ ॥

सर्वव्यापिनमात्मानं क्षीरे सर्पिरिवार्पितम् ।
आत्मविद्यातपोमूलं तद्ब्रह्मोपनिषत्परम् ॥
तद्ब्रह्मोपनिषत्परम् ॥ १६ ॥

tileṣu tailaṁ dadhanīva sarpir-āpaḥ srotaḥsvaraṇīṣu cāgniḥ,
evamātmātmani gṛhyate'sau satyenainaṁ tapasā yo'nupaśyati. (15

sarvavyāpinam-ātmānaṁ kṣīre sarpir-ivārpitam,
ātmavidyā-tapomūlaṁ tadbrahmopaniṣat-param.
Tadbrahmopaniṣat-param. (16)

तिलेषु – in sesamum; तैलम् – oil; दधनि – in yoghurt; इव – like; सर्पिः – butter; आपः – water; स्रोतःसु – in the (underground) rivers; अरणीषु – in the firewood; च – and; अग्निः – fire; एवम् – in the same way; आत्मा – the Self; आत्मनि – in oneself; गृह्यते – is realised; असौ – this; सत्येन – through truth; एनम् – this One; तपसा – through meditation; यः – one who; अनुपश्यति – sees (continuously)

सर्वव्यापिनम् – all-pervasive; आत्मानम् – the Self; क्षीरे – in milk; सर्पिः – butter; इव – like; अर्पितम् – seen; आत्मविद्या-तपोमूलम् – rooted in Self-knowledge and penance; तत् – that; ब्रह्म – Truth (Brahman); उपनिषद् – Upaniṣad; परम् – the highest; तत् – that; ब्रह्म – Truth (Brahman); उपनिषद् – Upaniṣad; परम् – the highest

15. Like oil in sesamum, butter in yoghurt, water in the underground rivers, and fire in the firewood, the Self is realised in oneself by him who sees this One person through truth and meditation.

16. The Self is seen to be all-pervasive like butter in milk, rooted in Self-knowledge and penance; that Truth is the highest Upaniṣad. That Truth is the highest Upaniṣad.

The previous mantra said 'one should see' (paśyet) the Truth. Once the Truth is realised it is seen always (anu-paśyati). For example, once I know that the object I hold in my hand is a book, I always see it as such. It would be impossible to see it as a watch or a television. Anupaśyati could also mean that the Truth even though ever present is seen only after (anu) we meditate regularly.

Right process and right instrument: A specific process and special instruments are required to manifest that which already exists in an unmanifest form. Sesamum seeds (tila), coconut or groundnuts are ground, crushed and pressed in special machines to extract oil from them. Milk is first made into curd or yogurt and then churned with a churner to extract butter. A well is dug or a bore well is drilled and the water is hauled out or pumped out from the underground spring. Wood is rubbed in the araṇi to kindle the sacred fire. Similarly 'the Self/Truth is gained through Self-knowledge with a body and mind well tuned by truthfulness, austerity and self-control.'[1]

[1] satyena labhyas-tapasā hyeṣa ātmā samyag-jñānena brahmacaryeṇa nityam – *Muṇḍakopaniṣad* 3.1.5

The oil potentially present in the sesamum seeds cannot be used to light a lamp and the butter in milk or yogurt as such cannot be used for cooking. The water in the underground spring cannot quench our thirst and the fire in the wood cannot light the fireplace and give us light and warmth. Similarly the Truth in Its unmanifest form cannot benefit us. We remain in ignorance of our blissful nature and suffer through life. Only when we realise the Truth/Self we are in Bliss Absolute.

In the Path of Devotion, it is said that the attributeless (nirguṇa) and formless (nirākāra) God/Truth cannot fill our hearts with love. Only when He incarnates in a particular form like Śrī Rāma or Śrī Kṛṣṇa, are we blessed and become full and fulfilled.

Preparing the instrument: A mind purified by truthfulness and austerity has the strength to abide in the Truth always (anupaśyati).

One who respects the false, never gains the Truth. An intellectual value for the artificial, illusory, apparent or virtual keeps us away from our nature – the real and actual. Truthfulness is to speak as thought of, seen or heard, in a pleasant manner for the benefit of all. We always have a choice in action and so to speak the truth should be chosen by those who seek the Truth.

An indulgent and extroverted lifestyle is unconducive for knowing the Truth within. Tapas is to live a simple and austere life or to follow specific penance to conserve and enhance our energy. 'Concentration of the mind is the highest tapas'[1] and also 'Deep contemplation or meditation is tapas.'[2]

Interestingly in all the above examples heat is needed and generated before the subtle form manifests. Even the well gets heated before the water is tapped from the spring. Similarly, the heat of sorrow in worldly pleasures, the intense desire for liberation, the thirst for knowledge and longing for God, precede the Realisation of God/Truth.

Seen differently, austerity is the outer means (bahiraṅga sādhanā) needed to prepare the mind and Self-knowledge (ātmavidyā) characterised by listening, reflection and meditation are the subtler means (antaraṅga sādhanā) for Self-realisation. The Truth is the source (mūla) for both.

It is interesting that the Truth (Brahman) itself is called Upaniṣad. The Truth is revealed by the Upaniṣad but Upaniṣad itself means knowledge of the Truth. The knower (Self), the known (Truth) and the revealer (Upaniṣad) are one and so the Truth is called Upaniṣad. The last line 'tad-brahmopaniṣad-param' is repeated twice to indicate the end of the chapter.

Summary of the chapter: Four topics are traditionally indicated in the beginning of any treatise. They are the qualification needed to study the treatise (adhikārī), the subject of the text (viṣaya), the result of the study (phala) and the relationship between the knowledge and the result

---

[1] aikāgryaṁ paramaṁ tapaḥ

[2] yasya jñānamayaṁ tapaḥ

(bodhya-bodhaka-sambandha). The first chapter deals with all the above in detail.

The qualified persons are the seekers of Truth (brahmavādinaḥ). The theme of the text is the oneness of the Truth and the Self (brahmātmaikya bodha) or Self-realisation, the result of which is the liberation from all limitation and bondage (jñātvā devaṁ mucyate sarvapāśaiḥ). Thus the first chapter by itself completes the study of the entire Upaniṣad.

Chapter 2

The mantras in this chapter are a little different in style and language and can be interpreted in different ways. The first six mantras appear in the ritual section of the Vedas (karma-kāṇḍa or saṁhitā) wherein their meaning has a ritualistic angle. Since they are included in the Upaniṣad here, some commentators have explained them from the standpoint of knowledge. Our interpretation is based on the commentary of Śaṅkarācārya which is both simple and clear.

The first chapter ended with the thought that God/Truth is hidden in our own heart and has to be realised through meditation (dhyāna-nirmathanābhyāsāt devaṁ paśyet nigūḍhavat). 'Meditation is the highest vocation in life' – Śrī Gurudev. This asks for an extraordinarily alert, concentrated, pure, subtle, strong and firm mind. A car may look sleek, but its engine has to be powerful enough to get us to the top of the mountain. We therefore need to make our mind 'meditation worthy' to enable us to reach the highest.

Prayer is one of the powerful means to do so. Human efforts are limited. God/Truth is infinite. Prayer invokes the infinite power of God and manifests as grace in all we do. Self effort manifests grace and grace strengthens self effort. The following three mantras are both a prayer for grace and a promise of self effort.

युञ्जानः प्रथमं मनस्तत्त्वाय सविता धियः ।
अग्नेर्ज्योतिर्निचाय्य पृथिव्या अध्याभरत ॥ १ ॥

युक्तेन मनसा वयं देवस्य सवितुः सवे ।
सुवर्गेयाय शक्त्या ॥ २ ॥

युक्त्वाय मनसा देवान् सुवर्यतो धिया दिवम् ।
बृहज्ज्योतिः करिष्यतः सविता प्रसुवाति तान् ॥ ३ ॥

yuñjānaḥ prathamaṁ manas-tattvāya savitā dhiyaḥ,
agnerjyotir-nicāyya pṛthivyā adhyābharata. (1)

yuktena manasā vayaṁ devasya savituḥ save,
suvargeyāya śaktyā. (2)

yuktvāya manasā devān suvaryato dhiyā divam,
bṛhajjyotiḥ kariṣyataḥ savitā prasuvāti tān. (3)

युञ्जानः – while engaging; प्रथमम् – first; मनः – the mind; तत्त्वाय – to seek Knowledge; सविता – the Sun-god; धियः – the senses; अग्नेः – of fire; ज्योतिः – the light; निचाय्य – having seen; पृथिव्या अधि – upon the earth; आभरत् – place it

युक्तेन – with that which has been fixed (on the supreme Self); मनसा – with the mind; वयम् – we; देवस्य – of God; सवितुः – of sun; सवे – with the blessings; सुवर्गेयाय – for the highest; शक्त्या – to the best of ability

युक्त्वाय – having united; मनसा – (with) the mind; देवान् – the sense organs; सुवर्यतः – turned towards the blissful Truth (Brahman); धिया – through right knowledge; दिवम् – the effulgence; बृहत् – the great; ज्योतिः – light; करिष्यतः – lead towards; सविता – the sun-god; प्रसुवाति – bless; तान् – them

1. May the Sun-god first engage my mind and the senses to seek Knowledge, and having seen the light of fire, place it upon the earth.

2. With the mind fixed (on the supreme Self), with the blessings of the Sun-god, we shall strive to the best of our ability for the highest.

3. May the Sun-god bless our mind and sense organs which are turned towards the blissful Truth (Brahman), and lead them through right knowledge towards the effulgence of the great light of Consciousness.

The Sun God: Every object has a gross, subtle and spiritual aspect – ādhibhautika, ādhidaivika and ādhyātmika. For example, when introduced casually, we see and know only the gross physical aspect of a person – his name and appearance. The employer needs to know his qualifications, skills, attitude, conduct and so on. This is subtler – related to the mind and intellect. The spiritual Master however sees that person as the Truth.

'God/Truth is one, though called by different names.'[1] Here the prayer is addressed to Savitā, the Sun-god. In Sanskrit, Savitā (like pitā) is a masculine noun. Girls are commonly named Savitā in India as it is a feminine noun in most Indian vernacular languages. The sun too has the three aspects. The sun we perceive (ādhibhautika) is the source of all energy and life on earth. Sun is also the presiding deity

[1] ekaṁ sat viprā bahudhā vadanti

(ādhidaivika) of light and hence of our eyes and all we see. Ultimately the sun stands for the supreme Consciousness, the very core of our existence (ādhyātmika). The prayer is addressed to all the three aspects of the sun.

The prayer: O Sun-god, do bless my mind with the right understanding of meditation. May conducive thoughts create a meditative mood. May my mind not get distracted and remain focussed within (yuñjānaḥ prathamaṁ manaḥ).

The word 'dhiya' refers to the sense organs of perception (eyes, ears, nose, tongue and skin), the five physiological functions (prāṇas), the mind and intellect. May all of these be vitalised and geared towards meditation. First we have to sit still, relax the body, steady the breathing, withdraw the senses, quieten the mind and then focus the intellect on the Truth within. Do bless these efforts (adhyābharat) so that I realise the Truth (tattvāya).

The Vedas say that every function is presided over by a presiding deity (devatā). For example, the sense organs of perception and action get their ability and energy from the respective presiding deities. The eyes can see only in the medium of light and the Sun-god is the presiding deity of light and the eyes. We pray to the respective presiding deities to bless the senses, prāṇas, mind and intellect. When we want to construct a building we have to get permission from various departments like the town planning department, water department and fire department. In case any of them create a problem, we need to approach a higher authority to clear the problem. In the same way, we pray to the Sun-god as the highest authority – supreme God – who would instruct all the presiding deities to empower our senses and mind. Generally our senses are extrovert, directed towards the material world (pṛthivi). We pray to the Sun-god and the presiding deities to help us withdraw from the external and turn inward.

With a mind thus blessed and empowered (yuktena manasā), we promise to put forth the maximum effort to the best of our ability (śaktyā). We shall strive with a firm resolve to realise the Truth (yatātmā dṛḍhaniścaya).

The Truth is here referred to as svarga or heaven. Etymologically svarga means 'there where one experiences bliss' (svar sukham gacchati iti svarga). The Truth/God alone is the source of all joy and therefore svarga here means the highest Bliss of the Self/Truth. *Kenopaniṣad* also uses the word svarga to indicate the blissful Truth in its last mantra. 'One who realises the Truth rejoices and is established in the eternal abode of Bliss.'[1]

God/Truth is called bṛhat-jyoti – the great light, as it is because of Consciousness we are able to see all physical lights, know our senses, organs and the subtle thoughts and ideas of our mind. It is the light of all lights.

'The senses are by nature extrovert.'[2] The mind finds a hundred reasons to be distracted. Old habits die hard. All this we discover whilst actually practising meditation. The third mantra is a prayer to the Sun-god to protect us and

---

[1] anante svarge loke jyeye pratitiṣṭhati – *Kenopaniṣad 4.9*

[2] parāñci khāni vyatṛṇat-svayambhūḥ-tasmāt-parāṅ-paśyati na-antarātman – *Kaṭhopaniṣad* 2.1.1

bless us as we struggle in the seat of meditation and lead us to the light of all lights. Knowing that the compassionate Lord is ever with us we can practice without fear and anxiety. The Lord too says, 'I take care of the needs of those who with an unswerving mind meditate on me.'[1]

The same thought expressed in these three mantras is brought out in the peace invocation – 'sahanāvavatu, saha nau bhunaktu, saha vīryaṁ karavāvahai.' – 'May you protect us... may we strive.' 'O Lord, please protect and empower us and thus protected and empowered by you, we will put forth maximum effort.'

[1] ananyāścintayanto māṁ ye janāḥ paryupāsate,
teṣāṁ nityābhiyuktānāṁ yogakṣemaṁ vahāmyaham – *Gītā* 9.22

Acknowledging the blessings of God, the following mantra urges the seekers to sing His praises.

युञ्जते मन उत युञ्जते धियो विप्रा विप्रस्य बृहतो विपश्चितः ।
वि होत्रा दधे वयुनाविदेक इन्मही देवस्य सवितुः परिष्टुतिः ॥ ४ ॥

yuñjate mana uta yuñjate dhiyo viprā viprasya bṛhato vipaścitaḥ,
vi hotrā dadhe vayunāvideka inmahī devasya savituḥ pariṣṭutiḥ. (4)

युञ्जते – yoke; मनः – the mind; उत – and; युञ्जते – yoke; धियः – the sense organs; विप्राः – seekers of Truth (Brahman); विप्रस्य – who is all-pervading; बृहतः – great; विपश्चितः – omniscient; होत्राः – the rites and rituals; वि दधे – has given (enjoined); वयुनावित् – knower of māyā; एकः – one alone (non-dual); इत् – thus; मही – mighty; देवस्य – of God; सवितुः – of sun; परिष्टुतिः – praise

4. Those who (try to) yoke their mind and the sense organs (to the blissful Self or Paramātmā) should thus sing mighty praises of the Sun-god who is all-pervading, great, omniscient, the knower of māyā and non-dual and has given the rites and rituals (yajñas).

This mantra is addressed to vipras or brāhmaṇas. 'Vipras are those who study the Vedas'[1] and 'Brāhmaṇas are those who know the Truth.'[2] Here the word refers to all spiritual aspirants who meditate on God/Truth by quietening their senses (yuñjate dhiyaḥ) and absorbing their mind in the Truth (yuñjate manaḥ).

[1] vedābhyāsāt bhavet vipraḥ

[2] brahma jānāti brāhmaṇaḥ

The seekers who are trying to meditate thus, should sing the praises of the Lord (savituḥ devasya pariṣṭutiḥ). He listens to their prayers, blesses them and strengthens their resolve. Even a worldly man thanks anyone who does him a favour. Should we not thank the Lord who has blessed us so much? The Lord also reveals many rituals to fulfill our worldly desires (hotrā vidadhe). We should therefore express our gratitude by singing His praise in full measure.

There is always an element of exaggeration in the praise of any worldly object or person. However the Lord has infinite and everlasting attributes in infinite measure. Any praise of Him is but less than what He is. The Lord is indeed all-pervading (vipra-viśeṣeṇa vyāpta), great (bṛhat) or the greatest, omniscient (vipaścitaḥ) and the knower of māyā (vayunāvit – māyā tu vayunāṁ jñānam). A hymn to the great Lord is indeed great (mahī pariṣṭutiḥ).

The intellect focusses on what it values and respects and the mind on what it loves. The more we know the greatness of God, the more we respect and love him and the more our intellect and mind remains fixed on Him. Remembering His glories is therefore an aid to meditation, besides being an expression of our gratitude.

The next mantra is a prayer addressed to the senses and their presiding deities.

युजे वां ब्रह्म पूर्व्यं नमोभिर्विश्लोक एतु पथ्येव सूरेः।
शृण्वन्तु विश्वे अमृतस्य पुत्रा आ ये धामानि दिव्यानि तस्थुः॥ ५॥

yuje vāṁ brahma pūrvyaṁ namobhir-viśloka etu pathyeva sūreḥ,
śṛṇvantu viśve amṛtasya putrā ā ye dhāmāni divyāni tasthuḥ. (5)

युजे – (we) absorb; वाम् – to you both (the senses and the presiding deities of the senses); ब्रह्म – Truth (Brahman); पूर्व्यं – ancient; नमोभिः – with many salutations; श्लोकः – hymn of praise; वि एतु – spread everywhere (in many ways); पथि – in the path; एव – verily; सूरेः – of the seers; शृण्वन्तु – listen; विश्वे – all; अमृतस्य – of Immortality; पुत्राः – children; ये – who; धामानि – abodes; दिव्यानि – celestial; आ तस्थुः – occupy

5. (O senses and the presiding deities of the senses), with many salutations we absorb our mind in that ancient Truth (Brahman). May this hymn of praise (stuti) verily spread everywhere in the path of the seers. Listen, O children of Immortality who occupy the celestial abodes!

Prayer: The mind and senses and their presiding deities play an important role in meditation. When they are well controlled they unite easily with God/Truth. We therefore pray to them with humility (namobhiḥ) to unite us with God (yuje vām) and enable us to realise the Truth (Brahman) which is ancient and eternal (pūrvyam).

In meditation we withdraw our attention from the body and the world of objects (ādhibhautika). The senses and the mind (ādhyātmika) and the presiding deities due to which they function (ādhidaivika) are to be united with God/Truth (yuje vām). This merging into oneness is meditation.

Prostrations: Just as hymns were recommended in the previous mantra as an aid to meditation, here we are asked to prostrate for union with God. Prostrations convey the recognition of our own limitations and acknowledging the glory of the higher force. It is the surrender to the higher power with humility. Many prostrations (namobhiḥ) or repeated prostrations bring humility and softens us. The bamboo which is flexible, bends low and weathers the most terrible storms, whereas the large and upright oak gets uprooted much more easily. Bending before a higher power with a humble attitude keeps us steady even as the storms of desire and disturbances pass over us in meditation.

May this hymn in praise of this knowledge (śloka) spread everywhere in many ways (vi-etu pathyeva) amongst the seers (sūreḥ). May the fame of this hymn and knowledge and the glory of one who has realised this knowledge spread far and wide especially amongst noble people so that they too are inspired to follow this path to the Truth.

The ancient call: The next line is very famous – śṛṇvantu viśve amṛtasya putrāḥ – 'Listen, O children of Immortality'. Sometimes the word 'sarve' is used instead of 'viśve'. This line has many connotations. It is addressed to the presiding deities who are the sons of the immortal creator (Lord Brahmā) and who reside in the celestial abodes in heaven (ye dhāmāni divyāni ātasthuḥ). 'May the glory of God sung by the seekers spread even to the heavenly abodes.' It also means – 'O celestial beings, the glory, eminence and bliss enjoyed by the one who realises the Truth is even greater than that enjoyed by you.' Brahmānanda is greater than svargānanda. It is also addressed to all of us as we too are children of Immortality. We are not born of sin, but indeed from the Immortal Truth and therefore Immortality is our birth right.

What happens when our mind is engrossed in rituals and when it is kept engaged in God is explained in the following mantra.

अग्निर्यत्राभिमथ्यते वायुर्यत्राधिरुध्यते ।
सोमो यत्रातिरिच्यते तत्र सञ्जायते मनः ॥ ६ ॥

agnir-yatrābhimathyate vāyuryatrādhirudhyate,
somo yatrātiricyate tatra sañjāyate manaḥ. (6)

अग्निः – the fire; **यत्र** – where; **अभिमथ्यते** – churned; **वायुः** – the wind; **यत्र** – where; **अधिरुध्यते** – controlled; **सोमः** – the soma juice; **यत्र** – where; **अतिरिच्यते** – flows excessively; **तत्र** – there; **सञ्जायते** – gets engrossed; **मनः** – the mind

6. Where the fire is churned, the wind is controlled, and where the soma juice flows excessively, there the mind gets engrossed.

When our mind is extrovert and we are always engaged and busy with activities – be they worldly or religious, we do get material results, but these create more desires and activities and bind us.

In this context, the churning of the fire (agnir-yatra-abhimathyate) refers to the performance of vaidika rituals where fire is kindled and offerings are made. These rituals also involve the worship of Wind-god, singing His praise and prāṇāyāma or breath control. The juice of the soma offered during the ritual is partaken as His gift – sometimes excessively. This can be understood to mean excessive indulgence. An extrovert and desire filled mind remains ever absorbed in activities unable to think of anything higher. For such people it is better to fulfill their desires through religious activities as it involves physical and mental discipline and a remembrance and worship of a higher power. This prepares the mind for higher spiritual pursuits.

For the spiritual seeker churning of the fire is the practice of meditation. Breath control is a means to concentrate, purify and control the mind and extracting of soma juice is the performance of penance to prepare the body and mind for meditation. The spiritual seeker remains ever absorbed in such activities.

This mantra can also be understood as an instruction for meditation. We are asked to absorb the mind there where speech ends (fire is the deity of speech), the breath slows down and thoughts end – in the experience of objectless bliss (somo yatra atiricyate).

The purpose of life is to realise the Truth. 'If we do so it is good, otherwise it is a great loss.'[1] *Bṛhadāraṇyaka Upaniṣad* says – 'One who realises the Truth and departs from this world is called a brāhmaṇa, a realised one. One who leaves the body without realising is kṛpaṇa, a pitiable person.' It is indeed a loss of a great opportunity – an opportunity to gain the infinite, lost in the pursuit of the finite.

---

[1] iha ced-avedīd-atha satyam-asti na ced-iha-avedīt mahatī vinaṣṭiḥ
– *Kenopaniṣad* 2.5

Having obtained the blessings of the deities, what then should be done by seekers on the spiritual path? The mantra says –

सवित्रा प्रसवेन जुषेत ब्रह्म पूर्व्यम्।
तत्र योनिं कृणवसे न हि ते पूर्तमक्षिपत्॥ ७ ॥

savitrā prasavena juṣeta brahma pūrvyam,
tatra yonim̐ kṛṇavase na hi te pūrtamakṣipat. (7)

सवित्रा – of the Sun-god; प्रसवेन – with the blessings; जुषेत – (must) worship; ब्रह्म – Brahman; पूर्व्यम् – eternal; तत्र – in That; योनिं कृणवसे – abide; न – not; हि – certainly; ते – you; पूर्तम् – the karmas; अक्षिपत् – bind

7. With the blessings of the Sun-god, you must worship the eternal Brahman and abide in it (That). Then certainly the karmas will not bind you.

Rituals like fire worship, idol worship and so on are called iṣṭa karma and social service activities like feeding the poor, tree plantation and so on are called pūrta. Here pūrta represents both types of activities. Interestingly some are interested in one and not the other and think of the other as a waste of time, money and effort.

Actions however noble bind man. Both actions and their results create attachments, pride, strengthen the notion of doership and generally cause disturbance in the mind –

especially during the practice of meditation. Try sitting for meditation in the middle of an extremely busy day!

In order to gain abidance (yoni) in meditation we should serve, worship and be devoted to the eternal and ancient God/Truth who exists before everything. Protection of God will free us from the bondage of action and help us to abide in the Truth.

In other words work done as worship of God will not create further desire prompted actions or disturbances in the mind.[1] Such a steady mind will abide in the Truth and of course Realisation of the Truth will free us from the bondage of action forever.[2]

The sum and substance of all the seven mantras is that we pray to God to bless us and empower us in the practice of meditation so that we realise the Truth.

---

[1] yajñārthāt karmaṇo'nyatra loko'yaṁ karmabandhanaḥ – *Gītā* 3.9
[2] jñānāgniḥ sarva-karmāṇi bhasmasāt kurute tathā – *Gītā* 4.37

The following three mantras give specific guidance for the practice of meditation.

त्रिरुन्नतं स्थाप्य समं शरीरं हृदीन्द्रियाणि मनसा सन्निवेश्य।
ब्रह्मोडुपेन प्रतरेत विद्वान् स्रोतांसि सर्वाणि भयावहानि ॥ ८ ॥

trirunnataṁ sthāpya samaṁ śarīraṁ hṛdīndriyāṇi manasā sanniveśya,
brahmoḍupena pratareta vidvān srotāṁsi sarvāṇi bhayāvahāni. (8)

त्रिः – the three; उन्नतम् – straight; स्थाप्य – keeping; समम् – erect; शरीरम् – the body; हृदि – into the heart; इन्द्रियाणि – the senses; मनसा – with the (help of the) mind; सन्निवेश्य – withdrawing; ब्रह्म-उडुपेन – with the boat of Brahman; प्रतरेत – crosses over; विद्वान् – the wise one; स्रोतांसि – waters; सर्वाणि – all; भयावहानि – fearsome

8. Keeping the three (head, neck and chest) up straight, the body erect, and with the help of the mind, withdrawing the senses into the heart, the wise one crosses over all the fearsome waters with the boat of Brahman (Oṁkāra).

Guidance in Meditation: The first instruction is to 'sit' for meditation. Standing or sleeping are not conducive postures for meditation as the mind is more rājasika and tāmasika whilst standing and lying flat respectively. The mind is more likely to remain calm and alert whilst sitting. One should not directly sit on the ground as our energy gets earthed. The seat (āsana) we sit on should be even and not too soft or hard so that the body remains erect and comfortable. One should sit cross legged in a comfortable posture (āsana) (sukhāsana, padmāsana...) with the head, neck and body held straight and erect, perpendicular to the base. The *Gītā* too says 'keep the head, neck and body in a straight line, still and steady, with the gaze steady (or eyes closed).'[1] Sitting thus, one should keep the body still and relaxed. Proficiency in this is called 'āsana siddhi'. If we are able to sit in meditation posture for forty-five minutes comfortably, without any strain, then we are said to have mastered it. In the beginning we should do it only for ten minutes and then increase the time gradually.

Thereafter with right understanding and the help of the mind we should withdraw the sense organs into the heart. This is called 'uparati' in Vedānta and 'pratyāhāra' in *Yoga Śāstra*. This means the mind should not prompt the eyes to see, ears to hear and so on, thereby all the activities of the senses stop. This is easier said than done.

To help us withdraw the senses and steady the mind we take the help of Omkāra. We must chant 'Om' repeatedly paying full attention to its sound. 'The long and repeated chanting of Om removes fluctuations of the mind.'[2] This helps to steady the senses and quieten the mind. When the mind is calm, we must contemplate on the meaning of Om – the letters A, U, M and the silence between two Om chantings. The silence is the attributeless Truth and the three letters represent the three states of consciousness (waking, dream and deep sleep) or the three bodies (gross, subtle

---

[1] samaṁ kāyaśirogrīvaṁ dhārayannacalaṁ sthiraḥ,
sampreksya nāsikāgraṁ svaṁ diśaścānavalokayan. – *Gītā* 6.13

[2] dīrghaṁ praṇavam-uccārya manorājyaṁ vijīyate – *Pañcadaśī* 4.62

and causal). 'I am the silence, the attributeless Truth that underlies the three states and three bodies.'

Thus with the boat (support) of Om, we can cross over the frightening undercurrents of our senses and mind and reach the banks of the supreme Truth. Instead of Om, any name of God can be used with the same effect. Here 'brahma-uḍupena' could also be interpreted as the support of the Guru and the knowledge of the Upaniṣads which helps us cross over the frightening and vast waters of transmigration (saṁsāra).

The next mantra speaks of the practice of breath-control (praṇayama).

प्राणान्प्रपीड्येह संयुक्तचेष्टः क्षीणे प्राणे नासिकयोच्छ्वसीत।
दुष्टाश्वयुक्तमिव वाहमेनं विद्वान्मनो धारयेताप्रमत्तः॥ ९॥

Prāṇān-prapīḍyeha saṁyuktaceṣṭaḥ kṣīṇe prāṇe nāsikayocchvasīta,
duṣṭāśvayuktamiva vāhamenaṁ vidvān-mano dhārayetāpramattaḥ. (9)

प्राणान् – breath; प्रपीड्य – having regulated; इह – in the seat of meditation; संयुक्तचेष्टः – one who is moderate in all activities; क्षीणे प्राणे – when the breath has become gentle; नासिकया – through the nostrils; उच्छ्वसीत – (should) breathe out; दुष्ट अश्वयुक्तम् – drawn by wild horses; इव – like; वाहम् – a chariot; एनम् – this; विद्वान् – the wise person; मनाः – mind; धारयेत – hold; अप्रमत्तः – alert

9. Moderate and disciplined in all his activities, the wise person regulates his breath (in the seat of meditation) and when it has become gentle, he breathes out through the nostrils. Like controlling a chariot drawn by wild horses, he holds the mind single pointed and alert.

Preparation for prāṇāyāma: Once we are seated in the meditation posture (āsana), still and steady, we proceed to the next step of regulated or controlled breathing (prāṇāyāma). This should be learnt from a competent teacher. *Yoga Śāstra* gives details on how it should be practiced. Śaṅkarācārya in his commentary emphasises the role of 'nāḍi śuddhi' cleansing of the system by simple breathing techniques as a necessary step before the practice of prāṇāyāma.[1] Lightness of the body, a natural glow, good digestion and good hearing indicate the cleansing of the body system.[2]

Prāṇāyāma: All prāṇāyāma practices start with breathing out. The breath is taken in (pūraka), held for a specific count as long as one feels comfortable (antaḥ kumbhaka) and then taken out slowly through the nostrils (recaka) and not through the mouth. The breath is held (bāhya kumbhaka) before the next round of breathing. If these practices are not done with proper guidance, one could even harm oneself.

However the simplest and harmless form is to observe our natural process of breathing (prāṇa vīkṣaṇa). This too can result in a concentrated, pure and subtle mind.

Pratyāhāra: After prāṇāyāma comes pratyāhāra – restraint of the senses, already discussed in the previous mantra. The senses are like untamed wild horses, ever ready to set off in different directions. 'The intellect through the reins of the mind, like an intelligent charioteer, must with an alert mind keep them in control.'[3] The meditator like the charioteer must be ever alert, calm and vigilant and keep the horses on track at all times. Ādi Śaṅkarācārya warns us that meditation must be practiced with 'great alertness and caution'.[4]

---

[1] prathamaṁ nāḍīśodhanaṁ kartavyaṁ, tataḥ prāṇāyāme adhikāraḥ

[2] śarīralaghutā dīptir-jaṭharāgni-vivardhanam,
nādābhivyaktir-ityetat liṅga tacchuddhi-sūcanam. – Śaṅkara Bhāṣyam

[3] susārathiḥ aśvān iva – *Śiva-saṅkalpa Sūkta*

[4] kuru avadhānaṁ mahad-avadhānam – *Bhaja Govindam* 30

Dhāraṇā: This practice of pratyāhāra leads to the next step dhāraṇā – deep concentration of the mind.

However the practice of meditation is possible and becomes effective only for one who leads a moderate life (saṁyukta ceṣṭa) – regular, disciplined and moderation in all activities – eating, waking, sleeping, entertaining or working.[1] An indulgent, hyper-active or excessively extrovert person will be restless in the seat of meditation.

[1] yuktāhāra-vihārasya yukta-ceṣṭasya karmasu,
yukta-svapnvābodhasya yogo bhavati duḥkhahā. *Gītā* 6.17

What is a good place to sit in meditation? The mantra says –

समे शुचौ शर्करावह्निवालुका-विवर्जिते शब्दजलाश्रयादिभिः।
मनोऽनुकूले न तु चक्षुपीडने गुहानिवाताश्रयणे प्रयोजयेत्॥ १०॥

same śucau śarkarā-vahni-vālukā-vivarjite śabda-jalāśrayādibhiḥ,
mano'nukūle na tu cakṣupīḍane guhā-nivātāśrayaṇe prayojayet. (10)

समे – even; शुचौ – clean; शर्करा-वह्नि-वालुका-विवर्जिते – free from pebbles, fire or sand; शब्दजल-आश्रयादिभिः – windy (or noisy) or near a water source or a public place; मनोऽनुकूले – conducive to the mind; न – not; तु – yet; चक्षु-पीडने – painful to the eyes; गुहानिवाताश्रयणे – in a shelter such as a cave, free from wind; प्रयोजयेत् – one should concentrate

10. Concentrate the mind in a place like a windless cave, a place that is clean, even, free from pebbles, fire or sand, which is not noisy or near a water source (public place), a place that is pleasing to the eyes and conducive to the mind.

Conducive place for meditation: Choose a place with a level or plain ground which enables us to sit erect. It should be pure, clean and preferably sacred. If it is a place associated with God or a saintly person the mind will get elevated naturally and spontaneously. Some places are pure, clean and holy by themselves. Otherwise we can make them so by cleaning and placing a picture or idol of God or Guru.

The place should not have any eatables – sugar (śarkarā) which will attract ants or other insects. The place should be without sharp pebbles which could prove quite painful. If the place is near a fire or if it is too hot, damp, sandy or dusty, it will be uncomfortable and difficult to meditate in. Of course such external factors do not affect great adepts like Ramaṇa Maharṣi. An ant hill had formed on Sage Vālmīki while he was in meditation and he was not even aware of it! In our case, even if there are no ants, we feel them crawling all over us!

The place we choose should not be noisy or a place where there is a lot of movement of people and commotion like a railway platform or an airport. Even in nature, a water hole where animals come and go constantly could prove a disturbance or dangerous. The place should be beautiful, pleasing to the eye and conducive to the mind.

Sant Jñāneśvara in his commentary on the sixth chapter of the *Gītā* discusses this subject in detail and describes an ideal place on the bank of a river with a small temple nearby, idyllic natural beauty with the occasional sweet cooing of a bird.

A cave which protects us from the winds and sounds, is secure and protected and free of disturbance, is suggested as an ideal place for solitude and meditation. Today, it is not necessary to go in search of a cave. We can meditate in our own home in our own room at a time when there is least movement and commotion in the home (early morning) – with the telephone switched off! In short the place must be conducive for the practice of meditation with minimum disturbance from external factors.

The signposts of experiences on the path of meditation are hereafter indicated.

नीहारधूमार्कानिलानलानां खद्योतविद्युत्स्फटिकशशीनाम् ।
एतानि रूपाणि पुरःसराणि ब्रह्मण्यभिव्यक्तिकराणि योगे ॥ ११ ॥

nīhāradhūmārkānilānalānāṁ khadyotavidyutsphaṭikaśaśīnām,
etāni rūpāṇi puraḥsarāṇi brahmaṇyabhivyaktikarāṇi yoge. (11)

नीहार-धूम-अर्क-अनिल-अनलानां – of mist, smoke, the sun, wind and fire; खद्योत-विद्युत्-स्फटिक-शशीनाम् – of firefly, lightning, crystal and moon; एतानि – these; रूपाणि – appearances; पुरःसराणि – precede; ब्रह्मणि अभिव्यक्तिकराणि – the manifestation of Truth (Brahman); योगे – in yoga

11. Mist, smoke, the sun, wind, fire, firefly, lightning, crystal, moon – these appearances precede the manifestation of Truth (Brahman) in yoga.

The likely signposts: According to the *Yoga Śāstras*, when the seeker starts practising meditation certain experiences are likely to arise. It is not necessary that they should happen and many more that are not described here could also occur. We may see mist, snow flakes or fog or see smoke, bright or soft light, feel a gush of cool wind or a gentle breeze passing through the spine or over the body, or feel hot air as in the proximity of fire within or outside the body. Some may see a light studded sky or streaks of light or sparks of light as from a crystal or bright light like the moon. These are sensory experiences without the use of the senses. Such extraordinary experiences of sounds, touch, forms, taste and smells are forerunners of the manifestation of the Truth. In fact all appearances are the Truth only manifesting as extraordinary sensual perceptions.

The significance: These experiences mentioned above indicate a state of deep concentration of the mind. It keeps away all ordinary worldly memories and disturbing thoughts at bay. The experiences depend on the nature of meditation and on which of the elements the practitioner is focussing his attention. For example, one focussing on the space element is likely to hear divine sounds or the sound of a conch or bell.

A caution: The seeker should be clearly aware that these experiences are just initial indicators that the practitioner is on the right path. They are by no means the goal of meditation and therefore we should not get attached and start longing for these experiences. 'The Self is beyond sound, touch, form, taste and smell.'[1] When these experiences happen, we should be a mere witness to them with the knowledge that 'I' am the experiencer and not the experienced.

---

1 aśabdam-asparśam-arūpavacca tathārasam nityam agandhavacca
– *Tapovana-ṣaṭkam* 4

These experiences are likely to disappear or be replaced with subtler and more wonderful experiences as the practitioner advances on the path of Yoga. This is explained in the following mantra.

पृथ्व्यप्तेजोऽनिलखे समुत्थिते पञ्चात्मके योगगुणे प्रवृत्ते ।
न तस्य रोगो न जरा न मृत्युः प्राप्तस्य योगाग्निमयं शरीरम् ॥ १२ ॥

pṛthvyaptejo'nilakhe samutthite pañcātmake yogaguṇe pravṛtte,
na tasya rogo na jarā na mṛtyuḥ prāptasya yogāgnimayaṁ
śarīram. (12)

पृथ्वि-अप्-तेज-अनिल-खे समुत्थिते – when the earth, water, fire, air and space are manifested; पञ्चात्मके योगगुणे प्रवृत्ते – when the fivefold attributes of yoga are experienced; न – no; तस्य – for him; रोगः – disease; न – no; जरा – old age; न – no; मृत्युः – death; प्राप्तस्य – for the one who has obtained; योगाग्निम् – made of the fire of yoga; अयम् – this; शरीरम् – body

12. When the earth, water, fire, air and space are manifested, and the fivefold attributes of yoga are experienced, the yogī obtains a body made of the fire of yoga, and no more does he have diseases, old age or death.

The elemental experience: Deeper meditation on the Truth with the support of the five elements and their subtle essence or qualities leads to subtler powers and experiences. For example, the meditator takes the support of the earth element and its essential quality of smell with the bīja mantra 'lam' with the thoughts, 'I am the Truth in the earth element which is in all things and beings in its gross and subtle form. I am the sacred smell that pervades everything.' Such meditation results in oneness with the earth element, power to control all that is created from it, experiences divine smells and so on. 'I am the sweet fragrance of the earth'[1], says Śrī Kṛṣṇa. Such meditation can take us closer to Realisation of the Truth which is the essence of all the elements, all its attributes and whole of creation.

The phenomenal body: In the advanced stage of practice the meditator experiences the essential qualities of the five elements and his body which is also made up of the five elements is transformed into a subtle form in the fire of yoga – the practice of meditation. The cells in our body too change every few years. The old ones wear out and are replaced by new ones. But we still age in time. However every cell in a yogi's body is renewed and he becomes younger. The process is completely different from what we experience. His body is no more prone to disease, old age or death. He can leave his body at will. I once met a saint who was 350 years old. Now he has given up his body. It is not easy to comprehend such a phenomenon. Meditation on the five elements as the Truth is given in great detail in the 'upaśama' section of *Yogavāsiṣṭha*, and the *Yoga Yājñavalkya Saṁhitā*.

[1] puṇyo gandhaḥ pṛthivyāṁ ca – *Gītā* 7.9

The indicators before a yogi attains this phenomenal transformation of the body are described in the next mantra.

लघुत्वमारोग्यमलोलुपत्वं वर्णप्रसादं स्वरसौष्ठवं च ।
गन्धः शुभो मूत्रपुरीषमल्पं योगप्रवृत्तिं प्रथमां वदन्ति ॥ १३ ॥

laghutvam-ārogyam-alolupatvaṁ varṇa-prasādaṁ svara-sauṣṭhavaṁ ca,
gandhaḥ śubho mūtrapurīṣam-alpaṁ yogapravṛttiṁ prathamāṁ vadanti. (13)

लघुत्वम् – lightness; आरोग्यम् – good health; अलोलुपत्वम् – non covetousness; वर्णप्रसादम् – glowing complexion; स्वरसौष्ठवम् – sweetness of voice; च – and; गन्धः – fragrance; शुभः – sweet; मूत्रपुरीषम् – urine and faeces; अल्पम् – scanty; योगप्रवृत्तिम् – of progress in yoga; प्रथमाम् – the first (signs); वदन्ति – (they) say

13. It is said that the first signs of progress in yoga are : lightness, good health, non covetousness, glowing complexion, sweetness of voice, sweet fragrance, and scanty output of urine and faeces.

The signposts: The following seven signs are indicative of the progress to the yoga practitioner much before his body is totally transformed:

a. **Lightness (laghutva):** The body becomes light and feels ever fresh and active. There is no trace of laziness, or lethargy.
b. **Health (ārogya):** The body becomes healthy and there is a sense of well-being. The mind generally

gets focused on pain. The yogi, being free from pain and disease is able to effortlessly lift his mind away from the body and focus on the Truth.

c. **Non coveteousness (alolupatva):** The habit of desiring to possess anything and everything makes people go on buying binges. The practitioner of yoga feels no craving for worldly possessions. The sense pleasures do not disturb or distract him during meditation or otherwise.

d. **Glowing complexion (varṇa prasāda):** Besides the glow due to good health, the skin of a yoga practitioner shines because of the joy, peace and beauty experienced within.

e. **Sweetness of voice (svara sauṣṭhava):** It does not mean that a yoga practitioner will start singing sweetly, but his voice becomes sweet and attractive as do his words and gestures. Even when gently and softly spoken, his words have a power and kindle joy, love and peace in the listener.

f. **Fragrance (śubha gandha):** It is said that an apple a day keeps a doctor away, but an onion a day would keep everyone away! Even in case of ordinary people, there is a noticeable difference in the body odour of the one who smokes, drinks alcohol and eats non vegetarian food and one who eats 'sāttvika' food. It is said that the heavenly deities do not stay long on earth as they cannot stand human odour! The body of the yogi does not bring out any bad odour, but emanates a fragrance. Many saints have been known to emanate fragrances like sandalwood and even objects touched by them would have the fragrance. Even their faecal matter would have no bad odor.

g. **Scanty urine and faeces (alpa mūtra-purīśa):** As the food intake decreases and digestion becomes strong, the urine and faeces decrease.

The Lord's creative power, māyā is twofold – the power of activity (kriyā śakti) and the power of knowledge (jñāna śakti).[1] Through the concentration on the prāṇas or vital air, the kriyā śakti is invoked and various extraordinary powers (siddhis) and various physical changes as described above can take place. If the practitioner focusses on the jñāna śakti, then the knowledge of the Truth takes place.

[1] citta-vāyavaścitkriyā-yutāḥ, śākhayor-dvayī śakti-mūlakā.
– *Upadeśa Sāraḥ* 12

The final goal of yoga is explained in the following two mantras:

यथैव बिम्बं मृदयोपलिप्तं तेजोमयं भ्राजते तत्सुधान्तम् ।
तद्वात्मतत्त्वं प्रसमीक्ष्य देही एकः कृतार्थो भवते वीतशोकः ॥ १४ ॥

यदात्मतत्त्वेन तु ब्रह्मतत्त्वं दीपोपमेनेह युक्तः प्रपश्येत् ।
अजं ध्रुवं सर्वतत्त्वैर्विशुद्धं ज्ञात्वा देवं मुच्यते सर्वपाशैः ॥ १५ ॥

yathaiva bimbaṁ mṛdayopaliptaṁ tejomayaṁ bhrājate tat-sudhāntam,
tadvātmatattvaṁ prasamīkṣya dehī ekaḥ kṛtārtho bhavate vītaśokaḥ. (14)

yadātmatattvena tu brahmatattvaṁ dīpopameneha yuktaḥ prapaśyet,
ajaṁ dhruvaṁ sarvatattvair-viśuddhaṁ jñātvā devaṁ mucyate sarvapāśaiḥ. (15)

यथा एव – just as; बिम्बम् – a disc; मृदया – with earth; उपलिप्तम् – covered; तेजोमयम् – as full of light; भ्राजते – shines; तत् – that; सुधान्तम् – when cleaned well; तत् वा – so too (in the same way); आत्मतत्त्वम् – the truth of the Self; प्रसमीक्ष्य – realising; देही – the embodied being; एकः – non-dual; कृतार्थः – fulfilled; भवते – becomes; वीतशोकः – free from sorrow

यदा – when; आत्मतत्त्वेन – as the Self (Ātmā); तु – verily; ब्रह्मतत्त्वम् – the Truth (Brahman); दीप-उपमेन – like a lamp (effulgent); इह – here (in meditation); युक्तः – yogī; प्रपश्येत् – realises; अजम् – unborn; ध्रुवम् – eternal; सर्वतत्त्वैः – from all modifications; विशुद्धम् – free; ज्ञात्वा – having known; देवम् – Divine Being; मुच्यते – released; सर्वपाशैः – from all bondages

14. Just as a (metal) disc covered with earth shines as full of light when cleaned well, so too the embodied being, realising the truth of the Self, becomes non-dual, fulfilled and free from sorrow.

15. When the yogī, with the mind absorbed here in meditation, realises the Truth (Brahman) verily as the Self (Ātman) like a lamp (effulgent), knowing the Divine Being as unborn, eternal and free of all modifications, he is released from all bondages.

The final goal: Extrasensory perceptions, extraordinary powers or transformation of the body is not the primary aim of yoga. If the meditator gets attached or takes pride in them, they become an obstacle in his spiritual journey. They are to be considered merely as signposts of progress on the path to the Truth. To realise the Truth as one's own Self (ātmatattvena) is the final goal of meditation.

The gold ore from the mine appears black. Layers of coverings are removed by many processes to bring out the natural shine of gold. Similarly the practice of meditation removes the layers of ignorance and false notions like 'I am finite' and 'I am the body' which covers the ever shining Self within.

The Truth (Brahman) is infinite, unborn, birthless and not preceded or caused by anything else. It is the uncaused cause of the whole universe. It is eternal and unchanging and free of all extraneous factors and free of ignorance and its effects. Just like the light of the lamp, the Truth or Self is self-evident and illumines all our thoughts and senses.

Here the words Truth (Brahman), Self (Ātmā) and Divine Being (Deva) are used for the Absolute One, with shades of meaning worth noticing. Ātmā indicates the subject 'I', the Knower, the Illuminator, the Consciousness in the individual body. Brahman indicates the infinite substratum of the entire universe. Deva indicates God (Īśvara), the Divine Being wielding the inscrutable power of māyā, the Lord of the universe who alone incarnates as Śrī Rāma or Śrī Kṛṣṇa. Brahman is the formless attributeless (nirguṇa nirākāra) Truth and Deva is the Lord with form and attributes (saguṇa sākāra). The seeker in meditation realises that the Self in me (Ātmā) is itself the substratum of the universe (Brahman) and the Divine Being (Deva) that assumes different forms (avatāras) at different times. When someone asked Tulasīdāsa, "Does God have a form, or is He formless?" He replied, "In the eyes He is with form, in the heart, He is formless." There is no conflict at all. Not understanding this, many say that Hindus believe in many Gods and some Hindus even get confused which God they must worship! However there need not be such confusion as Truth/God is one alone.

The result: To realise this Truth directly as our own Self brings total fulfilment as there remains nothing more to be gained in life. In the Realisation of Truth, the seeker becomes free from all bondages and sorrows.

People who climb the tall palm trees to pluck the palm fruit from which alcohol is made, are called pāśis. They tie their ankles with a rope (pāśa) to encircle the tree and also another rope around the waist which is tied to the tree. Thus yoked to the tree they make a strenuous climb upwards.

We too are tied with the ropes of ignorance, desires and attachments to the tree of life and make strenuous efforts for little fruits which are often illusive. Self-knowledge frees us from all bondages.

The next two mantras explain the immanent nature of the Truth.

एष ह देवः प्रदिशोऽनु सर्वाः पूर्वो ह जातः स उ गर्भे अन्तः ।
स एव जातः स जनिष्यमाणः प्रत्यङ्जनांस्तिष्ठति सर्वतोमुखः ॥ १६ ॥

यो देवो अग्नौ यो अप्सु यो विश्वं भुवनमाविवेश ।
य ओषधीषु यो वनस्पतिषु तस्मै देवाय नमो नमः ॥ १७ ॥

eṣa ha devaḥ pradiśo'nu sarvāḥ pūrvo ha jātaḥ sa u garbhe antaḥ,
sa eva jātaḥ sa janiṣyamāṇaḥ pratyaṅ-janāṁstiṣṭhati
sarvatomukhaḥ. (16)

yo devo agnau yo apsu yo viśvaṁ bhuvanam-āviveśa,
ya oṣadhīṣu yo vanaspatiṣu tasmai devāya namo namaḥ. (17)

एषः ह – this very; देवः – God; प्रदिशः – the directions; अनु – the intermediate (directions); सर्वाः – all; पूर्वः ह – as the first; जातः – was born; सः उ – He, again; गर्भे अन्तः – in the womb; सः – He; एव – verily; जातः – the one born; सः – He; जनिष्यमाणः – the one going to be born; प्रत्यङ् – within; जनाः – all beings; तिष्ठति – exists; सर्वतोमुखः – one who has faces everywhere

यः – one who; देवः – God; अग्नौ – in fire; यः – one who; अप्सु – in water; यः – one who; विश्वम् – entire; भुवनम् – creation; आविवेश – entered; यः – one who; ओषधीषु – in herbs; यः – one who; वनस्पतिषु – in trees; तस्मै देवाय – to that God; नमः नमः – salutations again and again

16. This very God is all the directions and all the intermediate directions. He was born as the first. He, again, exists in the womb. He, verily, is the one born; He is also the one going to be born. He exists in all beings; He has His faces everywhere.

17. Salutations again and again to that God who is in the fire, who is in the water, who has entered into the entire creation, who is in the herbs and who is in the trees.

God is everywhere: God/Truth pervades all the main and intermediate directions, above and below. He alone is born as Brahmā, the First born Creator, the father of all (paraṁ pitā). He alone is the father who then assumes the form of the foetus in the womb. A pregnant woman must understand that the Divine Being is in her womb. The *Aitareya Upaniṣad* (2.1.3) therefore urges the husband to take good care of the pregnant wife.[1] It is God alone who is born as the little baby and He alone will be born again and again in many forms in future, not only as a human child, but as every species. Puppies, kittens, calves, lion cubs and the young ones of all species look absolutely divine and it is easier to appreciate God in them.

God is indeed the inner Self of all beings. Since every face is His, He faces everywhere. A Marāṭhi song says, 'Lord Śiva is standing in front of me and also behind me. He looks at me from both sides.'[2] He alone looks at us through every face we see. But do we see Him?!

[1] sā bhāvayitrī bhāvayitavyā bhavati

[2] māge ubhā maṅgeṣa, puḍhe ubhā maṅgeṣa, donhi kaḍe deva mājhā pāhato āhe.

Not only is God within all, He is also outside as the five elements pervading the entire universe of countless cosmoses. He alone is present in the entire plant and animal kingdom, in everything inert and sentient.

That is why the Hindus worship everything – mountains, rivers, trees, plants, the sun, moon and the stars. They understand that 'whatever is seen or heard of in the world, both inside and outside, is pervaded by God.'[1] Not understanding this they were looked down upon as primitive stone worshippers or nature worshippers instead of enlightened ones.

With repeated salutations to the all-worshipful God who is everywhere, we come to the end of the second chapter of this Upaniṣad.

[1] yacca kiñcit jagat sarvaṁ dṛśyate śrūyate'pi vā.
antar-bahiśca tatsarvaṁ vyāpya nārāyaṇaḥ sthitaḥ.
– *Nārāyaṇa Sūktam* 1.10, 2.1

Chapter 3

In the famous statement 'That thou art' (tat tvam asi), 'that' refers to the true nature of the omniscient, omnipotent God, 'thou' refers to the true nature of the finite individual, you and me, and 'art' refers to their essential oneness. The first chapter revealed the main theme of the Upaniṣad which is to realise this oneness. The second chapter spoke about meditation as the means to realise this oneness. The third chapter now elaborates on God and His true nature (tat pada śodhana).

The first two mantras speak about the various powers of God.

य एको जालवानीशत ईशनीभिः सर्वांल्लोकानीशत ईशनीभिः ।
य एवैक उद्भवे सम्भवे च य एतद्विदुरमृतास्ते भवन्ति ॥ १ ॥

एको हि रुद्रो न द्वितीयाय तस्थुः य इमाँल्लोकानीशत ईशनीभिः ।
प्रत्यङ् जनांस्तिष्ठति सञ्चुकोचान्तकाले संसृज्य विश्वा भुवनानि गोपाः ॥ २ ॥

ya eko jālavān-īśata īśanībhiḥ sarvāṁllokān-īśata īśanībhiḥ,
ya evaika udbhave sambhave ca ya etad-vidur-amṛtāste bhavanti. (1)

eko hi rudro na dvitīyāya tasthuḥ ya imām̐llokān-īśata īśanībhiḥ,
pratyaṅ janāṁs-tiṣṭhati sañcukocāntakāle saṁsṛjya viśvā bhuvanāni gopāḥ. (2)

यः – one who; एकः – non-dual; जालवान् – possessor of the net (māyā); ईशते – rules; ईशनीभिः – through His divine powers; सर्वान् – all; लोकान् – the worlds; ईशते – rules; ईशनीभिः – through His powers; यः – one who; एव – alone; एकः – one; उद्भवे – when endowed with His glories; सम्भवे – at the time of creation; च – and; यः – one who; एतद् – this; विदुः – know; अमृताः – immortal; ते – they; भवन्ति – become

एकः – one; हि – only; रुद्रः – Rudra; न – no; द्वितीयाय – second; तस्थुः – remains; यः – one who; इमान् – these; लोकान् – worlds; ईशते – rules; ईशनीभिः – with His divine powers; प्रत्यङ् – in; जनान् – all beings; तिष्ठति – dwells; सञ्चुकोच – withdraws (them) into Himself; अन्तकाले – finally; संसृज्य – having created; विश्वा – all; भुवनानि – the worlds; गोपाः – protects

1. He who is non-dual and being the possessor of the net (māyā), rules through His divine powers. He rules over all the worlds through His powers and is the one alone endowed with glories at the time of creation. Those who know this become immortal.

2. There is only one Rudra and no second beside Him. He rules all these worlds with His divine powers. He dwells in all beings. Having created all the worlds, He protects them and then finally withdraws them into Himself.

God is one (eko deva): This statement is repeated often in many mantras in this Upaniṣad and also in all Hindu scriptures. Unfortunately the concept of many Gods has become so deeply entrenched in the psyche of some that reading, listening or intellectual understanding about God being one still does not remove the false notions.

God is infinite and infinity can be only one. All is included in infinity. Nothing can be added or subtracted from it. All names, forms, qualities, powers and concepts are included and possible in God. He naturally has none to oppose Him and there is no one equal or contender for Him, leave alone anyone greater than Him.

Those who know that one infinite God, want nothing else. They live for the sake of God alone. Mīrābāi, the great saint sings, 'For me there is only one God – Giridhara Gopāla and no one else (in this world).'[1] If someone says they want something apart from the infinite God, they have not understood God or Infinity.

It also means that all that the word God implies fits only one entity – God. For example, the word 'lamp' could mean a table lamp or an oil lamp. The word 'table' could imply the tabletop or the entire table or the word 'lion' could mean any lion in India or Africa. But God/Truth means only one entity – the One that can manifest as many without any intrinsic change.

God wields māyā (jālavān): God has infinite potential. He wields His inscrutable and infinite power of māyā which is like a net in which all beings get caught. A fisherman spreads his fishing net far and wide. He himself never gets caught, but hundreds of small and big fish get caught in the net. However one that swims near the feet of the fisherman is not trapped. The beings of the entire world seem enmeshed in māyā's net. 'Only those who surrender to Him are able to

[1] mero to giridhara gopāla dūsaro na koi

cross over this very evident and difficult to cross, māyā.'[1] God is like a magician (māyāvi), who casts His spell of magic (māyā) due to which we are unable to see Him and remain engrossed in His illusory and fascinating world.

God, the Ruler: God controls His various powers – the power of creation, sustenance and destruction or the power to bless, reward and punish (anugraha, nigraha). We too have these powers in limited measures, but we have little control over them. In fact we are controlled by them. Do we not unwittingly create disturbances or break relationships and neither our blessings nor curses are effective. If we say, "Go to hell", the other person replies, "Meet you there!"

At the individual level there is the power to see, hear, smell, talk, walk, think and so on. Through these powers, the Lord rules over the entire universe and all beings in it. Each cosmos (brahmāṇḍa) consists of many worlds or realms of experiences (lokas – bhūḥ, bhuvaḥ, suvaḥ, mahaḥ, janaḥ, tapaḥ, satyam, atala, vitala, sutala, talātala, mahītala, rasātala and pātāla). There are countless cosmoses with countless lokas. The Lord is the ruler of all the countless cosmoses of this universe with countless beings (ananta koṭi brahmāṇḍa nāyaka).

Each cosmos has its own in charges for production, maintenance and destruction departments (Brahmā, Viṣṇu, Maheśa). Through them He creates, sustains and destroys the worlds. His laws – the laws of nature, are infallible. Because of them, the wind blows, water flows, the planets,

[1] māmeva ye prapadyante māyāmetāṁ taranti te – *Gītā* 7.14

stars and galaxies revolve, the eyes see, the food gets digested and all beings live. He is endowed with all glory, splendour and majesty (udbhava) which manifests in full through the creation (sambhava) of this multifarious world. Remaining within all beings He controls man through his conscience and through circumstances and laws that govern his body and mind. For example, when we regularly overeat we become obese, the doctor warns us and our mind too tells us to stop.

God is Rudra: God earlier referred to as Savitā, the Sun, is now called Rudra. There are several meanings to this word.

1. Rudra is another name of Śiva – the auspicious One.
2. Rudra is 'One who makes others cry' – (rodayati iti). God gives the results of action (karma phala dātā). The evildoers cry when they receive the punishment for their evil deeds. Do not imagine a cruel God in heaven, punishing the wicked. It is God's law that we reap what we sow. Anger is its own punishment. It means that, His infallible laws, function in His presence.
3. Rudra is 'One who makes His devotees cry when their hearts are filled with love for Him.'
4. Rudra is 'One who removes (melts away) the disease of transmigration (saṁsāra).'[1] He is also called the doctor or medicine (cure) for the disease of saṁsāra – bhiṣaje bhavarogiṇām.

God is immortal: Those who realise God as their own inner Self also become immortal. Immortality is not just continuity

[1] rujaṁ drāvayati iti rudraḥ

in time. Becoming immortal does not mean that we retain our body and do not die. It would not be a very happy state to watch all our loved ones depart and live on without them! It means to know the Truth/God/Self to be beyond time and change. Its practical implication is to become free from fear of change and death. Immortality brings fearlessness (abhayaṁ pratiṣṭhāṁ vindate). It also means that the Realised one manifests the Lord's immortal and divine powers in his life.

The Cosmic Form of God is now briefly described.

विश्वतश्चक्षुरुत विश्वतोमुखो विश्वतोबाहुरुत विश्वातस्पात्।
सं बाहुभ्यां धमति संपतत्रैर्द्यावाभूमी जनयन्देव एकः॥ ३॥

viśvataś-cakṣuruta viśvato-mukho viśvato-bāhuruta viśvātaspāt,
saṁ bāhubhyāṁ dhamati sampatatrair-dyāvābhūmī janayan-deva ekaḥ. (3)

विश्वतः – everywhere; चक्षुः – eye; उत – and; विश्वतोमुखः – mouth everywhere; विश्वतः – everywhere; बाहुः – hands; उत – and; विश्वतस्पात् – feet everywhere; बाहुभ्याम् – with hands; सम् धमति – unites; संपतत्रैः – with feet and wings; द्यावाभूमी – the heaven and earth; जनयन् – having created; देवः – the Lord; एकः – one alone

3. His eyes are everywhere; His mouth, hands and feet are everywhere. This shining Lord who is one alone, having created the heaven and earth, unites (all beings) with hands, feet and wings.

viśvataścakṣu viśvatomukha: God has eyes and mouths everywhere. It means that all eyes and mouths in all living beings are His alone. Here eyes represent all perception and knowledge (jñāna) and mouth represents all enjoyments (bhoga). It is God alone who perceives all, knows all and enjoys all, through all living beings. We can see Him in the innocent gaze of a child, the powerful speech of an orator, or a hot meal enjoyed when hungry. Sipping a hot cup of coffee Śrī Gurudev once remarked, "Who says there is no Brahmānanda – the Bliss of God in coffee?" As long as our attention remains on the true source we will not get attached to any perception or enjoyments. The devotee therefore prays – May we always behold Thee everywhere and listen to and sing Thy glories.

viśvato-bāhu viśvatas-pāt: God has hands and feet everywhere. All hands and feet are His alone. They signify all action and movement. God can be seen in the leap of a frog, the firm grasp of an infant or the quick response of a touch-me-not.

bāhubhyāṁ saṁ-dhamati patatraiḥ: It is God alone who blesses all the beings in the world with the bodies to go through the results of their actions in the different realms of experiences like the earth and the heaven that He creates. He gifts hands and legs to humans and wings to the birds. The word 'patatra' means 'that which protects us from falling' (patantaṁ trāyate iti) which refers to both legs and wings without which animals and birds would fall to the ground.

The mention of hands has a special meaning. Animals walk on fours, but we stand on two legs and are gifted with hands with fingers and thumb due to which many more possibilities stand before us. Hands represent the capacity to think and act (karma śakti) and self effort (puruṣārtha) because of which we can progress and attain even divinity. We are therefore asked to look at our hands each morning and remember that Lakṣmī (wealth), Sarasvatī (knowledge) and Govinda (Lord Himself) reside in our hand.[1] We can work to get wealth, knowledge or Divinity. In essence God creates the world and all beings and endows them with special faculties. Human beings are specially endowed so that they can realise God.

[1] karāgre vasate lakṣmī karamadhye sarasvatī,
karamūle tu govindaḥ prabhāte karadarśanam.

Having had a glimpse of His cosmic form, the seeker prays thus:

यो देवानां प्रभवश्चोद्भवश्च विश्वाधिपो रुद्रो महर्षिः।
हिरण्यगर्भं जनयामास पूर्वं स नो बुद्ध्या शुभया संयुनक्तु ॥ ४ ॥

yo devānāṁ prabhavaścodbhavaśca viśvādhipo rudro maharṣiḥ, hiraṇyagarbhaṁ janayāmāsa pūrvaṁ sa no buddhyā śubhayā saṁyunaktu. (4)

यः – one who; देवानाम् – of all the deities; प्रभवः – origin; च – and; उद्भवः – source; च – and; विश्वाधिपः – the Lord of the entire universe; रुद्रः – Rudra; महर्षिः – all knowing; हिरण्यगर्भम् – Hiranyagarbha; जनयामास – brought into being; पूर्वम् – initially; सः – He; नः – us; बुद्ध्या – with thoughts; शुभया – (with) auspicious (or noble); संयुनक्तु – (may) endow

4. May Rudra who is the origin of all the deities and the source of all their powers, who is all knowing and the Lord of the entire universe, who initially brought into being Hiranyagarbha, do endow us with auspicious (noble) thoughts.

God (Rudra) the Creator of heavenly deities: God is the origin (prabhava) of all celestial beings and the presiding deities of all laws and departments that run this universe. He alone is the source of all their powers, might and glories (udbhava). In Kenopaniṣad there is a story that the fire god (agni devatā) could not even burn a blade of grass nor the wind god (vāyu devatā) blow it when challenged by God in the form of a Yakṣa. Śrī Gurudev would say, "They could not even dry the dew drop on the blade of grass with the force of a forest fire or a tornado." All power comes from Him alone. **God (Rudra) the Creator of the Creator:** He alone is the cause of all causes. He alone assumes the form of Hiraṇyagarbha, the Creator of the universe (hiraṇya – world + garbha – womb). Hiraṇya also means knowledge. Knowledge preceeds any creation. Even to make a good side dish, culinary knowledge is needed. God is the very womb of all knowledge.

Prayer to God: The intellect is what distinguishes us from other animals. It is gifted with choice, discrimination, understanding and ideals. However by its disuse or misuse we can bring about our own doom. Thoughts that take us away from goodness and our true nature bring sorrow. Hence the seeker prays fervently 'May we always entertain noble thoughts. May we be blessed with auspicious thoughts of serving others, improving ourselves, seeing the Lord in all and reaching the highest goal.' This prayer is important and therefore repeated in two more mantras in the next chapter. Lord Śrī Kṛṣṇa says, 'I unite you with such thoughts by which you can attain Me.'[1]

[1] dadāmi buddhiyogaṁ taṁ yena mām-upayānti te – *Gītā* 10.10

The following two prayer mantras also appear in the famous *Rudra Sūktam* which is found in the Saṁhitā portion of the Veda.

या ते रुद्र शिवा तनूरघोरापापकाशिनी ।
तया नस्तनुवा शन्तमया गिरिशन्ताभिचाकशीहि ॥ ५ ॥

यामिषुं गिरिशन्त हस्ते बिभर्ष्यस्तवे ।
शिवां गिरित्र तां कुरु मा हिंसीः पुरुषं जगत् ॥ ६ ॥

yā te rudra śivā tanūr-aghorāpāpakāśinī,
tayā nastanuvā śantamayā giriśantābhicākaśīhi. (5)

yāmiṣuṁ giriśanta haste bibharṣyastave,
śivāṁ giritra tāṁ kuru mā hiṁsīḥ puruṣaṁ jagat. (6)

या – that; ते – your; रुद्र – O Rudra; शिवा – auspicious; तनूः – form; अघोरा – gentle (not terrifying); अपापकाशिनी – which removes all sins; तया – with that; नः – us; शन्तमया तनुवा – with auspicious form; गिरिशन्त – O Giriśanta (Lord who while residing on a mountain spreads joy); अभिचाकशीहि – please look

याम् – which; इषुम् – arrow; गिरिशन्त – O Giriśanta (the Lord who while residing on a mountain spreads joy); हस्ते – in hand; बिभर्षि – (you) hold; अस्तवे – ready to shoot; शिवाम् – auspicious; गिरित्र – O Giritra (the protector of the mountain); ताम् – that; कुरु – do; मा – not; हिंसीः – to destroy; पुरुषम् – any person or creature (in this world); जगत् – this world

5. O Rudra! Please look at us with that form of yours that is gentle, auspicious, and removes all sins.

6. Please make the arrow which you hold in your hand auspicious and do not destroy this world or any person therein.

This is a prayer to God to manifest with form and special attributes (saguṇa sākāra).

Rudra as Aghora: Generally Rudra appears fierce and fiery, harsh and terrible as death and destruction, with eyes red and ready to kill. His form creates fear and terror in the hearts of all. However, His other form is calm, gentle (aghora) and beautiful. It is like the sea – sometimes rough and fierce, sometimes calm and serene. In India certain types of wandering mendicants are called aghoris, even though they appear just the opposite! We pray to Rudra to take a gentle form which instills peace, love and joy in our hearts.

Rudra as Śiva: When touched by divinity, everything becomes auspicious, sacred and glorious. A body without the spark of divinity, being lifeless becomes rigid, decomposes and stinks. It is then considered inauspicious and consigned to the fire. God is divine and auspicious. We pray to Him to manifest and fill our hearts with divinity and auspiciousness.

Rudra as Apāpakāśinī: Sins cause sorrow and good acts give joy. 'The mere remembrance of God removes all sins and manifests virtues.'[1] May His sight remove any desire within us to sin.

[1] smṛti mātra aghanāśinī puṇya abhivyaktikārī

Rudra as Giriśanta: Rudra is one who staying on the Kailāsa mountain spreads auspiciousness.[1] 'Seated in our speech and in the words of the Vedas, He spreads auspiciousness.'[2] May Rudra who is such, appear before me and bless me.

Abhicākaśīḥ: O Lord, please do look at us with love and compassion. May your mere look create love, joy, noble thoughts and wisdom in us.

Rudra as Giritra: 'Rudra is one who protects the Kailāsa mountain.'[3] Śiva always stays high up on the Himālayan peak of Mount Kailāsa which is always cold and snow-white. May He appear before us and protect us from the heat and sorrow of worldly existence, render us pure (white) and elevate our thoughts to divine peaks.

Rudra with weapons: Generally Rudra is ever ready to kill the wicked and destroy the world with His bow and arrow. The ṛṣi prays – 'Please do not be angry with me or kill me or anyone else. May you only kill our negativities and destroy our false notions. May your weapons be a blessing for all.'

[1] girau sthitvā śaṁ sukhaṁ tanoti iti

[2] giri vāci sthitvā vede tiṣṭhan artha rūpeṇa śaṁ tanoti iti

[3] giriṁ kailāsa ākhyaṁ trāyate pālayati iti

God's nature is further elaborated as:

ततः परं ब्रह्मपरं बृहन्तं यथानिकायं सर्वभूतेषु गूढम्।
विश्वस्यैकं परिवेष्टितारमीशं तं ज्ञात्वामृता भवन्ति॥ ७॥

tataḥ paraṁ brahma-paraṁ bṛhantaṁ yathānikāyaṁ sarvabhūteṣu gūḍham,
viśvasyaikaṁ pariveṣṭitāram-īśaṁ taṁ jñātvāmṛtā bhavanti. (7)

ततः परम् – above that; ब्रह्म – Truth (Brahman); परम् – that which is not subject to any limitation; बृहन्तम् – infinite; यथा-निकायम् – according to their body; सर्वभूतेषु – in all creatures; गूढम् – hidden; विश्वस्य – of this world; एकम् – one; परिवेष्टितारम् – all encompassing; ईशम् – Lord; तम् – whom; ज्ञात्वा – by knowing; अमृताः – immortal; भवन्ति – becomes

7. Above that is the infinite Truth (Brahman), who is hidden in all creatures according to their body, who is the one Lord encompassing this entire world, and knowing whom one becomes immortal.

God is beyond all names and forms: It means that God/ Truth is not limited by time, space or objects (deśa kāla vastu pariccheda śūnyam). That whose existence is impermanent, that which changes, which comes and goes, is limited by time. God/Truth is eternal and present at all times. That which is in a specific space is limited by space. God/Truth is all-pervading and unlimited spacewise. That which is an object with properties and form is limited by other objects. God/Truth is objectless, formless and attributeless and unlimited objectwise.

Take the example of a wave in the vast oceanic waters. It arises, grows and disappears – limited in time. It arises at a specific place – limited spacewise. The small wave is not the big wave, the droplet, foam or froth – limitation as an object. But the vast waters of the ocean do not have these limitations. The water is ever present, everywhere in all waves. It does not decrease or increase with the rise and fall of waves. Being waveless in essence, it is beyond all limitations of the waves.

God is 'the big': In life we want the largest profits, wear the biggest diamonds and own the biggest cars. We all wish to become big. The ṛṣi tells us that there is no need to become big, you are 'the big' as the infinite God/Truth is your own Self. Then why is 'the big' Self/God not seen?

God is hidden: Nikāya means an assemblage of various parts. The body is an assemblage of limbs (hands, legs ...), organs (heart, lungs ...) and matter (blood, bones ...). God/ Truth is hidden within this body because our attention remains only on its name, form and properties and not on the Truth that gives it life and existence. Is God/Truth only engulfed within this body?

God is all encompassing: In fact God/Truth is not just within the body, but He encompasses all bodies and the whole world. It is a very nice feeling to know that we are all in the loving embrace of the Lord.

How can death touch one who knows that he is beyond time, space and objects, 'the big' Truth which is within and beyond everything and all encompassing?

The same principle of the previous mantra is reaffirmed by the direct experience and bold declaration of Ṛṣi Śvetāśvatara in the next mantra. This is also the experience of all Realised Masters.

वेदाहमेतं पुरुषं महान्तम्-आदित्यवर्णं तमसः परस्तात्।
तमेव विदित्वाति मृत्युमेति नान्यः पन्था विद्यतेऽयनाय॥ ८॥

vedāhametaṁ puruṣaṁ mahāntam-ādityavarṇaṁ tamasaḥ parastāt,
tameva viditvāti mṛtyumeti nānyaḥ panthā vidyate'yanāya. (8)

वेद – know; अहम् – I; एतम् – this; पुरुषम् – Person; महान्तम् – great; आदित्यवर्णम् – resplendent like the sun; तमसः परस्तात् – beyond darkness; तम् – Him; एव – alone; विदित्वा – by knowing; मृत्युम् – death; अति एति – transcends; न – no; अन्यः – other; पन्था – way; विद्यते – there; अयनाय – for this (the highest state)

8. I know this great Person, resplendent like the sun, and beyond darkness. By knowing Him alone one transcends death, there is no other way for this.

The declaration of Realisation: Almost a replica of this mantra appears in the famous *Puruṣa Sūktam (7)*. The Sage says – 'I know this great Puruṣa'. Puruṣa means that 'Truth which is complete and infinite' (pūrṇatvāt) and 'resides in the hearts of all beings' (puri śayanāt). 'I see this Puruṣa as my own Self and the Self of all beings and as the very substratum of the whole universe. I know Him as the greatest, the self-effulgent Consciousness, the very source of all illumination, beyond the darkness of ignorance. I am that Puruṣa. I illumine even darkness and the thought of knowledge and ignorance.'

In the *Kenopaniṣad* the Master tells the disciple, 'If you say you know the Truth well, you know but a little of its nature.'[1] The disciple then meditates further and declares his Realisation in a classic manner. 'I do not say that I know the Truth well, nor do I say that I do not know It. Indeed I know It, yet know It not. He who knows It thus, knows It.'[2] It means that the Truth cannot be known as an object of knowledge, but as the very Self of the seeker. Knowing and not knowing are both thoughts of the mind. Realisation is to know the Truth that illumines all thoughts.

Once the great saint Uḍiyā Bābā said, "I am the infinite Truth." Someone remarked that such a statement sounded boastful. He said, "I do not want to say it, but what to do. I am the infinite Truth and I know it. That is a fact."

Transcending death: Death includes every change that takes place. Strangely enough, on the one hand we want change and on the other hand we are also afraid of it. Life would be boring if everything was static, yet we fear every kind of change. We dread bodily changes due to disease and old age. Change in our domestic set up or in our work environment like a new boss at the office, induces fear in us. Knowing the eternal and infinite God/Truth as our own

---

[1] yadi manyase suvedeti dabhramevāpi nūnaṁ tvaṁ vettha brahmaṇo rūpam – *Kenopaniṣad* 2.1

[2] nāhaṁ manye suvedeti no na vedeti veda ca,
yo nastadveda tadveda no na vedeti veda ca. – *Kenopaniṣad* 2.2

Self can make us fearless of every change, even the death of the body.

The only path: Some say there is one path to the Truth, some say that there are many, yet others say there is no path and some that it is a pathless path. Some prefer the easy path and some are stuck with 'my' path. Whatever be the religion, sect, ideology that a person believes in, Realisation of the infinite Truth as one's own Self is the only way to Liberation. The preparatory paths can be varied, but direct Realisation alone liberates (nānyaḥ panthā vidyate'yanāya).

Going to heaven (lokāntara prāpti), attaining heavenly body (dehāntara prāpti) or enjoying heavenly pleasures (bhogāntara prāpti) is not liberation. Liberation is to discard our false identity (with the not-Self) and abide in our true Self[1]. A person acting the role of a beggar got fixed with the thought that he actually is a beggar. The only way he will come out of his misery is by giving up the wrong notion that he is a beggar. If he is sent to heaven, he will start begging even there! Once, a beggar won a lottery. When asked what he would do with the money, he said, "Buy a golden begging bowl" Knowing the Truth alone liberates.

[1] muktirhitvā'nyathā rūpaṁ svarūpeṇa vyavasthitiḥ – *Bhāgavatam*

The next mantra too is popular amongst the students of Vedānta.

यस्मात्परं नापरमस्ति किञ्चित् यस्मान्नाणीयो न ज्यायोऽस्ति कश्चित्।
वृक्ष इव स्तब्धो दिवि तिष्ठत्येकस्तेनेदं पूर्णं पुरुषेण सर्वम्॥ ९॥

Yasmāt-paraṁ nāparamasti kiñcit yasmānnāṇīyo na jyāyo'sti kaścit,
vṛkṣa iva stabdho divi tiṣṭhatyekastenedaṁ pūrṇaṁ puruṣeṇa sarvam. (9)

यस्मात् परम् – beyond or higher than whom; **न** – nothing; **अपरम्** – different than; **अस्ति** – (there) is; **किञ्चित्** – whatsoever; **यस्मात्** – from or than whom; **न** – nothing; **अणीयः** – subtler; **न** – nothing; **ज्यायः** – greater; **अस्ति** – (there) is; **कश्चित्** – whatsoever; **वृक्षः** – tree; **इव** – like; **स्तब्धः** – unmoving; **दिवि** – in His own glory; **तिष्ठति** – stands or exists; **एकः** – one; **इदम्** – this; **पूर्णम्** – filled by; **तेन पुरुषेण** – by that Divine Being; **सर्वम्** – all

9. All this is filled by that Divine Being, higher or different than whom there is nothing else, subtler or greater than whom there is nothing else; He stands alone in His own glory, unmoving like a tree.

yasmāt na paraṁ na aparam: This is a powerful and deeply meaningful statement. Param means cause and aparam means effect. God/Truth has no cause or effect. The cause always exists before the effect. It means that nothing exists before God. This is accepted by all religions of world. However Vedānta also says that God/Truth is not the cause of anything. He is not the Creator! Nothing really comes from him, since nothing is different from him (aparaṁ nāsti kiñcit). God/Truth is neither a cause of anything nor an effect from anything. Nothing exists before Him or after Him, He is one without a second. The non-dual God/Truth alone exists (advaitaṁ paramārthatā). From the absolute standpoint God/Truth is not the Creator of the world. Concepts of cause and effect are superimposed on Him. Śaṅkarācārya urges us to meditate on that God/Truth who is distinct from cause and effect as one's own Self.[1]

yasmānna aṇīyo na jyāyo'sti: There is nothing greater or smaller than God/Truth. All religions again accept that nothing is greater than God. However Vedānta says that nothing is smaller than Him also. Neither the universe, heavens or earth, neither the heavenly beings, mortals or animals are smaller than Him as all is Him alone.

A stranger once entered the court of the king. The king in humility got up to receive the guest. To his utter surprise, the stranger walked right up to him and sat on his throne. The king in awe asked, "Who are you? Are you a king from another land, dressed in ordinary clothes?" The stranger said, "I am the king of all kings." The king then asked, "Are you Indra, the king of heaven?" The stranger said, "I am the God of all gods." The king said, "So you are God in human form?" The stranger said, "I am greater than God." The king spluttered, "But there is nothing greater than God." The saint replied, "I am that nothing which is greater than God." God/Truth is beyond all concepts of small or great, as all is Him alone. Even at the relative plane, God/Truth is subtler

[1] Kārya-kāraṇa-vilakṣaṇaṁ svayaṁ brahma tattvamasi bhāvayātmani
– *Vivekacūdāmaṇi* 260

than space which exists in the smallest atom and also engulfs the whole universe.

vṛkṣa iva stabdho divi tiṣṭhati ekaḥ: God/Truth shines alone in His own glory. A red wood tree stands for hundreds of years in all its majesty and might. God/Truth too stands immutable and alone in all His glory and divinity as Pure Existence-Consciousness pervading the entire universe.

Usually that which pervades and that which is pervaded are different like a carpet spread on the floor. But God/Truth pervades the world like the oceanic waters pervade all waves or the rope pervades the entire snake vision superimposed on it. God/Truth alone exists as the substratum and the world is merely an appearance.

Knowing God/Truth bestows immortality. But that seems a difficult task. What is the alternative? The mantra says –

ततो यदुत्तरतरं तदरूपमनामयम्।
य एतद्विदुरमृतास्ते भवन्ति अथेतरे दुःखमेवापियन्ति ॥ १० ॥

tato yaduttarataraṁ tadarūpam-anāmayam,
ya etadvidur-amṛtāste bhavanti-athetare duḥkham-evāpiyanti. (10)

ततः – than this (world); यद् – that (which is); उत्तरतरम् – higher; तद् – that; अरूपम् – formless; अनामयम् – free from diseases; यः – who; एतद् – this; विदुः – know; अमृताः – immortal; ते – they; भवन्ति – become; अथ – while; इतरे – others; दुःखम् – sorrow; एव – only; अपियन्ति – get

10. That which is higher than this (world) is formless and free from diseases. Those who know this become immortal, while others get only sorrow.

God is formless: Like space, the all-pervading God/Truth is formless. Beauty is the essence of the many beautiful objects, but beauty itself is one and formless. God/Truth is the one formless essence in all forms. That which is formless alone can assume all forms. Water takes on the form of the container. The formless God/Truth can assume any form and all forms.

God is free from disease: Naturally God/Truth is free from disease. A diseased God does not fit into anyone's concept of God. That which is formless, changeless and attributeless is free from disease as it is the body or mind which can have diseases. We all suffer from the spiritual disease of ignorance. Ignorance causes desires which give rise to desire prompted actions which give results, the enjoyment of which cause vāsanās or tendencies which in turn give rise to desires, actions and thus the cycle goes on. Ego, selfishness, anger, greed, jealousy and the like are the symptoms of the spiritual disease which in turn cause pain, anxiety, tension, fear, depression and so on.

Immortality or the alternative: Seekers who know God/ Truth as their immortal nature gain infinite Bliss. The ignorant ones remain immersed in sorrow. However happy a person may seem, the *Chāndogya Upaniṣad* declares that 'there is no real joy in finitude' (na alpe sukham asti). An addition and multiplication of finite numbers still gives a finite result. How can a man who is the inheritor of trillions be happy with a few hundreds!

The Ṛṣi again gives us a glimpse of His cosmic form in the next mantra.

सर्वाननशिरोग्रीवः सर्वभूतगुहाशयः ।
सर्वव्यापी स भगवांस्तस्मात्सर्वगतः शिवः ॥ ११ ॥

sarvānana-śirogrīvaḥ sarvabhūta-guhāśayaḥ,
sarvavyāpī sa bhagavāṁs-tasmāt-sarvagataḥ śivaḥ. (11)

सर्व-आनन-शिरो-ग्रीवः – who has all the faces, heads and necks; सर्वभूत-गुहाशयः – who resides in the core of all beings; सर्वव्यापी – all-pervading; सः – He; भगवान् – the Lord; तस्मात् – therefore; सर्वगतः – omnipresent; शिवः – auspicious

11. That Lord who has all the faces, heads and necks, who resides in the core of all beings, is all-pervading and therefore omnipresent and auspicious.

The stages of manifestation: God/Truth in His immaculate and absolute nature is nameless, attributeless and formless (nirguṇa nirākāra) and is generally referred to as Brahman. Associated with His infinite and inscrutable potential power (māyā or prakṛti) He is called Īśvara who is formless but with all attributes like omniscience and omnipotence in their latent form (saguṇa nirākāra). Then comes the manifestation of the Total Mind or the subtle world. God associated with the Total Mind is called Hiraṇyagarbha wherein the attributes get manifested as do the subtle forms (saguṇa sākāra). From this subtle state emerges the entire gross world of names and forms, the cosmic form of God which is then called Virāṭ. The countless cosmoses and all attributes like powers and knowledge are manifested in the cosmic form. God also manifests in specific forms as incarnations (avatāra) at different times out of compassion for the devotees[1]. Śrī Rāma and Śrī Kṛṣṇa are famous incarnations of God. It is difficult for most to comprehend Brahman, Īśvara, Hiraṇyagarbha or Virāṭ, whereas the beautiful form of Lord Śrī Kṛṣṇa, His divine life, work and elevating teachings become easy for all to love and follow.

sarva-ānana-śiro-grīva: He is all faces, heads and necks. All faces, heads and necks are His alone. After reading this we should be able to see God in all beings. Only then can we say that we have understood this mantra. When we see all as God, can we then label people as good, bad or ugly, friend or enemy? Is not the person we see as an enemy also God? He may consider us as his enemy, but should we? Saint Tulasīdāsa says, "I see the entire world as Lord Śrī Rāma and I bow down to all with folded hands."[2] We may understand this mantra intellectually, but it is not easy to get this divine vision.

'Ānana' also means mouth through which we enjoy food and hence represents the power to enjoy (bhoga śakti). Śira the head symbolises the power of knowledge (jñāna śakti) and grīva – the neck that supports the head represents the power that supports (ādhāra śakti). God's nature of Existence-Consciousness-Bliss manifests in this world and

[1] bhaktānukampinaṁ devaṁ jagatkāraṇamacyutam,
āvirbhūtaṁ ca sṛṣṭyādau prakṛteḥ puruṣātparam.

– *Gaṇapati Atharvaśīrṣam*

[2] siyārāma main saba jaga jāni karahuṁ praṇāma jori juga pāni

all beings as the power that supports – gives existence, knows and enjoys.

Bhagavān: This beautiful word is very commonly used for God by the Hindus. One with bhaga – fortune – is called Bhagavān. The six kinds of fortunes are lordship, righteousness, fame, wealth, knowledge and dispassion.[1]

God has all these in infinite measure. These divine powers are His very nature and not qualities which come and go, increase or decrease. The Lord's lordship is not because someone elected Him to power. He is the very embodiment of all virtues. His fame is such that His mere remembrance purifies the hearts of men. His is the world with all its wealth and knowledge. Knowing all and being all He is still untouched and beyond all. This is His dispassion. Anyone in the world who has a little of these or even one of these qualities is called fortunate indeed. When we understand that they are God's divine powers, we do not become proud of our wealth or envious of other's fame. That God (sa bhagavān) is the all-pervading auspicious One (Śivaḥ), the Self of all.

[1] aiśvaryasya samagrasya dharmasya yaśasaḥ śriyaḥ,
jñāna-vairāgyayoścaiva ṣaṇṇāṁ bhaga itīraṇā. – *Viṣṇu Purāṇa* 6.5.74

What does the Lord do seated within us? The mantra says –

महान्प्रभुर्वै पुरुषः सत्त्वस्यैष प्रवर्तकः ।
सुनिर्मलामिमां प्राप्तिमीशानो ज्योतिरव्ययः ॥ १२ ॥

mahān-prabhurvai puruṣaḥ sattvasyaiṣa pravartakaḥ,
sunirmalām-imāṁ prāptim-īśāno jyotiravyayaḥ. (12)

महान् – great; **प्रभुः** – Lord; **वै** – indeed; **पुरुषः** – the Puruṣa; **सत्त्वस्य** – of sattva; **एषः** – This; **प्रवर्तकः** – prompter; **सुनिर्मलाम्** – pure (state); **इमाम्** – this; **प्राप्तिम्** – attainment; **ईशानः** – the Ruler; **ज्योतिः** – the Light (of Consciousness); **अव्ययः** – immutable

12. Indeed this great Lord, the Puruṣa, the prompter of sattva in order to (help us) attain the pure state, is the Ruler, the Light (of Consciousness) and immutable.

God is great (mahān): God is great in every respect (mahān). God is great as He is the Lord of all fortunes. He is great in knowledge, stature, power, virtues – everything worthwhile. He is also the Master (prabhu), all capable and independent to do, undo or do otherwise. Nothing is impossible for Him. He is full and complete (Puruṣa), therefore without desires, yet capable of fulfilling all desires. We on the other hand feel incomplete and are full of desires and have little capacity in fulfilling them. Being so great, capable and complete, no wonder He is respected and worshipped.

God inspires (sattvasyaiṣa pravartakaḥ): Remaining within us He prompts sattva guṇa – noble qualities of goodness, selflessness, kindness and so on. 'Sattvasya' also means 'of the mind-intellect' as it is also made up of the sāttvika aspect of the five elements. He motivates us to improve ourselves, help others, gain purity and attain the Truth. His motivating power is felt more keenly as our tuning with Him increases. This can be seen in many ways. Sometimes when we are in a dilemma, intuitively we are impelled to act in the right way. We are often guided through difficult situations, though most of the time we are not even aware of it. The seeker therefore prays each day – dhiyo yo naḥ pracodayāt (Gāyatrī Mantra) 'May you enlighten our intellect.' Some in the world instigate us to do wrong and pull us downwards. Some motivate us and push us forward and some inspire us and uplift us. God is an eternal source of inspiration, the one who prompts us to attain the highest (sunirmalāṁ prāptiḥ), the state of pure Bliss.

The scriptures point out that we often experience a state free of all thoughts which is all bliss (nirvikalpa samādhi), but we do not know it, do not recognise it, leave alone abide in it. For example, in extreme anger we are paralysed, not aware of anything, not even of ourselves and for that moment, we are in a thoughtless state. It is later that thoughts that rouse action come in. In the same way, when we are struck suddenly by some calamity or tragic event, we are stunned into a thoughtless state. Moments of intense and extreme joy, fear, sorrow, physical pain, anger or love can catapult us into a thoughtless state. It may last for a fraction of a second before the sense of 'I' and 'my' come in. But for that brief moment, we are in touch with the Supreme, even though we are not aware of it.

It is quite difficult to conceive of God as infinite and all-pervasive. Can He not be thought of as something nearer to our size? The following echoes the mantra in *Kaṭhopaniṣad 2.3.17.*

अङ्गुष्ठमात्रः पुरुषोऽन्तरात्मा सदा जनानां हृदये सन्निविष्टः ।
हृदा मन्वीशो मनसाभिक्लृप्तो य एतद्विदुरमृतास्ते भवन्ति ॥ १३ ॥

aṅguṣṭha-mātraḥ puruṣo'ntarātmā sadā janānāṁ hṛdaye sanniviṣṭaḥ,
hṛdā manvīśo manasābhikḷpto ya etad-viduramṛtāste bhavanti. (13)

अङ्गुष्ठमात्रः – of the size of a thumb; पुरुषः – The Puruṣa; अन्तरात्मा – the indwelling Self; सदा – always; जनानाम् – of people; हृदये – in the heart; सन्निविष्टः – seated; हृदा – by the heart; मन्वीशः – The Lord of knowledge; मनसा – by the mind; अभिक्लृप्तः – hidden; ये – those who; एतद् – this; विदुः – know; अमृताः – immortal; ते – they; भवन्ति – become

13. The Puruṣa, the indwelling Self, of the size of a thumb, is always seated in the hearts of people. The Lord of knowledge is hidden by the mind and the heart. Those who know this, they become immortal.

God – the size of the thumb: The infinite God is available within the heart as the Self of the size of a thumb! Here the 'heart' does not refer to the physical heart that pumps our blood, but the spiritual heart, the very centre of our personality, the source from where the feeling of 'I'-ness arises. When asked where are you, universally we place our hand close to the physical heart. That can be said to be the location of spiritual heart (upalabdhi sthāna). We should not think that God is literally of the size of a thumb and that He is only in the heart-space. It is so considered, so that in meditation our mind can withdraw from the rest of the world and the body and focus at one place. This helps to concentrate the mind.[1]

It also means that even though God is great and infinite, He is available right here and now within each of us. It is generally very difficult to meet great people. We need to take an appointment and wait for long. However, great the person is he is easily available for his dear one and bends down to greet his little one. God is available at all times exclusively, right within us, in a conceivable form and size.

The infinite God alone appears in all shapes and sizes. Can He then not appear of the size of a thumb? When Aśvatthāmā shot the Brahmāstra to kill Parīkṣita in Uttarā's womb, Parīkṣita saw the Lord of the size of a thumb, in the womb, protecting Him.

God – the hidden Self: However, right now, even though God is ever available as our own Self, He is hidden from our sight. It often happens that the effects cover the cause. The mind-intellect which is the created effect covers our experience of its creator – the Lord like the clouds cover our vision of the sun. Desires make the mind agitated, likes and

[1] svaviṣayāsamprayoge cittasvarūpānukāra-ivendriyāṇāṁ pratyāhāraḥ – *Yoga Sūtra* 2.54,
deśabandhaścittasya dhāraṇā – *Yoga Sūtra* 3.1,
tatra pratyayaikatānatā dhyānam – *Yoga Sūtra* 3.2

dislikes colour the mind and the intellect creates its own doubts, confusions and concepts. All these do not allow us to see God/Truth. The layers of the food-sheath, vital-air-sheath, mental-sheath (manas), intellectual-sheath (manīṣā) and the bliss-sheath (hṛd) seem to completely cover the Self. Even though it is in His light alone are we aware of the three states, He seems hidden in the waking state by the intellect (manīṣayā), by the mental projections (manasā) in the dream state and by ignorance and the dormant vāsanās (hṛdā) in the deep sleep state, where all thoughts merge.

However, the beauty is that God is present in all of us as our own Self. None can claim that God forgot to put the Self in me. Can I exist without I? Can the pot maker forget to put mud in the mud pot? Those who have realised God within, have become free – they know that they were never bound and were always free.

The cosmic form of the Lord is again revisited through the following four mantras, wherein both the immanent and transcendental nature of God/Truth is explained. The first two mantras of the famous *Puruṣa Sūktam* are now given here.

सहस्रशीर्षा पुरुषः सहस्राक्षः सहस्रपात्।
स भूमिं विश्वतो वृत्वा अत्यतिष्ठद्दशाङ्गुलम्॥ १४॥

पुरुष एवेदगं सर्वं यद्भूतं यच्च भव्यम्।
उतामृतत्वस्येशानो यदन्नेनातिरोहति॥ १५॥

sahasra-śīrṣā puruṣaḥ sahasrākṣaḥ sahasrapāt,
sa bhūmiṁ viśvato vṛtvā-atyatiṣṭhad-daśāṅgulam. (14)

puruṣa evedaṁ sarvaṁ yadbhūtaṁ yacca bhavyam,
utāmṛtatvasyeśāno yad-annenātirohati. (15)

सहस्रशीर्षा – has a thousand heads; पुरुषः – The Puruṣa; सहस्राक्षः – having thousand eyes; सहस्रपात् – with thousand feet; सः – He; भूमिम् – the earth; विश्वतः – from all sides; वृत्वा – pervading; अत्यतिष्ठद् – extends beyond it; दशाङ्गुलम् – by ten fingers' breadth

पुरुषः – The Puruṣa; एव – alone; इदम् – this; सर्वम् – all; यद् – whatever; भूतम् – past; यद् – whatever; च – and; भव्यम् – future; उत – besides; अमृतत्वस्य – of immortality; ईशानः – the Lord; यद् – what; अन्नेन – with food; अतिरोहति – grows

14. The Puruṣa has a thousand heads, thousand eyes and thousand feet. He pervades the earth from all sides and extends beyond it by ten fingers' breadth.

15. All this is Puruṣa alone – whatever was in the past and what will be in the future and all that grows with food. Besides, He is also the Lord of immortality.

The *Puruṣa Sūktam*: It is a hymn in praise of God as the cosmic person. It is found in all the four Vedas with varying number of mantras. In the *Sāma Veda* and *Atharva Veda* there are four and five mantras, in the *Ṛg Veda* sixteen and in the *Yajur Veda* which we in the Chinmaya Mission study has eighteen mantras. Everyone in the ancient Gurukula system of education studied this right in the beginning.

It is very popular as in the sixteen step ritualistic worship (ṣoḍaśa upacāra pūjā), each step is performed with the chanting of one mantra and the entire hymn is chanted during the special ritualistic bath (abhiṣeka).

God – the immanent and transcendental: Since He is the Cosmic Person, all heads, eyes and feet are His alone. He naturally pervades everything. Is He only as much as is manifest as the unimaginably large, gross and subtle world? Beyond the manifest world is the infinite unmanifest potential of the Lord. He exists much beyond even this unmanifest potential state as the pure and absolute Truth. Ten inches beyond indicates this transcendental nature of the Lord. Ten inches does not mean that He transcends the world by a little; it means that His transcendental nature is beyond all conception. Elsewhere in the *Puruṣa Sūktam* it is said that only one-fourth of the Lord manifests as the world. Three-fourths remains untouched by māyā or its creation, in Its pure state.[1]

[1] pādo'sya viśvā bhūtāni tripādasyāmṛtaṁ divi – *Puruṣa Sūktam* 2

Another meaning is that God / Truth who is omnipresent and transcendental is also available in our heart as the Self, ten inches above the navel (nābhi). The president of a country lives in the Capital in his presidential palace far beyond the reach of most. But we do not have to undertake a long journey or struggle to get an audience with God. All we have to do is turn within. Maybe because He is so close, we miss Him and search for Him elsewhere. Kabīradāsa says – 'I feel amused that we like the fish in water complain of thirst.'[1]

God is all 'this': Everything – the world, body, emotions, thoughts, ignorance – that can be indicated as 'this' is God alone. There is no 'this' separate from 'I'. 'All is Me alone' is the Realisation of the seeker.

God – at all times: The cosmic form of the Lord is ever changing. Beings change forms, the realms of experiences change with the beings in them, the cosmoses are born and perish. However all that ever existed from beginningless time, all that exists and all that will exist is future in God alone. He alone existed in the past, exists in the present and will exist in the future. For example, the ocean alone is all the waves – those which arose in the past, are rising now and which will rise in future.

[1] pāni mein mīna piyāsi mujhe suna suna āvata hāṁsi

The same idea of the previous two mantras is now explained through the following mantras that also appear in the famous *Bhagavad Gītā (13.13).*

सर्वतः पाणिपादं तत् सर्वतोऽक्षिशिरोमुखम् ।
सर्वतः श्रुतिमल्लोके सर्वमावृत्य तिष्ठति ॥ १६ ॥

sarvataḥ pāṇipādaṁ tat sarvato'kṣi-śiromukham,
sarvataḥ śrutimalloke sarvam-āvṛtya tiṣṭhati. (16)

सर्वतः – everywhere; पाणि-पादम् – having hands and feet; तत् – It; सर्वतः – everywhere; अक्षि-शिरो-मुखम् – having eyes, heads and mouths; सर्वतः – everywhere; श्रुतिमत् – has ears; लोके – in the world; सर्वम् – all; आवृत्य – pervading; तिष्ठति – stands

16. It has hands and feet everywhere, eyes, heads and mouths everywhere, It has ears everywhere and It stands pervading all in the world.

The Vedas are the knowledge of the eternal truths that govern the world. 'They are the very breath of the Lord' (yasya niśvasitaṁ vedāḥ). The Lord Himself revealed this knowledge to Arjuna as the Divine Song – *Gītā*. Therefore the mantras of the Vedas do appear in the *Gītā* and other scriptures also.

A good teacher repeats the thought to emphasise its importance, to make the student reflect again and again till the full import of the knowledge sinks into the student's mind.

Implication of the cosmic vision: All hands, legs, eyes and heads are His alone. Then who am 'I' the individual? Is not the body and mind that I call mine, actually His? Understanding this will dissolve the sense of individuality into its infinite source - the Lord. Also understanding that all beings are His form alone makes us feel His presence at all times. We can then never feel lonely or afraid.

I, as an individual is finite and limited in my capacities. However when I identify with the totality, my capacities increase a millionfold as all hands and heads, all knowledge and powers become mine. I can then achieve anything as the totality will make it happen.

Let us take a practical example. In the Chinmaya Mission, as long as I remain identified with the entire organisation and do everything for the Mission, I have thousands of hands, legs and heads with which to accomplish the work. All members, all the centres, all the resources, everything is mine and at my disposal. As an individual, I have finite capacities and resources. As an individual if I ask for money, I will be directed to the bank! Not only me, for each member of the Chinmaya Mission, the hands, legs, heads and resources are available to achieve the work of the Mission. Wherever you go, the Chinmaya Family welcomes you in their fold. When you identify with the Mission, your strength and capacities multiply manyfold. Imagine what it will be like when we identify with God Himself!

When we read the scriptures we should not just focus on the translation or get overwhelmed by the principles.

We should also try and understand the implications of the knowledge in our day-to-day life.

The purpose of this study is to reduce our sense of 'I' and 'my', our sense of separateness and ultimately merge them with the Lord. The devotee says, "Everything is Your's, nothing is mine" and so his attachments drop off. Through knowledge or devotion, whatever be the method, selfishness, attachment, ego and possessiveness must reduce. They alone cause much sorrow in life. For transactional purpose we may use 'I' and 'my', but in our hearts we must understand that all is His alone. When we feel the presence of God all the time, all worries and anxieties drop away. My powers may be limited, but God is all powerful and He is there to protect me. Mīrābāi drank poison which turned to nectar as she considered her husband who sent it as God Himself. Such things happen to one who sees God everywhere. Even when the other person hates him due to ignorance, he does not hate anyone. Everyone is Nārāyaṇa – one is duṣṭa (wicked) Nārāyaṇa and another daridra (poor) Nārāyaṇa and yet another sādhu (good) Nārāyaṇa – but all are His form alone. He teases us, tests us and teaches us in many forms. In fact all is His divine play alone.

Like us, does God get caught up in His own creation? Do the individual's problems affect the Lord? Would He then not have innumerable problems as all individuals are Him alone? The mantra clarifies this doubt.

सर्वेन्द्रियगुणाभासं सर्वेन्द्रियविवर्जितम् ।
सर्वस्य प्रभुमीशानं सर्वस्य शरणं बृहत् ॥ १७ ॥

sarvendriya-guṇābhāsaṁ sarvendriya-vivarjitam,
sarvasya prabhum-īśānaṁ sarvasya śaraṇaṁ bṛhat. (17)

सर्वेन्द्रिय-गुणाभासम् – He appears to have all the qualities of the sense organs; **सर्वेन्द्रिय-विवर्जितम्** – (yet) He is devoid of all the sense organs; **सर्वस्य** – of all; **प्रभुम्** – the Lord; **ईशानम्** – the ruler; **सर्वस्य** – of all; **शरणम्** – refuge; **बृहत्** – mighty

17. He appears to have all the qualities of the sense organs, yet He is devoid of all the sense organs. He is the Lord of all, the ruler and the mighty refuge of all.

God – the spark in all: The first line of this mantra also appears in the *Gītā (13.14)*. 'Ābhāsa' means appearance. God appears to have the attributes and functions of all the instruments (sense organs of perception and action and the inner equipment of mind-intellect), but He is devoid of all attributes and equipments. He remains as the non-doer in whose presence everything gets done.

The example of electricity is very apt in this context. Electricity manifests as light in the bulb, heat in the heater and sound through the music system. Yet electricity is free from the bulb, heater or music system and all its limitation. When the music system breaks down, the electricity does not weep even if I who consider it as my music system may do so! None of the equipments can function without electricity, but electricity functions through all of them in whatever condition they may be.

God – the Lord of all: We often find that one who is capable (prabhu) may not have power and one with power (īśāna) may not be capable. For example, the master or boss could be inefficient and his servant or subordinate very efficient, but with no power. The Lord is both all-capable and all-powerful. He alone controls the whole universe and makes everything happen in it.

God – the great refuge: When a person is afflicted with adversity, he seeks refuge – shelter, support or help (śaraṇa).[1] The umbrella provides shelter from rain. However it is not large enough to shelter a group of people. It can protect us from a heavy shower, but not a gale or a storm. Some umbrellas are mere showpieces, not capable of protecting us even from a drizzle! The Lord is bṛhat śaraṇa – the huge and almighty shelter. He can shelter all beings, all the time, from all calamities.

In some readings we find the word suhṛt instead of bṛhat. This also gives a lovely meaning. Suhṛt means a good-hearted person, a well-wisher, one who is ready to help without any expectations (pratyupakāram anapekṣya

[1] ārti haraṇa sthāna

upakāra kartā). People help others, but generally they expect something in return or at least wish to be appreciated. A person may give refuge, but may not be good-hearted. He may in turn bind us for life for helping us. The help given by most is conditional. But the Lord is magnanimous, a true well-wisher and gives unconditionally to all. The *Gītā* says – 'When a person recognises God as his true friend and well-wisher, he finds great peace'[1] as he knows that God will always be with him in times of need.

[1] suhṛdaṁ sarvabhūtānāṁ jñātvā māṁ śāntiṁ-ṛcchati – *Gītā* 5.29

The next mantra gives a beautiful analogy of God's presence within us.

नवद्वारे पुरे देही हंसो लेलायते बहिः।
वशी सर्वस्य लोकस्य स्थावरस्य चरस्य च ॥ १८ ॥

navadvāre pure dehī haṁso lelāyate bahiḥ,
vaśī sarvasya lokasya sthāvarasya carasya ca. (18)

नवद्वारे पुरे – in the city with nine gates; देही – embodied; हंसः – the supreme Self; लेलायते – moves; बहिः – outwards; वशी – the master; सर्वस्य लोकस्य – of the entire world; स्थावरस्य – of the inanimate; चरस्य – of the animate; च – and

18. The supreme Self (God) who is the master of the entire world of animate and inanimate beings is embodied in the city with nine gates and moves outwards.

God is haṁsa: The word haṁsa has several meanings:

- **a.** Earlier this word referred to the individual being (jīva) who travels from one body to another and from one experience to another (hanti gacchati iti haṁsaḥ).
- **b.** Haṁsa means a swan. Monks too are called haṁsa or paramahaṁsa. Like the swan, the monk has a pure mind (white), can discriminate between the real and unreal (milk and water) and walks gracefully on the path of dharma.

c. God also is called haṁsa as He destroys ignorance and its effects (avidyāṁ tatkāryaṁ hanti nāśayati iti haṁsaḥ). He does so by bestowing the knowledge of Truth. The Guru too is called haṁsa or paramahaṁsa as he too gives knowledge and removes ignorance.

God – the city dweller: The body is like a city as it is filled with many facilities (pūryate anena iti puraḥ). The city has homes, schools, hospitals, jails, train stations, bus stations, gas stations and even police stations. This body is filled with the seven ingredients (pūryate sapta-dhātubhiḥ) – the skin, blood, flesh, fat, bone, marrow and semen. Or it is called a city as it has several limbs (pūrayate sarva aṅgaiḥ pratyaṅgaiḥ iti puram). Millions of individuals and species live in their respective city-like bodies going about their day-to-day activities. The body has nine gates – two eyes, two ears, two nostrils, the mouth, the genital organ and the anus, through which the individual transacts with the world. Elsewhere there is mention of ten gates. The tenth gate is the navel through which the foetus gets its nourishment. This gate is closed at birth. *Kaṭhopaniṣad 2.2.1* mentions eleven gates (puram ekādaśadvāram). The eleventh gate is the brahmarandhra on the crown of the head which for most of us is always closed. Only the great Yogis know how to open it and go out through it. The poet sings – 'In this bungalow there are ten gates and in the centre is a pillar of air. Nobody knows when the individual enters into this body and when he leaves. This wonderful bungalow is thus created and Bhagavān Nārāyaṇa has entered it.'[1] God as though enters this body as an individual and becomes very busy

[1] isa bangaleke dasa darvāje bīca pavana kā khambhā,
bangalā bhalā bana daraveśa isame nārāyaṇa paraveśa.

and extrovert. The individual is always up to something, remaining preoccupied, he restlessly moves about from place to place, seeking different kinds of pleasures and comforts. In the present day he is always occupied with either his mobile or computer. The *Gītā* says – 'The Lord dwells in the city of nine gates, doing nothing, nor prompting anything.'[1]

God the Master: An individual experiences finitude, helplessness and sorrow, but the Lord is the master of all (vaśī). Once, a king encountered a saint lying in the middle of the road. The saint refused to move when asked to do so and asked the king, "Who are you and what is your power?" The king replied, "I am the king of this land (rājā) and I can exile anyone from my kingdom. Who are you and what is your power?" The saint said, "I am a greater king (mahārājā). My kingdom is so vast, that there is no place outside it, so I cannot exile anyone." God is the supreme Master of the whole world. The inert objects and sentient beings, all are in His control. In the world we sometimes see the inert controlling the sentient (money controls man) or the gross controlling the subtler (the physically strong controlling the knowledgeable), but the Lord controls both – the sentient and the insentient, the gross and the subtle.

[1] navadvāre pure dehī naiva kurvanna kārayan – *Gītā* 5.13

The next mantra seems to contradict what was said often in earlier mantras about God's cosmic form.

अपाणिपादो जवनो ग्रहीता पश्यत्यचक्षुः स शृणोत्यकर्णः ।
स वेत्ति वेद्यं न च तस्यास्ति वेत्ता तमाहुरग्र्यं पुरुषं महान्तम् ॥ १९ ॥

apāṇipādo javano grahītā paśyatyacakṣuḥ sa śṛṇotyakarṇaḥ,
sa vetti vedyaṁ na ca tasyāsti vettā tamāhuragryaṁ puruṣaṁ mahāntam. (19)

अपाणिपादः – without hands and feet; **जवनः** – moves; **ग्रहीता** – grasps; **पश्यति** – sees; **अचक्षुः** – without eyes; **सः** – He; **शृणोति** – listens; **अकर्णः** – without ears; **सः** – He; **वेत्ति** – knows; **वेद्यम्** – to be known; **न** – no; **च** – and; **तस्य** – His; **अस्ति** – is; **वेत्ता** – knower; **तम्** – of Him; **आहुः** – speak; **अग्र्यम्** – the foremost; **पुरुषम्** – person; **महान्तम्** – the great

19. Without hands and feet, He moves and grasps; He sees without eyes and listens without ears; He knows whatever is to be known, but there is none who knows Him. He is said to be the foremost person, the great.

Kaivalyopaniṣad (2.2) has a similar mantra.

God – an enigma: The nature of God is truly mind-boggling. The earlier mantras said that all hands, feet and heads are His alone. He has eyes and faces everywhere. Here it is said that He has no hands yet grasps everything, has no ears, yet hears all (even the sound of a bell on the feet of an ant!), has no hands, yet catches all and has no feet yet moves everywhere.

Mantras like this cause confusion to those who read the literal meaning in translations without the help of a Guru or without any background or preparation. People ask why Upaniṣads use such paradoxical language. The language of paradox is meant to shatter any concept that the mind forms regarding the Truth and opens the path to direct Realisation.

So does He have hands or does He not? From His standpoint He has no hands, but from our standpoint, the standpoint of the world, all hands and legs are His alone. From His standpoint He is formless, but when the devotee worships Him as a form, for example as Śrī Kṛṣṇa, he is blessed by Him. The devotee begs forgiveness from God for three mistakes – 'Knowing that You are all-pervading, I still go for pilgrimages, knowing that You are beyond the mind, I still meditate with the mind and knowing that You cannot be described by the speech, I still sing your praises through hymns.'[1]

God has no conditionings (nirupādhika). Conditioning is that which remaining near, imposes its qualities on the other (upa samīpe sthitvā svaguṇa-dharmān anyasmin ādhatte iti upādhi). For example, the red cloth under the colourless crystal makes the crystal look red. However all conditionings – hands, legs, eyes or mind function only because of Him. The *Kaṭhopaniṣad* says – Seated He goes far

[1] tvadyātrayā vyāpakatā hatā te dhyānena cetaḥ paratā hatā te,
stutyanayā vāk paratā hatā te kṣamasva śambho trividhāparādhaḥ.

(āsīno dūraṁ vrajati). For example, when we travel in a car, we are seated in one place, but the car moves fast and far. From our standpoint we are in one place, but conditioned by the car, we are seen to be moving. So we generally say 'I travelled far.'

Without Existence and life, neither the hand can grasp nor the eyes see. Hence it is He alone that grasps and sees all. However, God/Truth has no hands or eyes. God/Truth is therefore called the ear of the ear and the mind of the mind (śrotrasya śrotraṁ manaso mano yat – *Kenopaniṣad 1.2*).

God – the unknown: Another interesting aspect of God is that He knows all and yet none can know Him. The Seer knows the seen, but the seen cannot know the Seer. For example, the eyes see objects but the objects cannot see the eyes. The mind knows what the eyes see, but the eyes cannot see what the mind knows. Similarly I the Self knows what the mind thinks and the eyes see, but neither the eyes nor the mind can know the 'I' that knows. The Self can never become an object of knowledge.

God is Himself enigmatic in nature and difficult to comprehend by the intellect. We generally know an object by objectifying it – as a vision, sound, smell, colour, form and so on. When we say the word 'cow', a mental image of a cow is formed. Anger, love, compassion are feelings known to us – objectified by us. Ideas are conceptualised – also objectified by us. Since we cannot objectify God/Self/Truth – as an image, emotion or a concept, He remains unknown to us.

No words can describe God/Truth, yet words have to be used to indicate God. Samartha Rāmadāsa says – 'Without becoming a thinker, think of that which cannot be thought of.' If this is grasped, the mind will merge in the Truth. Śrī Gurudev used to explain it this way. When we say 'table', the table image comes to mind. When we say 'infinite', 'immutable' or 'timeless' the intellect is unable to grasp its meaning, but it negates all that is finite, changing and time bound. Then whatever remains is the true meaning of 'infinite'. Then that what is indicated is Me, the infinite Truth.

God – the first (agryam): Chāndogya Upaniṣad says that the 'non-dual Existence existed before everything.'[1] From God/ Existence alone all names and forms emerged. Gold exists before all gold ornaments are made. Wherever you take the ornament, gold is always there. *Īśāvāsyopaniṣad* says that 'however fast one may run, God/Truth overtakes all, even the mind, and reaches before.'[2] It wins every race without any movement as He already exists everywhere.

[1] sadeva saumya-idam-agra āsīt-ekam-eva-advitīyam
– *Chāndogya-upaniṣad* 6.2.1

[2] anejad-ekaṁ manaso javīyo nainad-devā āpnuvan-pūrvamarṣat,
taddhāvato'nyān-atyeti tiṣṭhat-tasmin-apo mātariśvā dadhāti.
– *Īśāvāsyopaniṣad* 4

Then how is the enigmatic and unknowable God/Truth realised?

**अणोरणीयान्महतो महीयानात्मा गुहायां निहितोऽस्य जन्तोः।
तमक्रतुं पश्यति वीतशोको धातुः प्रसादान्महिमानमीशम्॥ २०॥**

*Aṇoraṇīyān-mahato mahīyān-ātmā guhāyāṁ nihito'sya jantoḥ,
tam-akratuṁ paśyati vītaśoko dhātuḥ prasādān-mahimānam-īśam. (20)*

अणोः – than the subtlest; अणीयान् – subtler; महतः – than the greatest; महीयान् – greater; आत्मा – the Self; गुहायाम् – in the cave of the heart; निहितः – seated; अस्य जन्तोः – of this creature; तम् – that Self; अक्रतुम् – desireless; पश्यति – sees; वीतशोकः – free from thoughts (sorrow); धातुः – of the pure mind; प्रसादात् – by the grace; महिमानम् – the greatness; ईशम् – the Lord

20. The Self is subtler than the subtlest and greater than the greatest. It is seated in the cave of the heart of all creatures. One who is free from thoughts and desires sees the greatness of the Lord through the grace of the pure mind.

This mantra is also found in the *Kaṭhopaniṣad (1.2.20)* with slight differences.

God – big or small? God is bigger than the biggest and smaller than the smallest. This idea was explained earlier also. God/Truth is all-pervading and formless and the substratum of everything, even the all-pervading space. Space exists in the minutest object of nano scale and also engulfs the countless cosmoses. Space must exist to be able to pervade and so God/Existence pervades even space.

Knowing God through grace (dhātuḥ prasādāt): Eyes reveal colours and forms. What is the valid means of knowing God/Truth? Self-knowledge as indicated in the Upaniṣads and revealed by the Guru (dhātā) is the valid means. The Guru's grace is very important as He is the one who reveals our infinite nature and helps us to drop the wrong identification with the body. Even the Lord when He incarnates goes to a Guru to learn about Self-knowledge. Lord Śrī Rāma went to Sage Vasiṣṭha and Lord Śrī Kṛṣṇa stayed in the hermitage of Sage Sāndīpanī.

Dhātā also means God – the sustainer and supporter of all. 'I am the father, mother, the sustainer and the grandsire of this world'[1] says Śrī Kṛṣṇa. It is God alone who manifests as the Vedas and the Guru who reveals the Truth. The entire world is sustained by His grace. All knowledge takes place through His grace. Self-knowledge which is otherwise so difficult to comprehend can only take place through His grace.

Dhātā also means the mind. Only a pure mind can realise God/Truth. Śrī Kṛṣṇa says that despite efforts, an impure mind cannot realise the Truth.[2] A mind preoccupied by sorrows and regrets of the past, fears and worries of the future and agitations and attachments in the present is unable to see the Truth. A mind free from these (vītaśoka)

---

[1] pitāhamasya jagataḥ mātā dhātā pitāmahaḥ – *Gītā* 9.17

[2] yatanto'pyakṛtātmānaḥ nainaṁ paśyantyacetasaḥ – *Gītā* 15.11

is a fit instrument to know the Truth which is beyond all sorrows. Again 'kratu' or desires alone agitate the mind and prompt us into action. A mind relatively free from desires (akratu) can know God/Truth who is full and complete and totally free from desires (akratu). It is interesting to note that in *Kaṭhopaniṣad* it is said that the desireless one sees the Truth (akratuḥ paśyati) and here it is said that the pure minded sees the desireless Truth (akratuṁ paśyati).

Hence the grace of God/Guru coupled with the grace of a pure mind can reveal the great and glorious Truth and make It our own direct Realisation.

Has anyone actually realised the Truth? The Ṛṣi asserts his own personal Realisation.

वेदाहमेतमजरं पुराणं सर्वात्मानं सर्वगतं विभुत्वात्।
जन्मनिरोधं प्रवदन्ति यस्य ब्रह्मवादिनो हि प्रवदन्ति नित्यम्॥ २१॥

vedāham-etam-ajaraṁ purāṇaṁ sarvātmānaṁ sarvagataṁ vibhutvāt,
janma-nirodhaṁ pravadanti yasya brahmavādino hi pravadanti nityam. (21)

वेद – know; अहम् – I; एतम् – this; अजरम् – ageless; पुराणम् – ancient; सर्वात्मानम् – one who is the Self of all; सर्वगतम् – omnipresent; विभुत्वात् – because of being all-pervasive; जन्मनिरोधम् – birthless; प्रवदन्ति – speak of; यस्य – regarding whose; ब्रह्मवादिनः – the knowers of Brahman; हि – indeed; प्रवदन्ति – speak of; नित्यम् – eternal

21. I know this ageless ancient One who is the Self of all, who is omnipresent because of being all-pervasive, who is indeed said to be birthless and eternal by the knowers of Brahman.

The Ṛṣi is doubtless in his Realisation and declares that he knows God/Truth. What is the nature of the Truth?

God is ageless and ancient: The body undergoes the six changes – existence in womb, birth, growth, maturity, decay and death (ṣaḍ vikāra). God is formless and thus ageless. Yet He is old, in fact the oldest, the most ancient as He existed before everything. In spite of being old, He is ever new and ageless. Actually God is unconditioned by time and so the idea of old and new do not apply to Him.

God is birthless: The ignorant identify with the body and consider that they are born and they shall die. But the Realised Masters know that they are birthless and deathless – the all-pervading, eternal Truth.

The third chapter thus ends with the direct experience of the Realised Master.

Chapter 4

The first three chapters have already expounded the subject matter of the Upaniṣad, but there are still three more chapters. Since the topic is profound and difficult to grasp, it has to be explained repeatedly. Also new aspects are revealed and deeper understanding takes place with each new mantra.

This is true even with secular knowledge. There is no end to the depth of each subject. Great musicians sometimes say that they have not understood the full reach of a rāga. A young graduate asked a renowned and aged astronomer, "What do you do?" He said, "I study astronomy". She remarked, "I finished studying it last year!" One may complete the syllabus and yet remain far from exploring the full depth of the subject. So the Sage begins the fourth chapter.

य एकोऽवर्णो बहुधा शक्तियोगाद् वर्णाननेकान्निहितार्थो दधाति ।
वि चैति चान्ते विश्वमादौ स देवः स नो बुद्ध्या शुभया संयुनक्तु ॥ १ ॥

ya eko'varṇo bahudhā śaktiyogād varṇān-anekān-nihitārtho dadhāti,
vi caiti cānte viśvam-ādau sa devaḥ sa no buddhyā śubhayā
saṁyunaktu. (1)

यः – one who; एकः – one; अवर्णः – without colours; बहुधा शक्तियोगाद् – through His multifarious powers; वर्णान् – colours; अनेकान् – innumerable or many; निहितार्थाः – one with a purpose known only to Himself; दधाति – creates or brings forth; वि एति – dissolves; च – [on whom it (the world or creation) rests in the middle also]; च – and; अन्ते – at the end; विश्वम् – the creation; आदौ – in the beginning; सः – that; देवः – Divine Being; (may); सः – He; नः – us; बुद्ध्या – with intellect; शुभया – with a pure; संयुनक्तु – endow

1. The Divine Being who is one and without colours, who creates, through His multifarious powers, innumerable colours in the beginning of creation with a purpose known only to Himself, and who dissolves the entire creation at the end - may He endow us with a pure intellect.

From one to many and many to one: The colourless beam of light passing through a prism disperses the seven colours of the spectrum. Similarly, the attributeless God/Truth, one without a second, united with His infinite and inscrutable power of māyā creates this multicoloured, multidimentional, multifarious and multiplying world. There seems no end to the multitude and it is difficult to imagine that it all comes from one Truth and even more difficult to imagine that it all winds up in that one Truth at the time of dissolution. On the streets of Indian villages, towns and cities, we see hawkers bring a bundle of their ware which they painstakingly spread out in the morning and neatly wind up in the same bundle in the evening, everyday throughout the year.

The meaning behind creation and dissolution (nihitārtha): Every object serves some purpose. Nothing is useless. An object discarded by one person may be very useful to another. Children are taught to make creative objects from waste products. Someone has said – 'There is no letter or sound which cannot become a mantra; there is no root or plant which has no medicinal value; there is no person who is unfit or useless – only it is difficult to find a person who understands their use and utilises them fully.'[1] A person who is considered physically challenged and incapable is really differently abled and can do unbelievable things.

There is a lot of meaning behind everything. Every event in our life has many lessons to teach. The more meaning we discover the more remains to be discovered. People ask, 'Why creation?' It can be answered with, 'Why not creation?' If the Lord so willed, why not. We can only guess at the meaning behind creation, but really speaking only God knows the purpose of His creation.

a. God has no selfish motive or hidden agenda behind creation. He creates spontaneously and effortlessly in a blink of an eye.

b. One can say that creation is for His recreation. Like a child plays with his own fingers, the Lord manifests in many forms and plays with Himself. For example, a person looks at himself in a hall of mirrors and gets entertained by the distorted images in the convex or concave mirrors.

c. God creates this world to give a chance to all the beings to exhaust their inherent desires so that they thereafter seek Him through His creation.

The seeking through prayer: There are many moods and feelings in prayer.

a. Some who understand that God is omniscient, omnipotent and compassionate, sit mute before Him in prayer.

[1] amantram akṣaro nāsti nāsti mūlam anauṣadham,
ayogyaḥ puruṣo nāsti yojakastatra durlabhaḥ.

b. Some ask for guidance and strength.

c. Some pray with the feelings – when will I become good or when will I turn to thee.' When will I become happy singing your name' prays Rāvaṇa to Lord Śiva.[1]

d. Some pray with longing to see the Lord, to gain liberation or with suffering in separation from the Lord.

e. Some looking at themselves feel they are even unfit to approach Him or ask for anything.

Here the seeker repeats his prayer to God to fill his mind with noble thoughts so that he can know the Truth.

[1] śiveti mantram uccaran kadā sukhī bhavāmyaham

A glimpse of His infinite variety in creation is given in three beautiful mantras.

तदेवाग्निस्तदादित्यस्तद्वायुस्तदु चन्द्रमाः ।
तदेव शुक्रं तद्ब्रह्म तदापस्तत्प्रजापतिः ॥ २ ॥

त्वं स्त्री त्वं पुमानसि त्वं कुमार उत वा कुमारी ।
त्वं जीर्णो दण्डेन वञ्चसि त्वं जातो भवसि विश्वतोमुखः ॥ ३ ॥

नीलः पतङ्गो हरितो लोहिताक्षस्तडिद्गर्भ ऋतवः समुद्राः ।
अनादिमत्त्वं विभुत्वेन वर्तसे यतो जातानि भुवनानि विश्वा ॥ ४ ॥

tad-evāgnis-tad-ādityas-tad-vāyus-tadu candramāḥ,
tadeva śukraṁ tadbrahma tad-āpastat-prajāpatiḥ. (2)

tvaṁ strī tvaṁ pumān-asi tvaṁ kumāra uta vā kumārī,
tvaṁ jīrṇo daṇḍena vañcasi tvaṁ jāto bhavasi viśvatomukhaḥ. (3)

nīlaḥ pataṅgo harito lohitākṣas-taḍidgarbha ṛtavaḥ samudrāḥ,
anādimat-tvaṁ vibhutvena vartase yato jātāni bhuvanāni viśvā. (4)

तद् – That; एव – alone; अग्निः – fire; तद् – That; आदित्यः – sun; तद् – That; वायुः – air; तद् उ – That; चन्द्रमाः – the moon; तद् – That; एव – indeed; शुक्रम् – pure; तद् – That; ब्रह्म – Truth (Brahman); तद् – That; आपः – water; तत् – That; प्रजापतिः – Creator

त्वम् – You; स्त्री – woman; त्वम् – You; पुमान् – man; असि – are; त्वम् – You; कुमारः – young boy; उत – or; वा – too; कुमारी – young girl; त्वम् – You; जीर्णः – old man; दण्डेन – with a stick;

वञ्चसि – tottering; त्वम् – You; जातः – born; भवसि – are; विश्वतोमुखः – one with faces in all directions

नीलः – blue; पतङ्गः – bee; हरितः – green; लोहिताक्षः – having reddish eyes; तडिद्गर्भः – the clouds (possessed of lightning in their womb); ऋतवः – the seasons; समुद्राः – the seas; अनादिमत् – beginningless; त्वम् – You; विभुत्वेन – on account of (Your) omnipresence; वर्तसे – exist (in varied forms); यतः – from whom; जातानि – are born; भुवनानि – the worlds; विश्वाः – all

2. That alone is fire, That is the sun, That is air and That is the moon. That, indeed, is pure, That is the Truth (Brahman), That is water and That is the Creator.

3. You are the woman, You are the man, You are the young boy and You are the young girl too, and You are the old man tottering with a stick. You are born with faces in all directions.

4. You are the blue bee, the green bird with the reddish eyes, the clouds, the seasons and the seas. You are beginningless and pervade everything, and from You are born all the worlds.

God as the vast cosmos (tadevāgni ...): He alone is the five elements and the sun, moon and stars made up from them. He alone is the laws of nature and the deities who govern these laws. He alone is the totality and the individuality. He is both global and local.

Is God a man or woman? (tvaṁ strī ...): This is a subject of a lot of debate. Since God is generally referred to as 'He', it creates reactions in a society which is sensitive to gender bias. However there need not be any controversy or heart burn in this regard as He alone manifests as all forms – man and woman – even though in His absolute nature He is formless, hence genderless.

It is God alone who manifests as a young boy and girl, an adult man and woman and as an aged man (as women never age!). He alone can be seen in the shyness of a girl, the femininity in a woman, the manliness in a man, the beauty of graceful aging, in the wizened face of a grandparent, or the unsteady gait of a senior citizen. How deceptive is God. Being timeless, He appears to be born growing and aging!

The scriptures therefore say that we should meet all with love and respect – as God is in all forms. In India the bride is looked upon as an embodiment of Divine wealth – Goddess Lakṣmī Herself and every young person bows down to those older than him.

God – the beauty in nature (nilaḥ pataṅgo ...): Some people are far removed from nature and some do not mind exploiting her for profit. Some enjoy an occasional week-end at the beach or a vacation skiing in the Alps. Some love nature deeply and live their life in harmony with her and are sensitive and concerned about her. However the scriptures ask us to look upon her as divine manifestation and worship her.

The Ṛṣi becomes poetic as he paints a picture of God's creation. God can be seen in the form of the beautiful blue bees and butterflies that flutter from flower to flower. He flies high and low and chirps and coos as hundreds of birds like the sparrows and the green parrots. He alone is seen as a multitude of creatures – both big and small in splendid colours and unbelievable shapes like the slithering shiny skinned serpent or the gigantic white whale.

The Lord is seen in the stormy clouds, changing of the seasons, various moods of the ocean and silence of the night. No two beings – even identical twins – are the same and the colours of the sunset or sunrise are never repeated. It is as though God breaks the mould after making each thing and being. If we can see Him in all, what love and joy there will be in life. Small things like the splash of water or the cool breeze caressing our skin could transport us into meditation.

Once upon a time there was a king who did not have an heir. He decided to hand over his kingdom to any young and intelligent man who could spot him in a crowd. He went to a huge fair in disguise. Thousands of people were there. Some made half-hearted efforts to search for him, before getting distracted by some tempting food or game. One young man remained focused and saw that one man alone did not indulge in any pleasures and sat watching others. He recognised the king and was later crowned to the throne. Similarly God too hides amongst us. One who searches for Him even in the midst of all worldly temptations is sure to find Him.

The next mantra illustrates the nature of Lord's māyā and her influence on the ignorant individual and the Realised one.

अजामेकां लोहितशुक्लकृष्णां बह्वीः प्रजाः सृजमानां सरूपाः ।
अजो ह्येको जुषमाणोऽनुशेते जहात्येनां भुक्तभोगामजोऽन्यः ॥ ५ ॥

ajāmekāṁ lohita-śukla-kṛṣṇāṁ bahvīḥ prajāḥ sṛjamānāṁ sarūpāḥ,
ajo hyeko juṣamāṇo'nuśete jahātyenāṁ bhuktabhogām-ajo'nyaḥ. (5)

अजाम् – birthless; एकाम् – one; लोहित-शुक्ल-कृष्णाम् – red, white and black in colour; बह्वीः – many; प्रजाः – offsprings; सृजमानाम् – who creates; सरूपाः – of its own kind; अजः – birthless; हि – indeed; एकः – one; जुषमाणः – being adored; अनुशेते – enjoys; जहाति – renounces; एनाम् – her; भुक्तभोगाम् – one who has been enjoyed; अजः – birthless; अन्यः – another

5. A birthless power, red, white and black in colour, who creates many offsprings like herself, is indeed adored and enjoyed by a birthless one, while another birthless one renounces her after having enjoyed her.

This mantra is often quoted by commentators and is quite famous.

The nature of māyā: God's indescribable divine power called māyā śakti or prakṛti was described earlier (1.2). This potential creative and deluding power of God is always with Him and is beginningless. Māyā has the three qualities of rajas, sattva and tamas, characterised by activity, knowledge and inertia and represented by red, white and black colours respectively. The three corresponding elements to the three qualities are fire (tejaḥ), water (āpaḥ) and earth (pṛthivī). Our body has a preponderance of inertness (tamas) and the earth element. The physiological functions (prāṇas) and sense organs of action have more rajas and the fire element. The mind and sense organs of perception have more sattva – the knowledge aspect and the element of water. The order of enumeration indicates the predominance of rajas, sattva and tamas in creation, sustenance and destruction – the three main functions of māyā.

In the presence of God, māyā manifests its full potential power and creates the gross and the subtle elements and the infinite variety of things and beings. The cause pervades the effect and therefore the three qualities pervade everything in creation.

The bondage of māyā: The finite individuals, you and me are also beginningless. We have been taking birth after birth from beginningless time. The ignorant individual identifies with māyā and its effects, the body-mind-intellect and thinks of it as 'me' and 'mine' and becomes the doer of actions and enjoyer of the world and the results of his actions.

In *Bhāgavatam* there is the popular story of King Purañjana who got so attracted and attached to Purañjanī that if she danced, he danced. When she sang, he sang. In her happiness, he smiled and in her sorrow he wept. This is the bondage of māyā. When the body suffers, I suffer, when the mind is happy, I am happy.

Attachments and bondages are often created through our relationships. Svāmī Akhaṇḍānanda would tell an interesting story to illustrate this. When bondage (bandhana) was created, he found no place to stay so he approached the Creator – Lord Brahmā and asked for accommodation. Lord Brahmā said, "Stay with any person you wish." He complained, "But no one wants me. They shut their door on my face." Lord Brahmā said, "Do not introduce yourself as 'bondage' (bandhana), disguise yourself and go as 'relationship' (sambandhana) and all will welcome you!" So he went and knocked on someone's door – 'Knock knock' 'Who is there?' "I am your friend" and the doors were thrown wide open! How easily we are bound by relationships.

Viṣṇu Purāṇa has a telling verse which means 'As long as man keeps forming relationships which please his mind, so long will his heart be pierced with the nails of sorrow.'[1]

Freedom from māyā: The intelligent individual understands well the binding nature of māyā, so does not get trapped even as he enjoys the world. He knows that māyā is not meant only for enjoyment, but also to recognise the Lord. Tamo guṇa of Māyā hides God and rajo guṇa projects what is not there. But sattva guṇa helps us to discriminate between the real and the false and frees us from false identifications and reveals the Truth. So the wise man gives up rajas and tamas and develops sattva guṇa and liberates himself.

There is also a subtle wordplay in this verse. 'Ajā' means a female goat and 'aja' a male goat. One male goat

[1] yāvataḥ kurute jantuḥ sambandhān manasaḥ priyān,
tāvanto'sya nikhanyante hṛdaye śokaśaṅkavaḥ.

gets fascinated and involved with the female goat and gives birth to a lot of progeny for which he becomes responsible. Another male goat leaves her well alone, as he sees the bondage in such pleasures. Śaṅkarācārya too says – Like an animal tied by rope, the individual identifies and gets attached to the body and the objects of the world by the ropes of māyā and its qualities. When he understands their binding (poisonous) nature and worthlessness, he becomes free.[1]

[1] dehādi-sarvaviṣaye parikalpya rāgaṁ badhnāti tena puruṣaṁ paśuvadguṇena, vairasyam-atra viṣavat-suvidhāya paścād-enaṁ vimocayati tanmana eva bandhāt.

– *Vivekacūḍāmaṇi* 173

The next two mantras give another beautiful analogy of the relation between the individual and God.

द्वा सुपर्णा सयुजा सखाया समानं वृक्षं परिषस्वजाते ।
तयोरन्यः पिप्पलं स्वाद्वत्त्यनश्नन्नन्यो अभिचाकशीति ॥ ६ ॥

समाने वृक्षे पुरुषो निमग्नोऽनीशया शोचति मुह्यमानः ।
जुष्टं यदा पश्यत्यन्यमीशमस्य महिमानमिति वीतशोकः ॥ ७ ॥

dvā suparṇā sayujā sakhāyā samānaṁ vṛkṣaṁ pariṣasvajāte,
tayoranyaḥ pippalaṁ svādvattyanaśnannanyo abhicākaśīti. (6)

samāne vṛkṣe puruṣo nimagno'nīśayā śocati muhyamānaḥ,
juṣṭaṁ yadā paśyatyanyamīśam-asya mahimānam-iti vītaśokaḥ. (7)

द्वौ – two; सुपर्णौ – birds of beautiful plumage; सयुजौ – (always) together; सखायौ – as friends; समानम् – the same; वृक्षम् – tree; परिषस्वजाते – sit upon; तयोः – of these two; अन्यः – one; पिप्पलम् – the fruit; स्वादु – of divergent tastes; अत्ति – relishes; अनश्नन् – without eating; अन्यः – the other; अभिचाकशीति – looks on

समाने – on the same; वृक्षे – on the tree; पुरुषः – the individual; निमग्नः – remains immersed; अनीशया – helplessly; शोचति – grieves; मुह्यमानः – being deluded; जुष्टम् – worshipped; यदा – when; पश्यति – sees; अन्यम् – the other; ईशम् – the Lord; अस्य – His; महिमानम् – glory; इति – so or thus; वीतशोकः – free of sorrow

6. Two birds of beautiful plumage (always) together as friends sit upon the same tree. One of them relishes the fruits (of divergent tastes) of the tree, while the other looks on without eating.

7. On the same tree, the individual remains immersed, helpless and grieving in delusion. When he sees the other, the Lord, and worships Him, He sees all as His glory and becomes free from sorrow.

One tree: Etymologically a tree is that which can be felled (vraścanāt vṛkṣaḥ). The body is like a tree since it perishes. Worldly existence (saṁsāra) is also compared to a tree as it can be felled by the sword of detachment and right knowledge.[1] The tree is samāna – with measurement. Like the tree, the body too is measured in terms of age, size, weight and such parameters.

Two birds: Two birds – the individual and God, both live on the same tree – in the body. They are both beautiful – with strong wings and beautiful plumage (suparṇā) with which they can fly far and wide. They are very closely connected with each other (sayujā). In fact they have always lived together from beginningless time even when the individual goes from body to body.

Some people may live together but may not be friends or friendly with each other. They may dislike the other or be indifferent towards the other. However the individual and God are fast friends (sakhāyā) and are always seen together (samāna khyāti). There where the individual is, God too is surely there and they love each other dearly.

The bird's eye-view: The individual (bird) indentifies with the body and attains finitude. He then always seeks to

[1] asaṅgaśastreṇa dṛḍhena chittvā - *Gītā* 15.3

become complete by eating the fruits of action – sometimes sweet, sometimes sour. He is always restless and desiring and searching for new ways to make himself happy, sometimes going to a movie theatre, sometimes vacationing in the Bahamas and sometimes engrossed in a game of football. Very often not getting what he desires, he experiences dejection and depression, which is the most common disease of modern times. He feels helpless and unable to give up either his wrong life style or his fascination for the world. In sorrow he cries, "My son is dead, my wife is gone, I am good for nothing."

In his quest for pleasure, the individual often forgets his friend, the Lord. But the Lord never forgets him. Sugrīva, when he got his kingdom after years of exile, got so engrossed in enjoyment that he forgot God and his promise to Lord Śrī Rāma to search for Sītā (true peace and love). Lakṣmaṇa (detachment) had to drag him away from pleasures and take him to God.

What does God (the other bird) do? He remains as a witness of both the body and the actions of the individual. In fact when we objectively observe the individual, it is quite entertaining to watch him flit from pleasure to pleasure. It is interesting to see an individual going after the same pleasure again and again, getting completely hooked by it – even when the fruit is no longer juicy. God always remains the witness Consciousness, the non-doer (akartā) and non-enjoyer (abhoktā).

However as a result of some previous meritorious deeds or the company of noble souls or the Grace of God, he turns towards God. Once in a while when he looks at God, he feels very happy and peaceful. But again some worldly temptation comes his way and he is off on a trip to the coffee shop. However after a time of going back and forth there comes a time when he moves closer and closer to God and finally realises God as his own Self. Thereafter he sees the whole world only as His glory. This puts an end to all finitude and sorrow.

As finite individuals we suffer in worldly existence. If we start looking for God in everything, even if we consider ourselves as individuals, we will still not be miserable. Liberation is assured for an earnest seeker. Seeing the firm determination of Naciketa, Lord Yama tells him that the gates of Truth are indeed open for him (*Kaṭhopaniṣad* 1.2.9).

The important thing is to take the first step and start worshipping God. Spend some time each day exclusively for God, sit in front of your altar and do whatever spiritual practice you love to do – repeat the Holy name, worship, meditation, talk to God, look at God, think of God ... or just sit with God. It is guaranteed that your mind will become quiet, solutions to problems will gradually come to you, you will feel the presence of God in your life and there will be an umbrella of His grace protecting you always. This will not happen overnight. It is a continuous process.

The Ṛṣi again urges us to know God through the study of the Vedas.

ऋचो अक्षरे परमे व्योमन् यस्मिन्देवा अधि विश्वे निषेदुः ।
यस्तं न वेद किमृचा करिष्यति य इत्तद्विदुस्त इमे समासते ॥ ८ ॥

ṛco akṣare parame vyoman yasmin-devā adhi viśve niṣeduḥ,
yastaṁ na veda kimṛcā kariṣyati ya ittad-vidusta ime samāsate. (8)

ऋचः – the Vedas; अक्षरे – in the imperishable; परमे – in the supreme; व्योमन् – in the space (of Consciousness); यस्मिन् – where; देवाः – the deities; विश्वे – all; अधि निषेदुः – dwell; यः – who; तम् – Him; न – not; वेद – know; किम् – what; ऋचा – with the Vedas; करिष्यति – will do; यः – who; इत् – thus; तद् – That; विदुः – know; ते – they; इमे – who; समासते – remain fulfilled

8. The Vedas reside in the imperishable supreme space (of Consciousness) where all the deities dwell. He who does not know That (Consciousness or Truth), what can Vedas do for him? Those who know It remain fulfilled.

What is the role of Vedas or the study of the Vedas in our life?

The Vedas dwell in God: Everything exists in God/Truth – all knowledge, powers and beings. Vedas are the knowledge of the external laws that govern the world and knowledge of the supreme Truth. They too naturally reside in Him. In fact they are revealed by Him alone.

Vedas – the mirror to God: Whether the Veda mantras speak of performance of rituals, attainment of heavens, worship of various deities or our true nature, their purport and purpose is in revealing the Truth as our own Self. They teach us to recognise the Lord in the hearts of all beings. If a person studies the Vedas and does not understand this, of what use is his study? It is not right to find fault with the Vedas, or study of the Vedas or the Guru who teaches the Vedas. It is aptly said, 'What can scriptures do for a person who does not have the intelligence to understand them? What use is a mirror to a blind person?'[1]

Scriptures are like a mirror that shows us the state of our life and lifestyle, our mind and its functioning and finally God as our own Self. People get impatient when they do not understand or when they are unable to see God/Truth and they give up the study. Don't give up the study; try again.

Some study the scriptures only for scholastic satisfaction, some only to teach others, some only commit the mantras to memory and some are engaged in scholastic discussions. Alas their knowledge of Vedas does not give them fulfilment (samyak āsate samāsate) that is promised in knowing God/Truth. Instead of carrying a load of trash, they are burdened with the load of gems.

[1] yasya nāsti svayaṁ prajñā śāstraṁ tasya karoti kim,
locanābhyāṁ vihīnasya darpaṇaḥ kiṁ kariṣyati.

The scriptures speak of various spiritual practices. What is their relation with God?

छन्दांसि यज्ञाः क्रतवो व्रतानि भूतं भव्यं यच्च वेदा वदन्ति।
अस्मान्मायी सृजते विश्वमेतत्तस्मिंश्चान्यो मायया सन्निरुद्धः॥ ९॥

chandāṁsi yajñāḥ kratavo vratāni bhūtaṁ bhavyaṁ yacca vedā vadanti,
asmān-māyī sṛjate viśvametat-tasmiṁścānyo māyayā sanniruddhaḥ. (9)

छन्दांसि – the Vedas; यज्ञाः – sacrifices; क्रतवः – spiritual practices; व्रतानि – vows; भूतम् – the past; भव्यम् – the future; यद् – that; च – and; वेदाः – the Vedas; वदन्ति – talk; अस्मात् – from It; मायी – the Lord of māyā; सृजते – creates; विश्वम् – world; एतत् – this; तस्मिन् – in that; च – and; अन्यः – another; मायया – because of māyā; सन्निरुद्धः – (remains) bound

9. The Vedas, sacrifices, spiritual practices, vows, the past, the future and all that the Vedas talk about are from It. The Lord of māyā creates this world. In that another remains bound because of māyā.

God – the means for purification: God manifests as the Vedas. The various spiritual practices revealed in the Vedas are a means to fulfill our desires or for purification of the mind. They are created by God for our well-being. The ritualistic fire sacrifices are called yajñas and other forms of rituals to fulfill our desires are called kratus. There are different types of vratas – vows that people take. Some are at the physical level like fasting, some are at the verbal level like observance of silence and some are at the mental level like avoiding anger. The mental ones are subtler, more difficult but the best. We can start with avoiding anger for just one day. And that day would seem to hold the maximum situations for us to get angry!

God – the right time: It is God alone who created the past and everything that happened, the present and all it holds and future with all its possibilities. Therefore all times are right and good.

God – the means to freedom: God is the weilder of māyā (māyī) and creates everything. He alone creates the means to liberation in the form of the Vedas and spiritual practices. The Vedas and scriptures are His books of instruction on how to use the God-given instruments (body and mind) and live happily in His creation. When we do not follow these instructions we get bound by māyā and suffer.

The next mantra throws more light on the relationship between God and māyā.

मायां तु प्रकृतिं विद्यान्मायिनं च महेश्वरम्।
तस्यावयवभूतैस्तु व्याप्तं सर्वमिदं जगत्॥ १०॥

māyāṁ tu prakṛtiṁ vidyān-māyinaṁ ca maheśvaram,
tasyāvayavabhūtaistu vyāptaṁ sarvam-idaṁ jagat. (10)

मायाम् – māyā; तु – surely; प्रकृतिम् – nature; विद्यात् – know; मायिनम् – the Lord of māyā; च – and; महेश्वरम् – Maheśvara; तस्य – His; अवयवभूतैः – by what are (His) limbs; तु – verily; व्याप्तम् – filled; सर्वम् – all or whole; इदम् – this; जगत् – world

10. Know that nature is surely māyā and the Lord of māyā is Maheśvara, the supreme Lord. This whole world is verily filled by His limbs.

The first line of this mantra is quite famous.

Māyā and prakṛti: Both are synonyms, however they have special connotations. Prakṛti is that power of the Lord which is capable of producing things (prakarṣeṇa kṛti yogyatvāt). It is the material cause and brings to mind the ever-changing aspect of creation.

Māyā refers more to the illusory aspect of creation and the power that deludes and eludes all. Māyā, like magic, makes everything appear without any real happening. That which is not, but appears to be there is called māyā (yā mā sā māyā). It makes the impossible possible (aghaṭita ghaṭanā paṭīyasī māyā). Saint Tulasīdāsa says that God paints the picture of this world on the canvas of void without hands or paint![1] Yet the painting appears so real and beautiful. However māyā has two aspects – vidyā māyā – which creates the world and helps us gain knowledge and avidyā māyā – which deludes and binds.

Lord – the Māyāvī: God is the Master, the controller or the wielder of māyā or prakṛti. It is confusing when we hear that prakṛti creates the world and then again we are told that God creates the world. Who actually creates? We must understand that 'Māyā presided over by God/Truth creates the world.'[2] By itself māyā can do nothing. The platoon was marching forward and neared the edge of a cliff. Not getting any order from the commander to turn, one officer said, "Please say something. At least say good-bye!" Māyā does nothing without the command of the Lord. When it is said God creates, it means God/Truth functioning through māyā creates the world. Without the power and potential to create, no creation is possible.

Is māyā real or unreal? How can God's power be unreal? How can māyā have any reality apart from God? If it does, God becomes unreal. It is answered thus – when we consider the world to be real, māyā, its cause appears real. From the standpoint of God, māyā does not exist. From māyā standpoint, it is both real and unreal, yet neither. Indescribable (anirvacanīya) indeed is māyā.

---

[1] śūnya bhitti par citra raṅga nahīn tanu binu likhā cittere – *Vinaya Patrikā*
[2] mayādhyakṣeṇa prakṛtiḥ sūyate sacarācaram – *Gītā* 9.10

What gives total peace in life? The mantra says –

यो योनिं योनिमधितिष्ठत्येको यस्मिन्निदं सं च वि चैति सर्वम्।
तमीशानं वरदं देवमीड्यं निचाय्येमां शान्तिमत्यन्तमेति ॥ ११ ॥

yo yonim̐ yonim-adhitiṣṭhatyeko yasminnidam̐ sam̐ ca vi caiti sarvam, tam-īśānam̐ varadam̐ devam-īḍyam̐ nicāyyemām̐ śāntim-atyantameti. (11)

यः – who; योनिं योनिम् – every womb; अधितिष्ठति – presides over; एकः – one; यस्मिन् – in whom; इदम् – this; सम् एति – exists; च – and; वि एति – dissolves or merges; सर्वम् – all; तम् – Him; ईशानम् – Lord; वरदम् – bestower of boons; देवम् – self-effulgent; ईड्यम् – adorable; निचाय्य – by realising; इमाम् – this; शान्तिम् – peace; अत्यन्तम् – supreme; एति – attains

11. By realising the one Lord who presides over every womb, in whom everything exists and merges, who bestows boons, and who is self-effulgent and adorable, one attains supreme peace.

God in every womb: It is God only who resides in every womb, presides over every womb and protects and supports every womb. The scriptures say there are 84 lakh different species and there are millions of creatures of each species and God is the indweller in all of them!

The phrase 'yonim yonim' also has another meaning. The unmanifest prakṛti is the womb of the entire creation. From that comes the manifest prakṛti made up of the five subtle and gross elements. The manifest prakṛti then becomes all things and beings. God presides over all wombs and the womb of all wombs (prakṛti).

God – the bestower of boons (varada): God gives liberally (varaṁ dadati iti varadaḥ). He gives what we desire. When He appears before the devotee as a result of worship, He always says, "Ask and it shall be granted." Nothing is impossible for Him to give as all is His alone. He therefore becomes adorable to many. Who will not adore someone who fulfills all they desire? However we do not know what to ask!

Once there lived a poor man who would spend his days in work and worship of God. He had no children and had to support his blind parents. Pleased by him, God appeared and offered him a boon. He was too overwhelmed and confused to ask and so consulted his intelligent wife. As advised by her he asked, "O Lord! May my old parents see with their own eyes their grandson drinking milk in a golden cup!" So at one shot he got vision for his blind parents, was blessed with a son and became prosperous enough to give him milk in a golden cup!

God – the Supreme Peace: External peace is the absence of sound. Internal peace is the flow of sāttvika thoughts or lesser number of thoughts or total absence of thoughts as when a person goes into samādhi (state of absorption of mind). However external and internal peace is not long lasting. It is very brittle. A slight sound or a passing thought of hatred can shatter it. To gain it takes effort, but to destroy it takes nothing. Supreme peace is everlasting and gained through Realisation of God who is one without a second and therefore of the nature of eternal peace.[1]

---

[1] teṣāṁ śāntiḥ śāśvatī netareṣām – *Kaṭhopaniṣad* 2.2.13

The next mantra is almost a repetition of an earlier mantra (3.4).

यो देवानां प्रभवश्चोद्भवश्च विश्वाधिपो रुद्रो महर्षिः ।
हिरण्यगर्भं पश्यत जायमानं स नो बुद्ध्या शुभया संयुनक्तु ॥ १२ ॥

yo devānāṁ prabhavaścodbhavaśca viśvādhipo rudro maharṣiḥ, hiraṇyagarbhaṁ paśyata jāyamānaṁ sa no buddhyā śubhayā saṁyunaktu. (12)

यः – who; देवानाम् – of deities; प्रभवः – origin; च – and; उद्भवः – the source; च – and; विश्वाधिपः – the Lord of the entire universe; रुद्रः – Rudra; महर्षिः – the great Seer (who is all knowing); हिरण्यगर्भम् – Hiraṇyagarbha; पश्यत – saw; जायमानम् – brought into being or emerging; सः – He; नः – us; बुद्ध्या – with thoughts; शुभया – with auspicious; संयुनक्तु – (may) endow

12. May Rudra who is the origin of all the deities and the source of all their powers, who is all knowing and the Lord of the entire universe, who initially brought into being Hiraṇyagarbha, endow us with auspicious (noble) thoughts.

The next mantra establishes God as the truly worshipful one.

यो देवानामधिपो यस्मिँल्लोका अधिश्रिताः ।
य ईशे अस्य द्विपदश्चतुष्पदः कस्मै देवाय हविषा विधेम ॥ १३ ॥

yo devānām-adhipo yasmiṁl-lokā adhiśritāḥ,
ya īśe asya dvipadaś-catuṣpadaḥ kasmai devāya haviṣā vidhema. (13)

यः – who; देवानाम् – of the deities; अधिपः – Lord; यस्मिन् – in whom; लोकाः – the worlds; अधिश्रिताः – rest; यः – who; ईशे – rules over; अस्य – this; द्विपदः – (of) the bipeds; चतुष्पदः – (of) the quadrupeds; कस्मै – to whom; देवाय – to the Lord; हविषा – oblations; विधेम – (we) offer

13. He who is the Lord of all the deities, He in whom rest all the worlds, He who rules over all the bipeds and quadrupeds, to that blissful Lord we offer our oblations.

God – the Lord of all: Some worship power like the power of a sole monarch or dictator of a land. Some respect lordship like lordship over a huge worldwide expanse of a multinational company. Some value the power of love that a Guru has over his followers. Some are fascinated by the control people have over animals like the man in a lion cage in a circus. But who will not revere God who has all of these? God is the Lord of all deities, human beings and animals.

God – the embodiment of Bliss: The word 'kasmai' means 'to whom?', but in this context the word 'ka' is interpreted as happiness or bliss. 'Kasmai devāya' then means to the blissful God/Truth. This small twist is delightful – instead of saying 'tasmai devāya' – to that God, it is said, 'kasmai devāya' giving it a beautiful double meaning. When such a God, personification of Bliss is there, which other deity will we worship? So both the meanings of kasmai come into play.

All are drawn to those who make them laugh and are fun to be with. But such joy is also conditioned. The person could one day even make you cry! But who will not want to serve and please God who is the very source of everlasting joy? Who will not worship one who fills us with love and joy always?

'Havis' is the oblation that is offered in the fire during the ritualistic fire worship (yajña). The seeker is asked to consider his work as an offering to God (karma yoga). At a subtler level, we are asked to offer our finite identity and become one with the Blissful Lord. Śrī Ramaṇa Maharṣi says, 'Realisation is oneself becoming food for God.'[1] It means to give up one's notion of doership and enjoyership and become one with God.

[1] svayaṁ tadannībhavanaṁ tadīkṣā – *Saddarśanam* 23

Can God be found in the midst of our chaotic and busy life? The mantra says –

सूक्ष्मातिसूक्ष्मं कलिलस्य मध्ये विश्वस्य स्त्रष्टारमनेकरूपम् ।
विश्वस्यैकं परिवेष्टितारं ज्ञात्वा शिवं शान्तिमत्यन्तमेति ॥ १४ ॥

sūkṣmātisūkṣmaṁ kalilasya madhye viśvasya sraṣṭāramanekarūpaṁ,
viśvasyaikaṁ pariveṣṭitāraṁ jñātvā śivaṁ śāntim-atyantameti. (14)

सूक्ष्मातिसूक्ष्मम् – subtler than the subtlest; कलिलस्य – of chaos; मध्ये – in the midst; विश्वस्य – of the universe; स्त्रष्टारम् – the Creator; अनेकरूपम् – appearing in manifold forms; विश्वस्य – of the universe; एकम् – one; परिवेष्टितारम् – who encompasses; ज्ञात्वा – having known; शिवम् – the Lord; शान्तिम् – peace; अत्यन्तम् – supreme; एति – attains

14. Knowing the Lord as one who is subtler than the subtlest, existing in the midst of chaos, the Creator of the universe, appearing in manifold forms and encompassing the entire universe, a person attains supreme peace.

God – subtler than the subtlest (sūkṣmātisūkṣma): The cause always has a subtle presence in the effect. The unmanifest prakṛti is subtler than the manifest prakṛti which is the cause of the names and forms in this world. God is the subtle presence even in the unmanifest prakṛti as the very Existence, which is subtler than the subtlest.

Subtlety is measured by pervasiveness. Space is subtler than air as it is more pervasive. God even illumines space and gives it existence and is therefore subtler than the all-pervading space. Then would it not be impossible to see such a subtle God, especially in the midst of our gross and chaotic world?

God – in the middle of chaos (kalilasya madhye): The word kalila has many meanings. One meaning is chaos, confusion or calamity. God is the silent presence in the midst of turbulence of daily life. He is the Consciousness connecting, illumining and in between our agitated and fast moving thoughts. Did not Arjuna find solace from Lord Śrī Kṛṣṇa in the middle of the Kurukṣetra battle field? God is the Truth between all our dancing thoughts as personified by Śrī Kṛṣṇa in the Rāsa Līlā standing in the midst of hundreds of Gopīs dancing around Him. Śaṅkarācārya explains that God or Consciousness illumines all thought modifications – even thoughts of ignorance (kalila).

The *Garbha Śāstra* gives a name for the foetus at different stages of its development in the womb. The foetus immediately after conception is called kalila. God is present even in that early stage of cell formation in our life!

God's all-encompassing embrace (pariveṣṭitāra): God embraces the whole universe. When He incarnates, He engulfs all in His love. It is said that Śrī Rāma and Śrī Kṛṣṇa had very long arms (ājānu-bāhu) – extending up to the knees. The saint explains that Śrī Rāma had long arms so He could embrace even His fattest devotee!

Reward of God-realisation (śāntim atyantameti): The beneficial effect, the measurable result, the attractive reward and the evident gain of God-realisation is pointed out time and again to inspire us towards it. Spiritual seekers must not seek material gains through spiritual pursuits, but measure their progress only in terms of inner gain. How much more spontaneous love do I feel? How much has anger and greed reduced? Am I willing to sacrifice more for the sake of another? Even supernatural powers should not be considered spiritual progress. Someone told Śrī Rāmakṛṣṇa Paramahaṁsa about a yogi who spent years in penance and could cross the river by walking on water. The saint remarked that it would have been better if he had paid a few paisa to the boatman and crossed with a boat instead of spending all those years for something the wood does naturally! The highest reward of God-realisation is to attain everlasting peace and bliss.

The next mantra gives examples of illustrious souls who have attained the Truth.

स एव काले भुवनस्य गोप्ता विश्वाधिपः सर्वभूतेषु गूढः।
यस्मिन्युक्ता ब्रह्मर्षयो देवताश्च तमेवं ज्ञात्वा मृत्युपाशांश्छिनत्ति ॥ १५ ॥

sa eva kāle bhuvanasya goptā viśvādhipaḥ sarvabhūteṣu gūḍhaḥ,
yasmin-yuktā brahmarṣayo devatāśca tamevaṁ jñātvā
mṛtyupāśāṁś-chinatti. (15)

सः – He; एव – alone; काले – at the appropriate time; भुवनस्य – of the world; गोप्ता – the protector; विश्वाधिपः – the Lord of the universe; सर्वभूतेषु – in all creatures; गूढः – hidden; यस्मिन् – in whom; युक्ताः – absorbed; ब्रह्मर्षयः – brahmarṣis; देवताः – the deities; च – and; तम् – Him; एवम् – thus; ज्ञात्वा – having known; मृत्युपाशाम् – the bondage of death; छिनत्ति – destroys

15. He alone is the protector of the world at the appropriate time. He is the Lord of the universe and remains hidden in all creatures. Knowing Him thus, in whom the brahmarṣis and deities are absorbed, one destroys the bondage of death.

God – the Protector (bhuvanasya goptā): Not only does God protect us when we are in trouble, but He alone protects the entire universe. The word 'kāle' means at the right time. Protection is valued only when it is timely. Of what use is the burglar alarm, if it rings after the thieves have departed, taking away all your wealth.

Lord Śrī Kṛṣṇa says that 'Whenever there is decline in dharma and increase in adharma, He incarnates to protect the world.'[1] He is indeed the 'protector of the eternal dharma.'[2] When dharma is protected, the whole world is protected. Dharma is the law of being. Dharma is that rhythm which maintains and sustains the world.

The phrase 'sa eva kāle' also means when the time is right for the creation to come into manifestation. Once the world is created, He protects it through the cycle of time, the law of karma, the various deities and so on. And when the time is right, He dissolves the entire creation.

God – unknown to the ignorant: God remains hidden in the hearts of the ignorant and the extrovert. He is veiled by the screen of our own desires. Many people think 'we will find God after retirement as now we have worldly duties to fulfill.' Some think that since He is always there in our heart, He can always be found later. It is better to work now for what is not there! Then when they seek Him, they discover that He is not so easily found!

God – known to the wise: The qualified and prepared seekers alone realise God as do great brahmarṣis and devarṣis. A brāhmaṇa who is a seer of mantras like Sage Vasiṣṭha is called a brahmarṣi and a celestial being who is also a seer of mantras like Sage Nārada is called a devarṣi. Viśvāmitra had to struggle for long years to qualify as a brahmarṣi.

---

[1] yadā yadā hi dharmasya glānirbhavati bhārata,
Abhyutthānam-adharmasya tadātmānaṁ sṛjāmyaham. – *Gītā* 4.7

[2] Śāśvata-dharma-goptā – *Gītā* 11.18

Freedom from death: Freedom from death is freedom from the fear of change – death being the ultimate change. Lord Yama says that death to a wise man is like pickle that enhances the taste of food (mṛtyuḥ-yasya-upasecanam – *Kaṭhopaniṣad 1.2.25*), a challenge that adds zest to life. Young Dhruva is said to have placed his foot on the head of Death and boarded the plane to Dhruva-loka – the Eternal Abode. Śrī Ramaṇa Maharṣi says, 'Those who surrender to God who is beyond death, become one with Him, thereafter how can there be any fear of death for them?'[1]

[1] mṛtyuñjayaṁ mṛtyubhiyāśritānām ahammatirmṛtyumupaiti pūrvam,
atha svabhāvādamṛteṣu teṣu kathaṁ punarmṛtyudhiyo'vakāśaḥ.
– *Saddarśanam* 2

The next mantra describes God as the very 'cream of life'.

घृतात्परं मण्डमिवातिसूक्ष्मं ज्ञात्वा शिवं सर्वभूतेषु गूढम् ।
विश्वस्यैकं परिवेष्टितारं ज्ञात्वा देवं मुच्यते सर्वपाशैः ॥ १६ ॥

ghṛtāt-paraṁ maṇḍam-ivātisūkṣmaṁ jñātvā śivaṁ sarvabhūteṣu gūḍham,
viśvasyaikaṁ pariveṣṭitāraṁ jñātvā devaṁ mucyate sarvapāśaiḥ. (16)

घृतात् – from ghee; परम् – subtle; मण्डम् – essence of ghee that rises to the surface; इव – like; अतिसूक्ष्मम् – extremely subtle; ज्ञात्वा – having known or realising; शिवम् – Śiva; सर्वभूतेषु – in all beings; गूढम् – hidden; विश्वस्य – of the universe; एकम् – one; परिवेष्टितारम् – which is all encompassing; ज्ञात्वा – having known; देवम् – God; मुच्यते – becomes free; सर्वपाशैः – of all bondages

16. Realising that Śiva to be hidden in all beings like the subtle essence of ghee that rises to the surface, knowing that God to be the one entity that encompasses the entire universe, one becomes free of all bondages.

God – the very cream of life: The extremely subtle nature of God (ati sūkṣma) is conveyed through a beautiful phrase 'like the cream over the clarified butter' (ghṛtāt paraṁ maṇḍam iva). When milk is boiled, the tasty cream floats on the top. Yogurt that is made from it is even more tasty and rich. The yogurt is churned and fresh butter, its essence, comes to the top which was the favourite of Lord Śrī Kṛṣṇa. When the butter is heated it forms clarified butter (ghṛtam) which again has a layer of crystallised clarified butter on it. That is called maṇḍam – the tastiest and richest aspect of milk, the very subtle essence free of all extraneous ingredients. This is a sheer delight for the connoisseurs (ati prīti viṣaya). Similarly God/Truth is the very essence of life, the subtlest core of our personality and the giver of immeasurable joy to the spiritual seekers.

The *Taittirīya Upaniṣad* says that God is Bliss Absolute (raso vai saḥ). That which adds spice to life, that which makes everything worthwhile and interesting. Were it not for the Blissful Lord who would even desire to live in this world! Happiness is the only goal of everyone. Even in times of sorrow, people continue to live in the hope that they will be happy later. Lord Śrī Kṛṣṇa, Bliss Incarnate, was the very life of all in Gokul. When He left Gokul, all lived only with the hope of His return. The Auspicious Lord (Śiva) is indeed the essence (sāra) of worldly existence (saṁsāra).

Knowing God: The word 'jñātvā' is repeated twice in this verse. It means knowing that one God (ekaṁ jñātvā) and knowing alone (jñātvā eva) can man free himself from bondage. It also means that our knowledge of God increases, as we come closer to Him (jñātvā jñātvā), our sorrows reduce and false notions loosen their hold on us.

Who is the great architect of this world? The mantra says –

एष देवो विश्वकर्मा महात्मा सदा जनानां हृदये सन्निविष्टः।
हृदा मनीषा मनसाभिक्लृप्तो य एतद्विदुरमृतास्ते भवन्ति ॥ १७ ॥

eṣa devo viśvakarmā mahātmā sadā janānāṁ hṛdaye sanniviṣṭaḥ,
hṛdā manīṣā manasābhikḷpto ya etad-vidur-amṛtāste bhavanti. (17)

एषः – this; देवः – effulgent one; विश्वकर्मा – the Creator of the entire universe; महात्मा – great or all-pervading; सदा – ever; जनानाम् – of all beings; हृदये – in the hearts; सन्निविष्टः – resides; हृदा – in the heart; मनीषा – by intelligence; मनसा – by the mind; अभिक्लृप्तः – well protected; यः – who; एतद् – this; विदुः – know; अमृताः – immortal; ते – they; भवन्ति – become

17. This effulgent and all-pervading Lord, the Creator of the entire universe, ever resides in the hearts of all beings, well protected by the mind and the intelligence which abides in the heart. Those who know this become immortal.

God – the Great Architect (Viśvakarmā): Viśvakarmā is the presiding deity of all construction. He is the celestial architect of Lord Brahmā. He is therefore propitiated by all construction labourers, artisans, artists, builders and architects in India. God is the original designer, planner and creator of countless cosmoses with countless Lord Brahmās and celestial and mortal artists and architects. We stand in admiration of the Taj Mahal or the wall of China. Imagine the creativity, dexterity and imagination of the brain behind all brains!

God – the Great Being (Mahātmā): One whose Self is big is called mahātmā[1]. God is the Self of all beings – indeed a big Self! Mahātmā also means one who is large-hearted – one who is not narrow-minded or petty-minded.'[2] A small-minded person thinks always in terms of 'me' and 'mine' whereas for a large-hearted person the entire world is his family.'[3] The whole world belongs to God and He has no prejudice, favouritism, likes or dislikes towards any thing or being. God does not stop the supply of oxygen to those who deny His existence. He remains as the Self of even such a person.

God – protected and revealed by the mind (manasā abhikḷptaḥ): God remains protected or hidden in the heart by the thoughts of the mind which are extrovert. Such a flow of thoughts, complains Arjuna, is fast, turbulent, strong, distracted and compulsive and difficult to control like a tornado.[4] But the same flow of thoughts when turned inward slows down and finally stops to reveal the God within.

---

1 mahān ātmā yasya iti mahātmā

2 akṣudra buddhiḥ ātmā yasya iti mahātmā

3 ayaṁ mama na mameti gaṇanā laghucetasām,
udāracaritānāṁ tu vasudhaiva kuṭumbakam.

4 cañcalaṁ hi manaḥ kṛṣṇa pramāthi balavaddṛḍham,
tasyāhaṁ nigrahaṁ manye vāyoriva suduṣkaram. – *Gītā* 6.34

The non-dual state of Realisation is revealed in the next mantra.

यदातमस्तन्न दिवा न रात्रिः न सन्न चासञ्छिव एव केवलः।
तदक्षरं तत्सवितुर्वरेण्यं प्रज्ञा च तस्मात्प्रसृता पुराणी ॥ १८ ॥

yadā-tamas-tanna divā na rātriḥ na sanna cāsañchiva eva kevalaḥ,
tad-akṣaraṁ tat-savitur-vareṇyaṁ prajñā ca tasmāt-prasṛtā purāṇī. (18)

यदा – when; अतमः – no darkness; तत् – then; न – neither; दिवा – day; न – nor; रात्रिः – night; न – neither; सत् – gross; न – nor; च – and; असत् – subtle; शिवः – the Auspicious One; एव – alone; केवलः – the absolute (one without a second); तद् – that; अक्षरम् – imperishable; तत् – that; सवितुः – by the sun; वरेण्यम् – worthy of adoration; प्रज्ञा – Knowledge; च – and; तस्मात् – from Him; प्रसृता – has spread; पुराणी – ancient

18. When there is no darkness, then there is neither day nor night, neither anything gross, nor subtle. There remains the Auspicious One alone, imperishable, worthy of adoration even by the sun. From Him has come the ancient Knowledge.

Neither day nor night (na divā na rātriḥ): The movement of the sun, moon and earth has created our concept of time which is measured as seconds, hours, days, months, years, decades and so on. It is experienced as days, nights and seasons. When the light of knowledge removes the darkness of ignorance, the Truth which is beyond time is experienced. In It there is no day or night. The world manifests in the day and is covered by darkness at night. In the state of Realisation there is no creation (day) or dissolution (night).

Neither gross nor subtle (na sat na asat): The Truth is beyond the gross world – body and the objects experienced through the senses and the subtle world of thoughts and emotions. Sat and asat also refer to all that is good and bad. God/Truth is beyond the concepts of good (sat) and bad (asat).

Śiva is non-dual (śiva eva kevala): Here Śiva does not refer to the Lord with form, the one who resides on the Kailāsa mountain, but the auspicious and non-dual Truth. In It there is no distinction, division, otherness or finitude.

Worshipped by the sun: Here the sun (sūrya devatā) could refer to the deity of light or sight or the intellect (prakāśa devatā, cakṣu devatā or buddhi devatā). The sun illumines the physical world, because of which the eyes can see. The sun deity also inspires our intellect to function (dhiyo yo naḥ pracodayāt). But the deity gets the power to preside from God/Truth, hence he too worships God. Here it means all the deities worship God. Also Consciousness illumines even the sun deity.

Here Lord Sun could also mean Hiraṇyagarbha, the Total Mind, the omniscient, omnipotent Lord of the universe. Sometimes we wonder what or on whom do Lord Sun, Lord Śiva, Lord Viṣṇu or Lord Kṛṣṇa meditate. Lord Sūrya meditates on the pure Self, the nameless, formless, attributeless God/Truth within and worships Him to get inspiration to create, sustain and dissolve the world.

The source of knowledge: God alone is the source of all knowledge, spiritual or secular. He is the first Guru, from whom starts the lineage of the teacher and taught (guru-śiṣya-paramparā). Indeed this lineage is very ancient (purāṇī). Āyurveda, the science of medicine was revealed by Dhanvantari who was the incarnation of God. All Sanskrit grammar rules, Māheśvara Sūtras emerged from the 'ḍamaru' of Lord Śiva.

Bhāgavatam says that Lord Kṛṣṇa is the first Guru of all fine arts (akhila kalādi guruḥ). It should be noted that Lord Kṛṣṇa, Lord Śiva and Lord Dhanvantari are not different, but the same Lord seen in different forms. If we too tune our mind and worship the Lord, we too will know the essence of everything and more importantly God, the very essence of life.

God is indeed unique. The mantra says –

नैनमूर्ध्वं न तिर्यञ्चं न मध्ये परिजग्रभत्।
न तस्य प्रतिमा अस्ति यस्य नाम महद्यशः॥ १९॥

nainam-ūrdhvaṁ na tiryañcaṁ na madhye parijagrabhat,
na tasya pratimā asti yasya nāma mahadyaśaḥ. (19)

न – not; एनम् – Him; ऊर्ध्वम् – above; न – nor; तिर्यङ् – across; च – and; न – nor; मध्ये – in the middle; परिजग्रभत् – can grasp; न – no; तस्य – His; प्रतिमा – likeness or comparison; अस्ति – is; यस्य – whose; नाम – name; महद् – Great; यशः – Glory

19. Nobody can grasp Him from above, nor across, nor in the middle. There is no comparison for Him whose name is Great Glory.

God is ingraspable (na parijagrabhat): Above, below, middle, across, left or right are space concepts. God is beyond space and therefore He has no front or back, above or below or left or right. When Arjuna saw the Lord's cosmic form, he said, 'Lord! I do not understand which is the beginning, middle or end of this cosmic form.'[1] Physically nobody can grasp God and intellectually no one can comprehend Him, as He is infinite.

Lord Brahmā and Lord Viṣṇu once got into an argument as to who was greater amongst them. Lord Śiva

[1] na-antaṁ na madhyaṁ na punastavādim – *Gītā* 11.16

appeared before them as a column of light. Both tried to find the beginning and the end of the column of light, but failed. They realised that Lord alone was the greatest, the infinite and ungraspable Truth.

God is incomparable (na tasya pratimā asti): In this context the word 'pratimā' or 'upamā' means comparison. God is unlike anyone or incomparable to anyone. There is no example available that can come even close to God. For the sake of our understanding of God, examples are given. For example, God is all-pervading like space or immeasurable like the ocean. However He is much beyond space and ocean.

The word 'pratimā' also means an idol or a statue. Even though God is aliṅga (one who cannot be indicated), again for our easy understanding, He is represented in idols like a śiva-liṅga. This line is cited by people who do not believe in worshipping God through idols. The point to note is that God is beyond form and manifests as all-forms, so he cannot be limited to exist only in one form. Worshipping God through idols serves its purpose of focusing our mind and meditating on the ideal symbolised by the idol.

God of great fame: Fame is one of His glories (ref. 3.11). He has infinite and everlasting fame due to His infinite and everlasting glories. Hence He is named mahad-yaśaḥ – Great Fame.

Has anyone perceived God/Truth in His incomparable formless form? The mantra says –

न संदृशे तिष्ठति रूपमस्य न चक्षुषा पश्यति कश्चनैनम्।
हृदा हृदिस्थं मनसा य एनमेवं विदुरमृतास्ते भवन्ति ॥ २० ॥

na sandṛśe tiṣṭhati rūpamasya na cakṣuṣā paśyati kaścanainam,
hṛdā hṛdisthaṁ manasā ya enam-evaṁ vidur-amṛtāste bhavanti. (20)

न – not; संदृशे – in the range of vision; तिष्ठति – remain or exists; रूपम् – form; अस्य – His; न – not; चक्षुषा – with the eyes; पश्यति – sees; कश्चन – nobody; एनम् – Him; हृदा – (absorbed) in the heart; हृदिस्थम् – existing in the heart; मनसा – with mind; यः – who; एनम् – Him; एवम् – as; विदुः – know; अमृताः – immortal; ते – they; भवन्ति – become

20. His form does not come witin the range of vision; no one sees Him with the eyes. Those who know Him as existing in the heart, with a mind absorbed in the heart, become immortal.

This mantra is also found in the *Kaṭhopaniṣad 2.3.9.*

God – the ever unseen: Someone may feel that I have not seen God, but surely someone, somewhere at sometime must have seen Him. The eyes have seen only a small part of the infinite world. There is an unimaginable expanse of creation which no mortal eye has seen. Maybe God exists in some remote place like the seventh heaven that no one has managed to see.

God/Truth does not become an object of perception to anyone, at anytime, anywhere. Devotees can only see His manifest form and never His formless form. He is the Consciousness behind all perceptions and not available to be seen, heard or felt.

God – the Seer: When the senses are withdrawn from all perceptions and the mind from all ideations, in that state of meditation, God/Truth, the Seer behind all thoughts and perception is realised as the very Self of the seeker. The seen changes whereas the Seer Self is unchanging and immortal.

Frightened of the pull of the world that prevents him from realising God, the seeker prays -

अजात इत्येवं कश्चिद्भीरुः प्रपद्यते ।
रुद्र यत्ते दक्षिणं मुखं तेन मां पाहि नित्यम् ॥ २१ ॥

ajāta ityevaṁ kaścid-bhīruḥ prapadyate,
rudra yatte dakṣiṇaṁ mukhaṁ tena māṁ pāhi nityam. (21)

अजातः – birthless; इति – since; एवम् – therefore or so; कश्चिद् – someone; भीरुः – one who is frightened; प्रपद्यते – takes refuge; रुद्र – O Rudra; यत् – that; ते – Yours; दक्षिणम् – that is turned southward; मुखम् – face; तेन – with that; माम् – me; पाहि – protect; नित्यम् – always

21. Since You are birthless, a person who is frightened (of saṁsāra) takes refuge in You. O Rudra, protect me always with Your face that is turned southward.

This is a prayer to Lord Rudra.

'I Surrender in fear': God is birthless and deathless. Lord Death is said to reside in the south direction. Rudra faces death – the south – fearlessly. He is therefore called Mṛtyuñjaya – one who has conquered death. The devotee or seeker who is frightened of sorrow, old age, disease and death which are the lot of worldly existence (saṁsāra) or even of the temptations of the world, turns to Rudra, who is immutable, immortal and all Bliss. Lord Śiva is said to have five faces – the one facing south is called Aghora – benign. Śaṅkarācārya says that the Lord facing south is benign and fills us with enthusiasm and bliss when meditated upon (utsāha-jananaṁ dhyāta-āhlāda-karam). Such a form of Lord Śiva is called Dakṣiṇāmūrti and is generally meditated upon by spiritual seekers, as He also represents the giver of the knowledge of Truth (Brahmavidyā).

Despite efforts when the seeker fails to 'see' God/ Truth, He prays in sheer helplessness, "Please remove my fear and let me merge my little self in You. You are immortal so I too shall become so. How can any fear then come to me the infinite Self?" This same meaning is conveyed in a beautiful verse by Śrī Ramaṇa Maharṣi quoted in an earlier mantra (4.15).

There is a story in the Purāṇa about Mārkaṇḍeya who came to know that he would die at an early age. He clung to the Lord in the form of a śivaliṅga. When Death came to take him, Lord Śiva protected him. This story does not mean that a person will never die physically. It means that the fear of death is removed in the knowledge of one's immortal nature.

The seeker not only prays for himself but also for the well-being of all who are dear to him.

मा नस्तोके तनये मा न आयुषि मा नो गोषु मा नो अश्वेषु रीरिषः।
वीरान्मा नो रुद्र भामितो वधीर्हविष्मन्तः सदमित्त्वा हवामहे ॥ २२ ॥

mā nastoke tanaye mā na āyuṣi mā no goṣu mā no aśveṣu rīriṣaḥ,
vīrānmā no rudra bhāmito vadhīr-haviṣmantaḥ sadamittvā havāmahe. (22)

मा – please do not; नः – our; तोके – children; तनये – grandchildren; मा – please do not; नः – our; आयुषि – lifespan; मा – please do not; नः – our; गोषु – cattle; मा – do not; नः – our; अश्वेषु – horses; रीरिषः – bring destruction; वीरान् – brave ones; मा – please do not; नः – our; रुद्र – O Rudra; भामितः – in your anger; वधीः – destroy; हविष्मन्तः – with oblations; सदम् – always; इत् – thus; त्वा – You; हवामहे – (we) worship

22. O Rudra, please do not bring destruction to our children or grandchildren, do not cut our lifespan, and do not harm our cattle and horses. In Your anger, please do not destroy our brave ones (servants). We worship You with oblations.

Prayer for the sake of others is always more effective.

O God! Please do not be angry (mā bhāmitaḥ): One aspect of Lord Rudra is ferocious and uncompromising in doling out punishment. However there is another aspect that is compassionate and eager to reward true devotion.

The prayer invokes His auspicious and compassionate form. Please do not get angry with our children and grandchildren. Sometimes our children do not behave well or our grandchildren are disrespectful or do wrong. We seek pardon on their behalf. Also we do not want a person we love to get angry with us. Sometimes people do foolish things then say, "Swamiji, please do not be angry with me!"

O God! Do not cut short our lifespan: May we not face untimely death. May we live the full lifespan allotted to us serving God (vyaśema devahitaṁ yadāyuḥ). A householder asked a visiting saint to bless him and his family. The saint said, "May your grandfather die, may your father die, may you die, may your son die, may your grandson die." The man was shocked at the words of the kind and saintly soul and asked to be explained this strange blessing. He was told that it meant that may none die an untimely death. It is indeed a great sorrow for a person to watch his own children or grandchildren die. So may each one live their full lifespan and die in sequence.

O God! Protect our wealth and helpers: Cows and horses represented wealth and vehicles of transport. May the brave and enthusiastic helpers too be protected. So the prayer addresses all aspects of a householder's life.

O God! Please accept our offerings: We propitiate you with what little we have. Be always pleased with our offerings and be always gracious on us. Look upon us always with love and compassion.

Tulasī Rāmāyaṇa narrates the story of Kākabhuśuṇḍī. In his previous birth he was a disciple of a great Guru. One day he was praying in the Śiva temple and his Guru came there to offer prayers. Even though he saw his Guru, in his arrogance, he did not get up to greet him. Lord Śiva got angry and reprimanded him. The Guru pleads for mercy and begs for forgiveness on behalf of the disciple. Even though the disciple's behaviour was inexcusable, the Lord forgives him in response to the Guru's prayer. Later Kākabhuśuṇḍī too became a great devotee of the Lord.

It is indeed because of God's infinite mercy and the prayers of great souls for our well-being that we are forgiven for our shortcomings. If God were to give us results solely according to our actions, we would be suffering much more. The Ṛṣi here prays out of compassion and for the welfare of all beings.

With this we come to the end of the fourth chapter.

Chapter 5

The first part of this chapter speaks more about the nature of God/Truth and the latter part about the individual. Underlying both is their essential oneness. To know that oneness is the purpose of the Upaniṣad.

Understanding the nature of Truth is important for realising the oneness and therefore the Ṛṣi says –

द्वे अक्षरे ब्रह्मपरे त्वनन्ते विद्याविद्ये निहिते यत्र गूढे ।
क्षरं त्वविद्या ह्यमृतं तु विद्या विद्याविद्ये ईशते यस्तु सोऽन्यः ॥ १ ॥

dve akṣare brahmapare tvanante vidyāvidye nihite yatra gūḍhe,
kṣaraṁ tvavidyā hyamṛtaṁ tu vidyā vidyāvidye īśate yastu so'nyaḥ. (1)

द्वे – two; अक्षरे – in the immutable; ब्रह्मपरे – in the supreme Truth; तु – verily; अनन्ते – in the infinite; विद्याविद्ये – knowledge and ignorance; निहिते – lie; यत्र – where; गूढे – hidden; क्षरम् – perishable; तु – while; अविद्या – ignorance; हि – indeed; अमृतम् – immortal; तु – verily; विद्या – knowledge; विद्याविद्ये – knowledge and ignorance; ईशते – rules; यः – He who; तु – indeed; सः – He; अन्यः – is different (from them)

1. Knowledge and ignorance verily lie hidden in the infinite, immutable supreme Truth. Knowledge verily is immortal, while ignorance is perishable indeed. He who rules over knowledge and ignorance is indeed different from them.

The two knowledges (vidyāvidye): *Muṇḍakopaniṣad* calls these two knowledges parā vidyā – supreme knowledge and aparā vidyā – lower knowledge. Here they are called 'vidyā' and 'avidyā'. Vidyā implies the knowledge of the supreme Truth (Brahmavidyā) and avidyā refers to all other knowledges – secular, religious or spiritual.

Both are inherent in God. Both are imperishable and eternal (akṣara and ananta). Knowledge really never perishes. It only goes from manifest to unmanifest condition. It always remains in its latent form, waiting to manifest or be discovered. Again it is only ignorance that ends, never knowledge.

Another meaning of vidyā and avidyā is knowledge and ignorance. Here both could also refer to the Truth – knowledge of the Truth and ignorance of the Truth.

Even though of opposite nature, both reside in God who is unfathomable, imperishable and infinite. It is difficult to understand the nature of both ignorance and knowledge as they are deep (gūḍha). In trying to gain Self-realisation, some get stuck to scholastic study of scriptures, some to intellectual understanding, some become proud and some even imagine they have become realised. They are still caught up in the net of ignorance which is difficult to understand.

Ignorance is perishable (kṣaraṁ tu avidyā): Ignorance of the Self or any subject ends with knowledge and is therefore perishable (kṣaram). Also secular knowledge or religious knowledge keeps changing (kṣaram). Scientific theories are at times modified or proved wrong with the passage of time. Also no object or being of the world remains the same. Everything changes in time. Therefore its knowledge also changes and so we have to keep upgrading our knowledge. This is especially experienced in modern days when technology changes so fast that knowledge becomes obsolete by the time you manage to master it.

Knowledge is immortal (amṛtaṁ tu vidyā): However, knowledge of the Truth is immortal (akṣaram) as Truth is immortal. Also once the ignorance of the Truth/Self is dispelled, it never comes back. The state of Realisation never ends into a state of ignorance. Phrases like 'amṛtaṁ tu vidyā' – knowledge is immortal and 'vidyayā vindate amṛtam' (*Kenopaniṣad 2.4*) – 'Knowledge bestows immortality' are famous and become the mottos of many education institutions in India.

God is different from both (so'nyaḥ): God rules over both knowledge and ignorance, knowledge of the Truth and all other knowledges with their branches. He encompasses both, yet remains beyond both. As Consciousness, the very knowledge principle, He is different from all, subjects and objects of knowledge or the thoughts of ignorance and knowledge of objects.

The next mantra reasserts that right from the beginning of creation, all beings and all knowledges come from God only.

यो योनिं योनिमधितिष्ठत्येको विश्वानि रूपाणि योनीश्च सर्वाः।
ऋषिं प्रसूतं कपिलं यस्तमग्रे ज्ञानैर्बिभर्ति जायमानं च पश्येत्॥ २॥

yo yonim̐ yonim-adhitiṣṭhatyeko viśvāni rūpāṇi yonīśca sarvāḥ,
ṛṣim̐ prasūtam̐ kapilam̐ yastam-agre jñānair-bibharti jāyamānam̐ ca paśyet. (2)

यः – who; योनिं योनिम् – every womb; अधितिष्ठति – presides over; एकः – the one; विश्वानि – all; रूपाणि – forms; योनीः – wombs; च – and; सर्वाः – all; ऋषिम् – the sage; प्रसूतम् – was born; कपिलम् – Kapila; यः – who; तम् – him; अग्रे – in the beginning; ज्ञानैः – with knowledge; बिभर्ति – filled; जायमानम् – as he was being born; च – and; पश्येत् – saw

2. He is the one who presides over the origin of every creation, over all forms and wombs. From Him came the Sage Kapila in the beginning and He gave the knowledge to him, the all-knowing, and saw him being born.

The first one fourth part of the mantra is repeated (4.11) and the phrase 'yonim yonim' was explained therein.

The innumerable species and beings (viśvāni rūpāṇi yoniśca sarvaḥ): According to the Vedas there are 84 lakh different species with millions of beings in each species. The species were categorised as:

a. udbhija: Those born from seeds which germinate and sprout like trees and plants.

b. svedaja: Those born of sweat or humidity like lice and fungus.

c. aṇḍaja: Those born from eggs like amphibians, reptiles and birds.

d. jarāyuja: Those born from a womb like monkeys or human beings.

God presides over the creation of all beings of every species. What a task!

The First Born: Kapila here refers to Hiraṇyagarbha the Total Mind which is the source of the entire creation. It is God from whom the omniscient and all-shining Kapila (kanaka varṇam) was born. He was the witness to the birth of the Creator. It means that God exists before creation and is the origin of all that exists.

Kapila could also refer to Sage Kapila the incarnation of Lord Viṣṇu who was born to Sage Kardama and who imparted the knowledge of the Truth (Brahmavidyā) to His mother, Devahūti. God naturally exists before He manifests as His incarnations.

For how long has this cycle of creation and dissolution been going on? The mantra says –

एकैकं जालं बहुधा विकुर्वन्नस्मिन्क्षेत्रे संहरत्येष देवः।
भूयः सृष्ट्वा पतयस्तथेशः सर्वाधिपत्यं कुरुते महात्मा ॥ ३ ॥

ekaikaṁ jālaṁ bahudhā vikurvannasmin-kṣetre saṁharatyeṣa devaḥ,
bhūyaḥ sṛṣṭvā patayastatheśaḥ sarvādhipatyaṁ kurute mahātmā. (3)

एकैकम् – each; जालम् – net; बहुधा – multifarious; विकुर्वन् – making; अस्मिन् – in this; क्षेत्रे – in the world; संहरति – destroys; एषः – this; देवः – effulgent one; भूयः – once again; सृष्ट्वा – having created; पतयः – the rulers; तथा – as before; ईशः – the Lord; सर्वाधिपत्यम् कुरुते – presides over (them); महात्मा – the great Self

3. This effulgent deity makes each net multifarious in this world and then destroys it. The Lord, the great Self, once again creates the rulers and presides over them all.

The world wide web: Earlier it was said that the Lord is jālavān – weilds the great net of māyā (3.1) from which the world emerges. Here it is said that each category of species is like a net from which innumerable variety of beings emerge. For example, there is a breathtaking variety of trees, bushes, creepers, flowering and non-flowering plants, crops, vegetables – all born from seeds. There are amazing creatures like the variety of tiny birds, insects, to the huge dinosaurs born from eggs. There are a variety of celestial beings like devatās, gandharvas, kinnaras, yakṣas, apsarās or siddhas about which we have only heard in the scriptures. In the modern times human beings too have created a world wide web of knowledge with an intricate communication network which connects people all over the world and keeps many caught up day and night. Bombarded by information from all sides and various web-sites (aneka jālam) the modern man is even socialising most of the time in a virtual world like on the Face Book. Unfortunately the modern man finds it impossible to withdraw from his self-created net connections. God's web is spread all over the universe studded with the beings woven into an intricate pattern which is withdrawn back at the time of dissolution.

The endless cycle: This is not the first creation, nor will it be the last. The word 'kṣetra' is used, which means 'a field or farm land'. Like crops that grow in fields and are cut and grow again and again, creation comes into being and is destroyed again and again.[1] And so far the Lord has not got tired! No wonder He is called Mahātmā – the Great Being.

[1] Sasyam-iva martyaḥ pacyate sasyamivājāyate punaḥ – *Kaṭhopaniṣad* 1.1.6

Who illumines this beginingless cycle and this endless expanse of creation?

सर्वा दिश ऊर्ध्वमधश्च तिर्यक् प्रकाशयन्भ्राजते यद्वनड्वान्।
एवं स देवो भगवान्वरेण्यो योनिस्वभावानधितिष्ठत्येकः ॥ ४ ॥

sarvā diśa ūrdhvam-adhaśca tiryak prakāśayan-bhrājate yadvanaḍvān,
evaṁ sa devo bhagavān-vareṇyo yonisvabhāvān-adhitiṣṭhatyekaḥ. (4)

सर्वाः – all; दिशः – the directions; ऊर्ध्वम् – above; अधः – below; च – and; तिर्यक् – across; प्रकाशयन् – illumining; भ्राजते – shines; यत् उ अनड्वान् – just as the sun; एवम् – in this way; सः – He; देवः – the effulgent one; भगवान् – the Lord; वरेण्यः – adorable; योनिस्वभावान् – the source and its effects; अधितिष्ठति – presides over; एकः – alone

4. Just as the sun shines, illumining all the directions, above, below and across, the effulgent and adorable Lord Himself presides over the source (prakṛti) and all its effects.

The self-effulgent light: 'Anaḍvān' is also the name of sun. The physical world is illumined by the sun in all directions – above, below, horizontally and across. It is self-evident and brilliant. Similarly God, the supreme Consciousness is self-effulgent and lights up the entire universe for our perception. Vareṇyam means both adorable and eminently fit to be chosen (varaṇīya) amongst all the other things of the world. The word Bhagavān means the Lord of all fortunes as explained earlier (3.11). He is varaṇīya and vareṇya because He is Bhagavān.

The natural cause (yoni-svabhāva): Prakṛti, God's power is the cause (yoni) of the whole world. It is the very nature (svabhāva) of prakṛti to produce the world. The Lord presides over prakṛti and all that is born from it like the five elements and its grosser forms.

The next mantra describes God as the Great Cook.

**यच्च स्वभावं पचति विश्वयोनिः पाच्यांश्च सर्वान्परिणामयेद्यः ।
सर्वमेतद्विश्वमधितिष्ठत्येको गुणांश्च सर्वान्विनियोजयेद्यः ॥ ५ ॥**

yacca svabhāvaṁ pacati viśvayoniḥ pācyāṁśca sarvān-pariṇāmayed-yaḥ,
sarvametad-viśvam-adhitiṣṭhatyeko guṇāṁśca sarvān-viniyojayed-yaḥ. (5)

यत् – who; **च** – and; **स्वभावम्** – the nature of each thing; **पचति** – ordains or bestows; **विश्वयोनिः** – the source of the entire creation; **पाच्यान्** – the mutable (things created); **च** – and; **सर्वान्** – all; **परिणामयेद्** – modifies; **यः** – who; **सर्वम्** – all; **एतद्** – this; **विश्वम्** – whole universe; **अधितिष्ठति** – presides; **एकः** – alone; **गुणान्** – qualities; **च** – and; **सर्वान्** – all; **विनियोजयेद्** – endows; **यः** – who

5. The Lord, who is the source of the entire creation, who ordains the nature of each thing, who modifies the things thus created, who endows them with qualities and He alone presides over this whole universe.

The cause of all: Various causes can be found for the different things, situations and beings experienced in this world like matter and energy, the elements and nature (1.2). God is the cause of all causes, the source of the entire creation.

The cause of each nature: Every element of nature has its own special characteristic. Everything in the world has its innate nature. For example, heat in fire and sapidity in water. It is God who has endowed each with this inherent nature (svabhāva). We know that fire is hot, but nobody knows why it is hot. We know how it burns but we do not know why it burns. The literal meaning of the word 'pacati' is 'cooks'. But here it means God bestows or endows each object with its special qualities.

Śrī Gurudev would tell an interesting story. A child would come back from school and open the fridge and find his meal each day. The child began to think that the food comes from the fridge. One day he told his mother, "I think I don't need you anymore. The fridge gives me a variety of food each day." In same way, the scientists open the door, see some things and call it scientific discovery. They start feeling they know a lot and give no credit to God. The point is that we may discover the gravitational force but we do not know why it works the way it does.

Not only does He endow everything with its inherent nature, but He also strengthens their nature and does not allow it to be otherwise. Fire cannot change its nature and become cold. The Upaniṣad says, 'The fire emits heat out of fear of the Lord.'[1]

The cause of all modifications: Milk has its inherent quality of colour, taste, fluidity and so on. When mixed with yeast it curdles to become yogurt which again has its own special colour, texture and taste. It is God who endows milk with the ability to curdle. Hydrogen is a gas, oxygen is a gas and

[1] Bhayāt-asya-agnistapati – *Kaṭhopaniṣad* 2.3.3

when they combine we get water. Hydrogen is a gas that burns, oxygen helps in burning but when they combine to form water, it puts out fire! Two parts of hydrogen with one part of oxygen becomes H_2O – water with which we wash our hair. But two parts of hydrogen with two parts of oxygen becomes H_2O_2 – hydrogen-peroxide which bleaches your hair. God presides over all these permutations, combinations, mutations and modifications of the world and all the qualities born thereof.

The cause of utility of each quality: Each quality of each and everything is meant for a purpose which it fulfills. Sattva guṇa understands, rajo guṇa activates and tamo guṇa gives rest. Therefore in the world we see the strong labour, the smart create resources, the brave defend and the brainy discover. It is the Lord that puts each quality to good use. A good boss utilises the special talent of each employee. The Big Boss of creation puts each quality in everyone to good use and therefore fire burns and the wind blows and not vice versa.

When milk, sugar, coffee powder and water are mixed in the right proportion and heated, each substance imparts its special quality to form the special concoction we call coffee. The Great Cook, the Lord creates different ingredients, each with its special quality, mixes them in different pots in different combinations to create this great feast called creation.

The glory of Brahmavidyā – the knowledge of the Truth is revealed thus –

तद्वेदगुह्योपनिषत्सु गूढं तद्ब्रह्मा वेदते ब्रह्मयोनिम्।
ये पूर्वं देवा ऋषयश्च तद्विदुस्ते तन्मया अमृता वै बभूवुः ॥ ६ ॥

tad-veda-guhyopaniṣatsu gūḍhaṁ tad-brahmā vedate brahmayonim,
ye pūrvaṁ devā ṛṣayaśca tadviduste tanmayā amṛtā vai babhūvuḥ. (6)

तत् – That; वेदगुह्योपनिषत्सु – lies in the Upaniṣads which are the mystical parts of the Vedas; गूढम् – hidden; तत् – That; ब्रह्मा – Lord Brahmā; वेदते – knows; ब्रह्मयोनिम् – which can be known only through the Vedas; ये – who; पूर्वम् – ancient; देवाः – the deities; ऋषयः – the Seers; च – and; तत् – That; विदुः – knew; ते – they; तन्मयाः – became one with It; अमृताः – immortal; वै – indeed; बभूवुः – became

6. That (Truth) lies hidden in the Upaniṣads which are the mystical parts of the Vedas. Lord Brahmā knows that (Truth) which can be known only through the Vedas. Those ancient deities and Seers who knew It indeed became one with It and became immortal.

The Vedas and Upaniṣads: The Vedas are the eternal truths discovered by great Seers in their seat of meditation. Their main theme is knowledge of Dharma – how to live a happy and fulfilled life here and hereafter and knowledge of Brahman the Truth – how to liberate oneself from the here and hereafter. The knowledge of Dharma too is meant to prepare us for the knowledge of Brahman. The Upaniṣads primarily propound the knowledge of Brahman. This knowledge is deep, mystical and difficult to understand, especially for an unprepared mind. The Upaniṣads are the valid means for this knowledge. Here the word Brahma also means Vedas and yoni means – valid means. The Vedas (Upaniṣads) are the valid means of knowing the Truth. Bhagavān Veda Vyāsa too says the same.[1]

The glory of Brahma Vidyā: Lord Brahmā the creator, the ancient deities, the great Seers like Sage Atri and Sage Vasiṣṭha realised the Truth through the Vedas. Becoming one with the Truth they gained immortality. Brahmā also means the Veda mantras. The Veda mantras know the Truth or reveal the Truth. Anyone who realises this Truth, even in this age, shall become immortal – that is the promise of the scriptures. The Truth is our own Self and available to all. This gives hope to all of us, that we too can realise the Truth and become liberated.

This knowledge is indeed great. It has stood the test of time. Even today we study it. So many branches of knowledges have disappeared, so many species have become extinct, so many great empires and cultures are in ruins, yet the knowledge of the Vedas has remained. Invaders have burnt our books but they could not destroy this knowledge. Modernisation has changed our lifestyle, but there still remain seekers of Truth and this knowledge. The great Seers, the exalted beings, saints and sages through the ages gave

[1] śāstra yonitvāt – *Brahma Sūtra* 3

top priority to this knowledge. So when we understand how precious it is, we too will strive to know it.

When we read all this, we think of Śrī Gurudev and all that he has done for us. He expounded this great knowledge in a language that the modern man can understand. He gave this knowledge unstintingly to everyone and left it as a legacy for all of mankind. Our grateful prostrations to him.

As the Ṛṣi spoke about the nature of God / Truth (tat pada), he kept emphasising on the essential oneness of the individual and God. Now begins an interesting description of the nature of the individual being (jīva) – tvam pada śodhanam.

गुणान्वयो यः फलकर्मकर्ता कृतस्य तस्यैव स चोपभोक्ता ।
स विश्वरूपस्त्रिगुणस्त्रिवर्त्मा प्राणाधिपः सञ्चरति स्वकर्मभिः ॥ ७ ॥

guṇānvayo yaḥ phala-karma-kartā kṛtasya tasyaiva sa copabhoktā,
sa viśvarūpas-triguṇas-trivartmā prāṇādhipaḥ sañcarati
svakarmabhiḥ. (7)

गुणान्वयः – endowed with qualities; यः – who; फलकर्मकर्ता – performer of actions leading to results; कृतस्य – of the result of the action that has been done; तस्य – of that; सः एव – himself; च – and; उपभोक्ता – the enjoyer; सः – he; विश्वरूपः – one who has many forms; त्रिगुणः – having the three qualities; त्रिवर्त्मा – has three paths; प्राणाधिपः – master of the vital force; सञ्चरति – moves; स्वकर्मभिः – due to (his) own actions

7. Endowed with qualities, he (jīva) is the performer of actions that lead to results and he himself becomes the enjoyer of their results. He has many forms, has three qualities and three paths, is the master of the vital force and moves due to his own actions.

The individual – endowed with qualities (guṇānvayaḥ): Guṇa here means vāsanās. It also means ropes. We are tied by the ropes of our vāsanās or inherent tendencies formed through past actions. For example, the angry person through frequent anger bouts has mastered getting angry and compulsively and helplessly gets angry at the slightest provocation. Driven by our vāsanās, we feel that what we do is important and right. The angry man thinks that the other person deserves to be shouted at and abused. He should be taught a lesson and if not by me, then by who else? Vāsanās take the lead and one becomes their faithful follower (anu-aya). The drinking vāsanā leads one to the bar everyday to knock oneself senseless!

The individual – performs actions for results (phala-karma-kartā): We perform actions which give rise to results of joy or sorrow. We always do actions for desired results. Most of our actions are prompted by selfish motives which is a sure way to get bound by the results – be it a success or failure.

The doer becomes the enjoyer (kṛtasya tasyaiva sa copabhoktā): We do not remember all our past actions and are not able to connect them with the results that we get in the present. But we are receiving results – good, bad or indifferent, desired (iṣṭam), undesired (aniṣṭam) or mixed (miśram) – based on what we have done. The kartā alone becomes the bhoktā. It cannot happen that I get the good or bad result of someone else's action or someone enjoys the fruits of my hard work. The fruits he is enjoying right now were sown by him some time earlier!

A man who met with an accident asked a saint, "What have I done to deserve a broken leg. It was not even my fault. He came at me as though he was after my life." The saint said, "Think what good karma you must have done that you so miraculously escaped death." When we are faced with problems and difficulties we should not complain. The sins of the past come back to us in the form of diseases or other problems.[1]

In *Tulasī Rāmāyaṇa* we find that Guha blamed Kaikeyi for the plight of the crown prince of Ayodhyā, Śrī Rāma and His beloved wife Sītā sleeping on a makeshift bed of straw. Lakṣmaṇa then said, 'Dear brother, no one is responsible for our joys and sorrows. We are all enjoying or suffering the results of what we have done.'[2]

The individual takes many forms (viśva-rūpa): How many roles do we play during our lifespan and everyday of our life – a son, husband, father, employer, and so on. It is interesting to watch a person lord over his employee and the next moment become meek and henpecked before the wife!

The individual is tied by three qualities (triguṇa): Here guṇa means the qualities of sattva, rajas and tamas. We are controlled by our moods which vary with time and situation. When in a sāttvika mood we become meditative and before we can settle in, restlessness (rajo guṇa) catches up or more often sleep (tamo guṇa) overwhelms us. Sometimes we entertain noble desires, sometimes selfish and sometimes downright bad ones. The three qualities indeed have us well tied.

The individual takes three paths to his destinations (trivartmā): Our actions lead us to different destinations or

---

[1] pūrva-janmakṛtaṁ pāpaṁ vyādhi-rūpeṇa jāyate

[2] Kāhu na kou sukha dukha kara dātā nija kṛta karama bhoga sabu bhrātā
– *Ayodhyā Kāṇḍa 91*

results. We may follow the path of action (karma), worship or devotion (upāsanā or bhakti) or knowledge (jñāna). The three paths can also mean the two nobler paths of uttarāyaṇa or devayāna which leads to Brahmaloka, and dakṣiṇāyana or pitṛyāna which leads to the world of ancestors. The third path is the lower path which takes us to mortal existence on earth or even lower realms. What this means is that our future destination is decided by our own actions in the present.

The individual controls his prāṇas (prāṇādhipa): This is explained beautifully also in the *Gītā* by Lord Śrī Kṛṣṇa. 'Taking charge of his subtle body the individual leaves the gross body like fragrance carried away by breeze, and moves to yet another body.'[1] We thus move from womb to womb taking different forms as determined by our own actions.

[1] śarīraṁ yadavāpnoti yaccāpyutkrāmatīśvaraḥ,
gṛhītvaitāni saṁyāti vāyurgandhānivāśayāt. – *Gītā* 15.8

The next two mantras discuss the size of the individuality that dwells in this body.

अङ्गुष्ठमात्रो रवितुल्यरूपः सङ्कल्पाहङ्कारसमन्वितो यः ।
बुद्धेर्गुणेनात्मगुणेन चैव आराग्रमात्रो ह्यपरोऽपि दृष्टः ॥ ८ ॥

वालाग्रशतभागस्य शतधा कल्पितस्य च ।
भागो जीवः स विज्ञेयः स चानन्त्याय कल्पते ॥ ९ ॥

aṅguṣṭha-mātro ravitulya-rūpaḥ saṅkalpāhaṅkāra-samanvito yaḥ,
buddher-guṇenātmaguṇena caiva ārāgra-mātro hyaparo'pi dṛṣṭaḥ. (8)

vālāgra-śatabhāgasya śatadhā kalpitasya ca,
bhāgo jīvaḥ sa vijñeyaḥ sa cānantyāya kalpate. (9)

अङ्गुष्ठमात्रः – of the size of a thumb; रवितुल्यरूपः – bright like the sun; सङ्कल्पाहङ्कारसमन्वितः – associated with wishful thinking and individuality; यः – who; बुद्धेः – of the intellect; गुणेन – with the qualities; आत्मगुणेन – with the qualities of the mind and the body; च – and; एव – alone; आराग्रमात्रः – like the tip of a goad; हि – even though; अपरः – different; अपि – as if; दृष्टः – seen

वालाग्रशतभागस्य – of the size of the tip of a hair divided into hundred parts; शतधा – a hundred times; कल्पितस्य – imagined; च – and; भागः – of the size; जीवः – the individual being; सः – he; विज्ञेयः – to be known; सः – he; च – and; अनन्त्याय – for infinity; कल्पते – fit or capable

8. Of the size of a thumb and bright like the sun, associated with wishful thinking and individuality, and also with the qualities of the intellect, the mind and the body, the jīva is seen as if different, like the tip of a goad.

9. The jīva, the size of the tip of a hair imagined to be divided into a hundredth of its hundredth part, is capable of infinity and is to be known.

The individual – the size of a thumb: It was earlier said that God/Truth is seated in the heart-space and is the size of the thumb (viz. 3.3). He is of the nature of pure Consciousness and illumines the mind and the senses. Now it is said that the individual being is also of the size of the thumb and is self shining like the sun. How can two entities of the same size occupy the same space simultaneously? It means that they are essentially one and one is only superimposed on the other. What is the difference between them?

The finite individual: God/Truth is infinite, whereas the individual becomes finite because of its association with saṅkalpa and ahaṅkāra. Saṅkalpa means fanciful thinking or wishful thinking like – how nice would it be if I have a chocolate, isn't this movie great, how happy it made me. The individual sometimes imagines things which are not even there like 'a cigarette solves all problems, or when I smoke I become creative'. From saṅkalpa arise desires which make us perform actions. Ahaṅkāra comes into play when I own every saṅkalpa, desire, or memory like 'I wish', 'I want', 'I remember'. The ahaṅkāra identifies with the finite body, mind and senses to give rise to the individuality. It expresses itself also as superiority or inferiority complexes like 'I am the greatest' or 'I am good for nothing'. Here the word ātma-guṇa means the qualities of the body and senses. Identified with the body the individual says, 'I am tall or short, fat or thin, fair or dark, man or woman'. Owing to the intellect it says – 'I understand', 'I am peaceful' or 'I am agitated'.

The size of a tip of a goad: In ancient days the cattle and horses were kept in control with a stick which had a sharpened end fixed with a metal tip (āra-agra). This goad was used to prod the cow or horse. The Self/God residing within all of us is all-pervading and infinite and now due to this false identification, it appeared as a small, finite being, the size of the goad tip or needle tip.

The size of thousandth fraction of a hair tip: If the tip of the hair is imagined to be split into hundred parts, one hundredth of its size is imagined to be the size of the individual. Not being satisfied with the tip of the needle the Ṛṣi wishes to show how very small, we have made ourselves – the infinite reduced to a dot of nothing.

This individuality is a subtle and tricky entity – difficult to catch and pin down. It is purely notional, an appearance of a thought. It defies perception and the minutest analysis. It changes its identity in a fraction of a second from being bad to sad, to glad, to mad.

What is the size of the wave or a bubble compared to the size of the mighty ocean. The individual is like a wave rising and falling and yet this tiny entity gives endless trouble to everyone.

The infinite possibility: However being essentially infinite, it can by giving up its finitude realise its infinite Self. The size of the individual is initially said to be of the size of a thumb and later the tip of a needle and finally the thousandth part of a hair tip. As the mind tries to conceive its size, the mind and the individuality disappear in the Realisation of the infinite Self.

What is the gender of the individuality? The mantra says –

नैव स्त्री न पुमानेष न चैवायं नपुंसकः ।
यद्यच्छरीरमादत्ते तेन तेन स रक्ष्यते ॥ १० ॥

naiva strī na pumān-eṣa na caivāyaṁ napuṁsakaḥ,
yadyaccharīramādatte tena tena sa rakṣyate. (10)

न – not; एव – surely; स्त्री – woman; न – not; पुमान् – man; एषः – this; न – not; च – and; एव – surely; अयम् – this; नपुंसकः – eunuch; यत् यत् – whichever; शरीरम् – body; आदत्ते – takes up; तेन तेन – by those (very bodies); सः – it; रक्ष्यते – protected

10. This (jīva) is surely not a woman, nor a man and surely not a eunuch. Whichever body it takes up, it is protected by those (very bodies).

Neither a woman nor a man: In an earlier mantra (4.3) the Ṛṣi said that God is a man, woman, boy and girl. In fact He is all beings – plant, animal and human. This mantra says that God even as an individual is neither a man, or a woman nor a eunuch. As explained earlier, from the standpoint of God/Truth, He is only Existence-Consciousness-Bliss, unconditioned by any body. From the standpoint of the world He manifests as all forms – man, woman or child. But is not the individual a man or a woman?

The individual becomes what it identifies with: By itself the individuality (jīva) has no form. It takes on the form of what it owns. 'I am' has no form. It becomes 'I am a man' when it owns a man's body. The individuality is indeed strange. It does not mind identifying with any body. In one life it becomes a dog, in another a divine being and in yet another, a monster.

The biography of every individual (jīva) is beautifully given by Bhagavān Ramaṇa Maharṣi – 'The individuality' (ahaṅkāra or jīva), itself being formless, is born when it owns a form, it stays within the assemblage of form, it eats forms and gives up and takes on forms all the time. When enquired into its true nature, it runs away like a ghost.'[1]

[1] rūpodbhavo rūpa-tati-pratiṣṭho rūpāśano dhūtagṛhīta-rūpaḥ,
svayaṁ virūpaḥ svavicārakāle dhāvatyahaṅkāra-piśāca eṣaḥ.
– *Saddarśanam* 27

The story of the individuality – you and me continues.

सङ्कल्पनस्पर्शनदृष्टिमोहैर्ग्रासाम्बुवृष्ट्या चात्मविवृद्धिजन्म ।
कर्मानुगान्यनुक्रमेण देही स्थानेषु रूपाण्यभिसम्प्रपद्यते ॥ ११ ॥

saṅkalpana-sparśana-dṛṣṭi-mohair-grāsāmbu-vṛṣṭyā
catma-vivṛddhijanma,
karmānugānyanukrameṇa dehī sthāneṣu
rūpāṇyabhisamprapadyate. (11)

सङ्कल्पन-स्पर्शन-दृष्टि-मोहैः – by wishful thinking and the desire to touch and see and delusion; ग्रासाम्बुवृष्ट्या चात्मविवृद्धिजन्म – just as the body is nourished by the food and water that is showered into it; कर्मानुगानि – according to its deeds; अनुक्रमेण – in succession; देही – the embodied one; स्थानेषु – in different places; रूपाणि – different forms; अभिसम्प्रपद्यते – assumes

11. Just as the body is nourished by the food and water that is showered into it, the embodied one is also nourished by the wishful thinking, the desire to touch and see and delusion, and according to its deeds, successively it assumes different forms in different places.

The individuality's nourishment: Our body is kept well nourished by food and water. Our solid and liquid intake may be healthy or unhealthy. We may drink fresh juices, soft drinks or hard drinks. The body becomes according to what we nourish it with.

Similarly the individual being (jīva) grows and is strengthened by saṅkalpas – fanciful thinking. These saṅkalpas may be righteous or unrighteous like 'let me help my friend' or 'how good it would be if the other person dies'. Animals and birds live a simple and natural life guided by their instincts. Human beings imagine and attribute attractive qualities to the objects of their choice. This then prompts man to hear, see, touch, smell or taste the objects of desire. This sensual experience he wants to repeat again and again and thereby he gets attached to the objects. Touch (sparśanam) and sight (dṛṣṭiḥ) are specially mentioned as they are powerful causes for attachment. Many fall in love at first sight. The miser counts his money again and again never wanting to part with it. It is said in jest that if a man opens the door of the car for his wife, either his car is new or the wife is new! The scriptures say that if one is intensely attached to someone or something, then in the next life one becomes that. A man who is deeply attached to a woman is likely to be born as a woman in future lives. Sage Bharata got attached to a deer and became a deer in his next life. The individuality is indeed strengthened by every desire and sensory experience.

The individual being's endless journey: Nourished by our imaginations, desires, enjoyments and attachments, we take different forms in different worlds in accordance with our actions. Thus life after life the story of the individual continues.

The factors that decide the type of form that the individual gets are enumerated.

स्थूलानि सूक्ष्माणि बहूनि चैव रूपाणि देही स्वगुणैर्वृणोति ।
क्रियागुणैरात्मगुणैश्च तेषां संयोगहेतुरपरोऽपि दृष्टः ॥ १२ ॥

sthūlāni sūkṣmāṇi bahūni caiva rūpāṇi dehī svaguṇair-vṛṇoti,
kriyāguṇair-ātmaguṇaiśca teṣāṁ saṁyogahetur-aparo'pi dṛṣṭaḥ. (12)

स्थूलानि – gross; सूक्ष्माणि – subtle; बहूनि – many; च एव – and; रूपाणि – forms or bodies; देही – the embodied being; स्वगुणैः – by its own tendencies; वृणोति – adopts or assumes; क्रियागुणैः – by quality of actions; आत्मगुणैः – by the quality of the mind; च – and; तेषाम् – their; संयोगहेतुः – cause of the union; अपरः – another; अपि – also; दृष्टः – seen

12. The embodied being assumes many bodies, gross and subtle, chosen by its own tendencies, actions and quality of mind. Another cause for this union (with various bodies) is also seen.

The individual's choice (dehī vṛṇoti): It is we alone who have chosen to be born in the body we now have and we will also choose all future bodies. Some are born in grosser bodies (animal or human) and some are born with subtle bodies (deities and other celestial beings). We choose the form we get according to our vāsanās – good or bad, formed in previous births (svaguṇaiḥ). They in turn were formed by the combination of the quality of actions (kriyā-guṇaiḥ) and quality of mind (ātma-guṇaiḥ).

God's grace: The other cause which connects the individual with the body is God. God presides over all actions and enjoins results according to our actions (karmādhyakṣa and karma-phala-dātā). 'Ordered by God, man gets the result of his actions as actions by themselves are inert.'[1] For one who has strong swimming vāsanās, the body of a water creature would seem more appropriate. It is He who knows which is the appropriate body needed to fulfill the vāsanās of the individual.

---

[1] kartuḥ-ājñayā prāpyate phalam,
karma kiṁ paraṁ karma tajjaḍam. – *Upadeśa Sāraḥ* 1

Does the individual's story ever end? The mantra says –

अनाद्यनन्तं कलिलस्य मध्ये विश्वस्य स्रष्टारमनेकरूपम्।
विश्वस्यैकं परिवेष्टितारं ज्ञात्वा देवं मुच्यते सर्वपाशैः॥ १३॥

anādyanantaṁ kalilasya madhye viśvasya sraṣṭāram-anekarūpam,
viśvasyaikaṁ pariveṣṭitāraṁ jñātvā devaṁ mucyate sarvapāśaiḥ. (13)

अनाद्यनन्तम् – without beginning and end; कलिलस्य – of chaos; मध्ये – in the midst; विश्वस्य – of the universe; स्रष्टारम् – the creator; अनेकरूपम् – in many forms; विश्वस्य – of the universe; एकम् – one; परिवेष्टितारम् – encompassing or pervading; ज्ञात्वा – knowing; देवम् – the Lord; मुच्यते – released; सर्वपाशैः – from all bondage

13. Knowing the Lord in the midst of the chaos (of saṁsāra), the one without beginning and end, the creator of the universe, in many forms, the one pervading the entire universe, one is released from all bondage.

The compassionate Lord who unites the individual to the results of his actions is also the cause for his liberation. It is He who unites the individual with his Guru, who gives him knowledge and inspiration to start the inward journey.

The journey's end: Just as in the outside world, the individual initially finds only chaos and confusion within. The inward journey seems more difficult and obstacle ridden than the outward journey, he was going through life after life. However with persistence and sincerity, when he wades through his inner turmoil he reaches the shore which is beginningless and endless, which is effulgent and all-engulfing. He meets the Lord, the creator of all whom he then recognises in all forms and most importantly as his own Self. Realising that he is birthless and deathless, he is liberated from the cycle of birth and death and reaches the end of his journey.

What happens to the body when the individual realises the Truth? Does he give up the body? The mantra says –

भावग्राह्यमनीडाख्यं भावाभावकरं शिवम्।
कलासर्गकरं देवं ये विदुस्ते जहुस्तनुम्॥ १४॥

bhāvagrāhyam-anīḍākhyaṁ bhāvābhāvakaraṁ śivam,
kalāsargakaraṁ devaṁ ye viduste jahus-tanum. (14)

भावग्राह्यम् – realised through devotion; अनीडाख्यम् – who is the bodiless (devoid of a body); भावाभावकरम् – who creates and destroys; शिवम् – pure; कलासर्गकरम् – the projector of the sixteen parts; देवम् – God; ये – who; विदुः – know; ते – they; जहुः – (they) give up; तनुम् – the body

14. Those who know this God who can be realised only through devotion, who is devoid of a body, who creates and destroys this world, who is pure, who projects the (sixteen) parts – they give up the body.

The nature of Truth to be realised is described as –

bhāvagrāhyam: Bhāva means feelings. Here it means devotion. The Truth is known by a heart filled with love for God, the Guru and the scriptures. Single pointed devotion and faith is the key to God-realisation. Śaṅkarācārya says that God is realised by a pure hearted person. Śrī Ramaṇa Maharṣi also says that supreme Devotion or God-realisation arises from intense 'bhāvanā'.[1]

[1] bhāvanābalāt-bhaktiruttamā – *Upadeśa Sāraḥ* 9

Devoid of body (anīḍākhyam): Nīḍa means a nest. Anīḍa means one who is homeless. Here it means God is bodiless. He does not have a particular physical or subtle body. He does incarnate in a special body for some time, but in His absolute nature, He is formless.

Creator and destroyer (bhāvābhāvakaram): Here bhāva means creation and abhāva, the absence of creation or dissolution. God is the creator, sustainer and destroyer of this world and always remains as pure Consciousness (śivam).

Projector of sixteen parts (kalā-sargakaram): Kalā means phases or aspects. *Praśnopaniṣad* (6.4) enumerates sixteen kalās or aspects of God. They are the five elements, faith, prāṇa, senses, mind, strength, food, penance, mantra, realms of experience and name. These aspects itself hide the True nature of God and hence they are called kalā.[1] They divert our attention away from God and keep it engaged in their attributes and modifications.

The Realised One gives up his body (ye viduḥ te jahus-tanum): God is bodiless. Realising oneness with God, the seeker also becomes bodiless. Here giving up body means giving up identification with the body.

The ignorant individual gives up identification with the gross body when he dies, but carries the subtle and causal bodies with him. Prompted by his desires and vāsanās he is born again and again. At the end of his lifespan when the Realised One departs from the gross body, the subtle body

[1] kaṁ brahma līyate ācchādayate yayā iti kalā

merges with the subtle elements. The individuality has already merged in the infinite Truth, so there is no one left to be reborn.[1] He is liberated from the cycle of birth and death.

With this we come to the end of the fifth chapter.

[1] na tasya prāṇāḥ utkrāmanti

Chapter 6

The last chapter not only discusses the true nature of God/ Truth and the individual, but also expounds various means of Realisation.

The Upaniṣad began with a discussion amongst the seekers of knowledge about the nature of the Truth, the cause of the Universe, and so on. Now, after due reflection and meditation they are clear and sure in their understanding of the Truth. They assert –

स्वभावमेके कवयो वदन्ति कालं तथान्ये परिमुह्यमानाः ।
देवस्यैष महिमा तु लोके येनेदं भ्राम्यते ब्रह्मचक्रम् ॥ १ ॥

svabhāvam-eke kavayo vadanti kālaṁ tathānye parimuhyamānāḥ,
devasyaiṣa mahimā tu loke yenedaṁ bhrāmyate brahmacakram. (1)

स्वभावम् – inherent nature; एके – some; कवयः – learned people; वदन्ति – say; कालम् – time; तथा – similarly; अन्ये – others; परिमुह्यमानाः – being under delusion; देवस्य – of God; एषः – this (world); महिमा – glory; तु – verily; लोके – in the world; येन – by whom; इदम् – this; भ्राम्यते – rotates; ब्रह्मचक्रम् – wheel of world (saṁsāra)

1. In their delusion, some learned people say that it is inherent nature and others say it is time. The world verily is the glory of God. By Him does the wheel of this world (saṁsāra) rotate.

Conclusive discussion: Discussion with co-seekers is a good way to arrive at the nature of Truth. Reflection in groups and reflection alone both serve the purpose of clarity in thinking and right understanding.

In the beginning of the Upaniṣad (1.2) many factors like time, inherent nature, chance and fate were considered to be the cause of creation. All of these factors are rejected as it was realised that they were part of creation. And a part of creation cannot be the cause of creation as the cause must always precede the effect.

It is now concluded that God alone is the ultimate cause of creation and that creation is the manifestation of His glory alone. The wheel of creation described in detail earlier (1.4) moves only because of God.

Having concluded that God/Truth is the cause of the world, the wise seekers now contemplate on how He creates.

येनावृतं नित्यमिदं हि सर्वं ज्ञः कालकारो गुणी सर्वविद्यः।
तेनेशितं कर्म विवर्तते ह पृथ्व्यप्तेजोऽनिलखानि चिन्त्यम्॥ २॥

yenāvṛtaṁ nityam-idaṁ hi sarvaṁ jñaḥ kālakāro guṇī sarvavid-yaḥ,
teneśitaṁ karma vivartate ha pṛthvyaptejo'nilakhāni cintyam. (2)

येन – by whom; आवृतम् – pervaded; नित्यम् – ever; इदम् – this; हि – indeed; सर्वम् – all; ज्ञः – knower; कालकारः – the creator of time; गुणी – possessed of qualities; सर्वविद् यः – He who is omniscient; तेन – by Him; ईशितम् – willed; कर्म – the entire activity (of creation); विवर्तते – appear; ह – well known; पृथिवि-अप्-तेज-अनिल-खानि – earth, water, fire, air and space; चिन्त्यम् – has to be contemplated upon

2. *He, by whom indeed all this is ever pervaded, who is the knower, the creator of time, who possesses qualities and is omniscient – willed by Him the entire well known activity of creation, i.e, earth, water, fire, air and space appear. This has to be contemplated upon.*

God the Existence-Consciousness behind creation: The material cause always pervades the thing created like the mud pervades the mud-pot. Prakṛti is the material cause of this world; however Existence exists before prakṛti. Therefore Existence always pervades all that can be indicated as 'this' – the inert. This includes countless cosmoses, the body, senses, vital air, mind, the elements and the unmanifest prakṛti.

God is also the sentient cause of the creation. Consciousness alone illumines all in general and its functioning through the Total Mind. He is the omniscient Lord (sarvajña) who knows every individual's thoughts (sarvavit). For example, the light of the sun illumines everything in general but reflects specially on all reflecting surfaces like a mirror or water.

God – the changeless creator of time and qualities: Time is an imperceptible factor, known only through change in objects. We realise how much time has passed when we observe the wrinkles on our face reflected in the mirror. In fact only when our thought changes or the object of our thought changes, do we perceive time. *The Yoga Śāstra* explains that in the deep sleep state the same thought of the absence of objects alone exists and so we are unable to perceive the passage of time. God/Truth is the changeless substratum of all changes which we call time.

Wielding His great potential power, He is the treasure house of all attributes and virtues (sarva-kalyāṇa-guṇa-nidhāna). He is omniscient, omnipotent, omnipresent, presiding over all actions, giver of all results, compassionate, gracious and forgiving. He is the abode of all love and joy which sustains creation.

Creation an appearance (vivarta): Whenever the material and the sentient cause is the same, the thing created is an illusion. For example, the waking mind alone provides both the material and knowledge for the dream world which is only an appearance. Similarly God is both the material and sentient cause of creation and so creation is only an appearance (abhinna nimitta-upādāna-vivarta kāraṇa). Vivarta means to appear different (viparīta vartanam). The Existence-Consciousness God/Truth appears as this changing world of names, forms and qualities without undergoing any change like the appearance of the snake vision on the rope.

Contemplation – the means: The seekers understood the nature of God/Truth and creation as His glory through discussion and realised that meditation is the means to know the Truth as one's own Self.

Once, one man concluded that he was 99% realised. God is beyond everything and remains unaffected by anything. He too remains unaffected by anything that happens in the world. But he is affected when any small or big thing happens to him so he is 99% realised. This is no Realisation. The Truth has to be contemplated upon to be realised.

The seekers now contemplate further how God/Truth creates this world.

तत्कर्म कृत्वा विनिवर्त्य भूयस्तत्त्वस्य तत्त्वेन समेत्य योगम्।
एकेन द्वाभ्यां त्रिभिरष्टभिर्वा कालेन चैवात्मगुणैश्च सूक्ष्मैः ॥ ३ ॥

tatkarma kṛtvā vinivartya bhūyas-tattvasya tattvena sametya yogam, ekena dvābhyāṁ tribhir-aṣṭabhirvā kālena caivātmaguṇaiśca sūkṣmaiḥ. (3)

तत्कर्म – that work; कृत्वा – having done; विनिवर्त्य – having examined; भूयः – again; तत्त्वस्य – of principle; तत्त्वेन – with principle; समेत्य – having brought about; योगम् – association; एकेन – with one; द्वाभ्याम् – with two; त्रिभिः – with three; अष्टभिः – with eight; वा – or; कालेन – with time; च एव – as well; सूक्ष्मैः आत्मगुणैः – with subtle qualities (of the internal organs); च – and

3. Having finished that work, He examines it and brings together one principle with another – one, two, three or eight – in association with time and the subtle qualities.

The Grand Mixer: The previous mantra explained that God/Truth creates the five great elements. He examines His creation and finds it lacking in spirit. Without the spirit that enlivens matter, creation is lifeless and uninteresting. So He combines the matter and the spirit – the inert and the sentient and thus this interesting and mind-blowing creation comes about.

The spirit or sentient principle is one alone. However prakṛti can be seen as one, two, three or eight. Seen as one, God creates with the combination of the sentient principle and the primordial matter (avidyā). Seen as two, He combines the spirit with the merits and demerits or righteousness and unrighteousness (dharma and adharma) of previous creations, giving rise to the present variety in creation. Or, God combines the spirit with the three inherent qualities of prakṛti (sattva, rajas and tamas) to create the world. Alternately it is to be understood that God combines the spirit with the eight-fold prakṛti (space, air, fire, water, earth elements, the mind, intellect and I sense or ego) to create the world.

A chef once advised his friend never to eat the 'Monday Special' as it was usually the mix of the Saturday and Sunday leftovers! Creation is a delicious feast of the Grand Mixer of matter and spirit.

The phrase 'tat karma kṛtvā vinivartya bhūyaḥ' has another beautiful understanding of God's nature. Having created the world, having allotted all the duties and positions, created all the laws and rules, the beings, instruments and the materials necessary to run the world, He withdraws and silently watches. The world then functions automatically in His mere Existence and Awareness. This is indeed a sign of efficient management!

After having created this great grand creation what does the Lord do? The mantra explains –

आरभ्य कर्माणि गुणान्वितानि भावांश्च सर्वान्विनियोजयेद्यः ।
तेषामभावे कृतकर्मनाशः कर्मक्षये याति स तत्त्वतोऽन्यः ॥ ४ ॥

ārabhya karmāṇi guṇānvitāni bhāvāṁśca sarvān-viniyojayed-yaḥ,
teṣām-abhāve kṛtakarma-nāśaḥ karmakṣaye yāti sa tattvato'nyaḥ. (4)

आरभ्य – having begun; कर्माणि – works; गुणान्वितानि – associated with the qualities (of prakṛti); भावान् – effects; च – and; सर्वान् – all; विनियोजयेत् – employs; यः – who; तेषाम् – their; अभावे – absence (when they wear out); कृतकर्मनाशः – that which was created vanishes; कर्मक्षये – when the creation is dissolved; याति – reaches (abides); सः – He; तत्त्वतः – from prakṛti; अन्यः – distinct

4. Having begun the work (of creation) associated with the qualities (of prakṛti), He employs all the effects (of prakṛti), and when they disappear (wear out), that which was created vanishes. When the creation is dissolved, He abides in His own Self (which is distinct from prakṛti).

Dissolution follows creation: What begins must end. Taking recourse to the power of māyā which has the qualities of sattva, rajas and tamas, the Lord creates this wonderful creation which manifests the various effects of māyā. When the total inherent tendencies which triggered this creation and set it in motion get exhausted, creation comes to an end. The karmas of all beings which are to be manifested in this cycle of creation are the momentum that keeps this creation going. Once they are over that particular creation is wound up and that is called dissolution. The fan blades keep rotating till electricity propels it. Once the fan is switched off, the blades slowly loose their momentum and finally stop moving altogether.

God/Truth in His absolute nature, nameless and formless, existed before creation. He appears as the world and when this appearance also disappears, He remains as always, in His absolute pure nature as Existence-Consciousness-Bliss.

This verse can also be seen from the standpoint of an individual and his journey.

The return journey: The vāsanās that we are born with creates desires and prompt actions. That is what gives momentum to all we do. Actions done with ego and ego-centric desires for selfish gains and for pleasure alone keep us in bondage by multiplying our desires and creating more vāsanās. However actions done as a worship of God without likes and dislikes, selflessly with love and dedication, purify the mind. They exhaust existing vāsanās and do not create new vāsanās. This is also called karma yoga. Śrī Kṛṣṇa says, 'Whatever action you do – mundane, religious or social, offer them to Me and all those results will free you from the bondage of action.'[1] When the mind is thus

[1] yat-karoṣi yadaśnāsi yajjuhoṣi dadāsi yat,
yat-tapasyasi kaunteya tat-kuruṣva madarpaṇam.
śubhāśubha-phalair-evaṁ mokṣyase karma-bandhanaiḥ. – *Gītā* 9.27,9.28

purified and the vāsanās are exhausted, it turns within. 'The individual cuts the knots of the heart (ignorance), dispels all doubts, and exhausts all vāsanās when he finally abides in the Self within.'[1]

The individual's heart is filled with many vāsanās. How can we exhaust them one by one? How do we come to know that a particular vāsanā is exhausted. When our dependence on the object vanishes, there is no more craving to gain it or an excitement or thrill on gaining it or desire to repeat the pleasure, we can safely say that the vāsanā has exhausted. For example, the sight of marbles no longer excites us. Some vāsanās get exhausted with age, some by right thinking and many through dedicated actions and all through knowledge of the Truth.

[1] bhidyate hṛdayagranthi-chidyante sarvasaṁśayāḥ,
kṣīyante cāsya karmāṇi tasmin-dṛṣṭe parāvare. – *Muṇḍakopaniṣad* 2.2.8

In the previous mantra karma yoga (dedicated actions) was the means recommended to lighten the load of vasanas. The present mantra suggests the subtler means of upāsanā (worship and meditation).

आदिः स संयोगनिमित्तहेतुः परस्त्रिकालादकलोऽपि दृष्टः।
तं विश्वरूपं भवभूतमीड्यं देवं स्वचित्तस्थमुपास्य पूर्वम्॥ ५॥

ādiḥ sa saṁyoga-nimitta-hetuḥ parastrikālād-akalo'pi dṛṣṭaḥ,
taṁ viśvarūpaṁ bhavabhūtam-īḍyaṁ devaṁ svacittastham-
upāsya pūrvam. (5)

आदिः – primordial being; सः – He; संयोगनिमित्तहेतुः – the cause for the union; त्रिकालात् परः – beyond the three periods of time; अकलः – devoid of parts; अपि – also; दृष्टः – recognised; तम् – Him; विश्वरूपम् – with the universal form; भवभूतम् – who has become the whole world; ईड्यम् – adorable; देवम् – effulgent; स्वचित्तस्थम् – present in one's own heart; उपास्य – having worshipped and meditated; पूर्वम् – earlier

5. He is the primordial being, the cause for the union (of matter, spirit etc.), beyond the three periods of time and also devoid of parts. This effulgent and adorable Lord with the universal form, who has become the whole world, can be recognised as He is present in our own heart as worshipped and meditated upon earlier.

God unites (saṁyoga-nimitta-hetuḥ): The primordial being, the cause of all, God is the great uniting factor in the world. He unites matter with spirit, the various causes with each other and with their effects, the action with the result, the doer of action with the enjoyer of the result, one thought with another and so on. God is love and love is the greatest uniting factor between any two objects or beings.

It is He alone who brings together the disciple and the Guru, connects the seeker with the spiritual practices needed to progress, brings about the urge for noble actions and unites us with noble thoughts and virtues. Ultimately it is He alone who connects us with Him through Self-knowledge and Self-realisation.

God is adorable (īḍya): Even though He is timeless (trikālāt para) and partless (akala), He alone has become the world and all its names, forms and qualities just to bless us. Seated in our heart as our own Self, He is naturally the most loved and adored.

Worship and meditation (upāsya): The means to realise this adorable God is to always remember Him and be aware of His presence through all our activities. 'Citta' specifically means the faculty of remembering. 'Sva-citta-stham' is to keep Him always in our memory. Being near God (upa-āsana) being connected to Him through our thoughts, words and deeds makes us pure and virtuous like Him. With such a mind, meditation on His true nature further is easier and it strengthens our connection. Thereafter through Realisation we become one with Him.

This mantra again extols the glory of God/Truth.

**स वृक्षकालाकृतिभिः परोऽन्यो यस्मात्प्रपञ्चः परिवर्ततेऽयम्।
धर्मावहं पापनुदं भगेशं ज्ञात्वात्मस्थममृतं विश्वधाम ॥ ६ ॥**

*sa vṛkṣakālākṛtibhiḥ paro'nyo yasmāt-prapañcaḥ parivartate'yam,
dharmāvahaṁ pāpanudaṁ bhageśaṁ jñātvātmastham-amṛtaṁ
viśvadhāma. (6)*

सः – He; वृक्ष-काल-आकृतिभिः – by the tree, time and form; परः – beyond; अन्यः – different (not affected); यस्मात् – because of whom; प्रपञ्चः – the universe; परिवर्तते – revolves; अयम् – this; धर्मावहम् – the source of virtue; पापनुदम् – the remover of sins; भगेशम् – the lord of all fortunes; ज्ञात्वा – having known; आत्मस्थम् – seated in one's own heart; अमृतम् – immortal; विश्वधाम – supporter of the whole universe

6. He, because of whom this phenomenal world revolves, is beyond the tree (of saṁsāra), time and form, and is different from these. He is the source of virtue, the remover of sins, the lord of all fortunes and the supporter of the whole universe. Knowing Him seated in one's own heart, one becomes immortal.

Beyond and different (paro'nyaḥ): The word 'beyond' signifies that God is unaffected by the world and the word 'different' signifies He is neither finite nor has other characteristics of the world.

The world is called prapañca as it is made up of the five elements. Even though He is the root cause (mūla) of the tree of worldly existence (saṁsāra vṛkṣa), which is conditioned by time, names and forms, He remains unaffected and unconditioned (ūrdhva) by them. The world revolves around Him and because of Him, yet He remains the unmoving centre of its existence.

The remover and bestower (pāpanudam, dharmāvaham): God removes our sins and bestows us with virtues. Only when the house is swept free of the trash and the stink, the fragrance of incense can be enjoyed. How can a mind full of resentment and revenge experience the joy of kindness and forgiveness? He is the Lord of the six fortunes (bhageśa) spoken of earlier (3.11) which He bestows on the deserving. The highest fortune He bestows is the knowledge that makes the individual immortal.

This mantra asserts God's absolute Lordship as realised by the Masters.

तमीश्वराणां परमं महेश्वरं तं देवतानां परमं च दैवतम्।
पतिं पतीनां परमं परस्ताद्-विदाम देवं भुवनेशमीड्यम्॥ ७ ॥

tam-īśvarāṇāṁ paramaṁ maheśvaraṁ taṁ devatānāṁ paramaṁ ca daivatam,
patiṁ patīnāṁ paramaṁ parastād-vidāma devaṁ bhuvaneśam-īḍyam. (7)

तम् – Him; ईश्वराणाम् – of the lords; परमम् – supreme; महेश्वरम् – Lord; तम् – Him; देवतानाम् – of the deities; परमम् – great; च – and; दैवतम् – God; पतिम् – the Ruler; पतीनाम् – of the rulers; परमम् – higher; परस्तात् – than the highest; विदाम – (we) know; देवम् – the effulgent one; भुवनेशम् – the Lord of the universe; ईड्यम् – adorable

7. We know Him, the effulgent one who is the supreme Lord of all lords, the great God of all deities, the Ruler of all rulers, beyond the highest, adorable and the Lord of the universe.

The supreme Ruler of rulers (īśvarāṇāṁ paraṁ maheśvaram): Īśvara means a ruler. There are many rulers in the world – kings, sultans, presidents, prime ministers or heads of huge organisations. Even in the animal world we see a lion as the king of the jungle and commanding his pride of lions and cubs. Then there are rulers who rule other realms of experiences (lokas) like heaven (svarga-loka) like

Indra. Each cosmos also has its own Creator, Sustainer and Destroyer – Lord Brahmā, Lord Viṣṇu and Lord Śiva – who are indeed powerful. Being a part of God/Truth all these rulers enjoy but a small part of this lordship and power. God is the supreme Ruler of Rulers, the Lord of countless cosmoses (ananta-koṭi-brahmāṇḍa-nāyaka).

The Chief Deity (devatānāṁ paraṁ daivatam): Every law and every function by which God governs His creation has its own presiding deity who is appointed by Him. For example, Aśvini-kumāras preside over hearing. Then of course we have our own grāma devatās who preside over the village (Mumba devi is the presiding deity of Mumbai). Kula devatās preside over our family lineage, sthāna devatās preside over a particular place. Each river, mountain range and elements are presided over by their respective deities like Gaṅgā devi over Ganga river, Himavān over the Himālayas and Agni devatā over the fire element. The scriptures say that there are 33 crore such deities. God is the one who presides over all of them. Were it not for Him, fire could not burn, nor the wind blow. We invoke the blessings of these deities to help us function well and they in turn worship God for strength and ability to function.

The supreme Lord of lords (patiṁ patīnāṁ paramam): Commonly the word pati is used for a husband. However etymologically it means one who protects. It means one who guides and protects 'dharma' or righteousness. God appoints certain souls like Manu, to take care of dharma in each Manvantara, who in turn appoints Dakṣa Prajāpati and others to help him.

In each country we have law upholders, Gurus and kings (bhūpati). The president of a country is called Rāṣṭrapati. Similarly we have words like aśvapati, gajapati, vidyāpati, vācaspati for those who are masters of horses, elephants, knowledge and speech respectively. God is the Lord of all those who guide and protect others. He is the supreme Lord.

Yudhiṣṭhira asks Bhīṣma-pitāmaha, "Who is the one supreme God, whom we should worship?"[1] He was told, "Worship that God who is the Chief deity and the imperishable Lord of all beings."[2]

[1] kimekaṁ daivataṁ loke kiṁ vāpyekaṁ parāyaṇam – *Viṣṇu-sahasranāma.2*

[2] daivataṁ devatānāṁ ca bhūtānāṁ yo'vyayaḥ pitā – *Viṣṇu-sahasranāma.10*

People become great because of what they do and what they have. What does God do and what does He have that makes Him the Lord of all?

न तस्य कार्यं करणं च विद्यते न तत्समश्चाभ्यधिकश्च दृश्यते ।
परास्य शक्तिर्विविधैव श्रूयते स्वाभाविकी ज्ञानबलक्रिया च ॥ ८ ॥

na tasya kāryaṁ karaṇaṁ ca vidyate na tatsamaścābhyadhikaśca dṛśyate,
parāsya śaktir-vividhaiva śrūyate svābhāvikī jñānabalakriyā ca. (8)

न – neither; **तस्य** – his (he has); **कार्यम्** – a body; **करणम्** – organ; **च** – and; **विद्यते** – is there; **न** – none; **तत्समः** – equal to Him; **च** – and; **अभ्यधिकः** – surpass; **च** – and; **दृश्यते** – seen; **परा** – supreme; **अस्य** – His; **शक्तिः** – power; **विविधा** – manifold; **एव** – indeed; **श्रूयते** – heard (said); **स्वाभाविकी** – spontaneous (natural); **ज्ञान-बल-क्रिया** – knowledge and power of control; **च** – and

8. He has neither a body nor any organ. None is seen to equal Him, leave alone surpass Him. His powers are heard (said) to be supreme and manifold indeed. His knowledge and power of control is spontaneous and natural.

He has no body or senses (na tasya kāryaṁ na karaṇam): God has neither a body (kāryam) nor the outer instruments (bahiḥ karaṇam) of sense organs of perception or actions or the inner equipment of the mind-intellect (antaḥ karaṇam). How can one do anything without the body or the outer and inner instruments? So He is not the doer of any action (akartā).

It means that God's greatness is not dependent on what He does or what He has. He is great because He is what He is.

Another meaning is that He has no kāryam or duties. Being full and complete He has nothing to be gained by doing anything. So He has no need for any instruments (karaṇam) by which He can attain it. We are troubled by a sense of incompleteness and to feel fulfilled we need to do something. God is ever full and fulfilled.

There is none equal to Him nor greater (na tat-samaḥ-ca-abhyadhikaḥ): Earlier it was said that 'God is incomparable' (na tasya pratimā asti – 4.19). There is none even equal to Him leave alone someone greater than Him. Pauṇḍraka tried to copy Lord Śrī Kṛṣṇa and pretended to be the original Vāsudeva Kṛṣṇa and became the laughing stock of the town. Rāvaṇa thought he was God and got killed. Hiraṇyakaśipu thought he was greater than God and came to a sad end. A woman when asked for a reason for divorce said, "We have major religious differences. We believe in different Gods. He thinks He is God!" Who can equal infinity or exceed infinity? When the great devotees Manu and Śatarūpā asked God to bless them with a child like Him, the Lord said, "Since there is none like Me, I alone shall incarnate as your son."

God's natural powers (svābhāvikī): God's māyā śakti or prakṛti, His inherent and inscrutable power manifests in manifold ways. Just as the ability to cool or heat or rotate are manifestations of the power of electricity through the cooler, heater or fan, God's great power manifests as the ability to see or hear in the eyes and ears and the power to know, energise, function and so on in the mind and the body.

A nouveau rich person boasts about his wealth and dresses flashily. One born with a golden spoon has a natural air of wealth and power about him which he is quite unaware of. God's unbelievable powers are natural (svābhāvika) to Him. Political power can be snatched away, our power of seeing may fade away with age, but God's powers always remain with Him in full measure.

Knowledge, strength and action (jñāna-bala-kriyā): Amongst other powers there is a special mention of these three. It indicates that to attain any amount of lordship and success we need all three. Thoughtless actions and actionless thinking bear no fruits. A nation should have 'knowledge' – its own vision and knowhow, 'might' – ability to defend itself and political and economic power and 'action' – must be dynamic and progressive. Such a nation can stand on its own and help others.

The thought of the previous two mantras is further elaborated.

न तस्य कश्चित्पतिरस्ति लोके न चेशिता नैव च तस्य लिङ्गम्।
स कारणं करणाधिपाधिपो न चास्य कश्चिज्जनिता न चाधिपः॥ ९॥

na tasya kaścit-patirasti loke na ceśitā naiva ca tasya liṅgam,
sa kāraṇaṁ karaṇādhipādhipo na cāsya kaścijjanitā na cādhipaḥ. (9)

न – no; तस्य – His (of Him); कश्चित् – any; पतिः – master; अस्ति – is; लोके – in the world; न – nor; च – and; ईशिता – ruler; न – no; एव – indeed; च – and; तस्य – with regard to Him; लिङ्गम् – ground of inference; सः – He; कारणम् – the cause; करणाधिपाधिपः – the Lord of the master of the sense organs; न – none; च – and; अस्य – His; कश्चित् – any; जनिता – creator; न – nor; च – and; अधिपः – overlord

9. In this world, there is no master to lord over Him, nor is there any ruler to rule over Him. Indeed there is no sign by which He can be inferred. He is the cause (of everything) and the Lord of the master of the sense organs. There is none who created Him nor anyone above Him.

na tasya pati na īśitā: God is the protector and Lord of all and also the controller of all, but there is none to Lord over or to control Him. Viṣṇu-sahasranāma has one name 'anīśa' for God which means one who has no Lord above Him. In *Tulasī Rāmāyaṇa* Sage Nārada tells the Lord, "You are supremely independent with none over Your head" (parama svatantra na sira para koi).

Does God need any protection? Being omnipotent He can well take care of Himself and all of us. In the world we see that power corrupts and total power corrupts totally. A teenager who rides his father's high-powered car may loose control or a dictator may become blind with power. Power controls the immature. God is always in full control of His power and so there is no question of His power controlling Him. God manifests His powers only in the welfare of all beings as He is the very source of righteousness (dharmāvahaḥ).

However in *Bhāgavatam* the Lord says, 'I remain in the control of my devotee' (ahaṁ bhakta-parādhīnaḥ). This is the beauty of the Path of Devotion. The Lord, who is above everything, dances to the tune of His devotee. But we must remember that it is by His own will. If someone thinks that He can control God by becoming His devotee, it will not work. Mother Yaśodā could tie baby Lord Śrī Kṛṣṇa easily. The devotees also know that the Lord is only allowing them to do it. This fills the devotee's heart with greater humility and love for God.

na tasya liṅgam: Liṅgam means a sign. God has no sign or indication by which we can recognise Him. Fire is inferred by its liṅgam – smoke. God is nameless, formless and attributeless and so has no sign by which He is known. It means that He is not available for direct perception or inference. That is why many people deny the very existence of God. Logic which is based on direct perception and inference can neither conclusively prove nor disprove the existence of God. The scriptures on devotion therefore say that God is revealed only to those to whom God reveals Himself.

sa kāraṇaṁ karaṇādhipa-adhipaḥ: He is both the cause and the master of all living beings. Karaṇādhipaḥ refers to the individual (jīva) who owns his outer and inner instruments. The individual may not have mastery over them, but he does employ them to function in this world. God is their master.

na tasya kaścit janitā: No one has created God. Children also ask this question often, "Who is God's father and mother?" The question itself is wrong. When we say that God is the ultimate cause and thereafter ask for His cause, we have in effect made Him an effect. If we continue to posit a cause, it will lead to the fallacy of regress ad infinitum (anavasthā doṣa). He is self-existent (svayambhūḥ) and there is no other cause above Him. He is the ultimate cause.

The next mantra is a prayer for abidance in God/Truth.

यस्तन्तुनाभ इव तन्तुभिः प्रधानजैः स्वभावतो देव एकः स्वमावृणोत्।
स नो दधाद्ब्रह्माप्ययम्॥ १०॥

yastantunābha iva tantubhiḥ pradhānajaiḥ svabhāvato deva ekaḥ svam-āvṛṇot,
sa no dadhāt-brahmāpyayam. (10)

यः – who; तन्तुनाभः – spider; इव – like; तन्तुभिः – with its web; प्रधानजैः – with the products of nature; स्वभावतः – spontaneously; देवः – Lord; एकः – one; स्वम् – Himself; आवृणोत् – covers; सः – He; नः – us; दधात् – (may) grant; ब्रह्माप्ययम् – absorption in Truth/Brahman

10. May the one Lord who covers Himself spontaneously with the products of nature just as a spider covers itself with its web, grant us absorption in Truth/Brahman.

God is the web-master (tantunābhaḥ iva): The spider weaves a web from its own secretions. With the thin threads that come from his navel, he makes a beautiful web and then hides behind it. Once the insect is trapped in it, he swallows up both the insect and the web. In the same way God creates the great grand world-web, from Himself, His own inherent power, also called pradhāna (māyā śakti is also called pradhāna as it has the seed of the entire creation in it). This most intricate and widespread web seems to hide God and we the individuals caught in this web are unable to see Him.

The Prayer – 'sa no dadhāt-brahma-apyayam': 'Like the spider who swallows the insect trapped in the web, O Lord! Grant us absorption in the Truth.' Apyayam means dissolution. O Lord, may we become one with You. May our ego that separates us from You, merge in You. May we become Your food and dissolve in You. The apple eaten by us does not regain its original form ever. May we too ever abide in You – the Truth which is our own Self.

The following is a beautiful mantra for meditation.

**एको देवः सर्वभूतेषु गूढः सर्वव्यापी सर्वभूतान्तरात्मा ।
कर्माध्यक्षः सर्वभूताधिवासः साक्षी चेता केवलो निर्गुणश्च ॥ ११ ॥**

*eko devaḥ sarvabhūteṣu gūḍhaḥ sarvavyāpī sarvabhūtāntarātmā,
karmādhyakṣaḥ sarvabhūtādhivāsaḥ sākṣī cetā kevalo nirguṇaśca. (11)*

एकः – one; देवः – God; सर्वभूतेषु – in all beings; गूढः – hidden; सर्वव्यापी – all-pervasive; सर्वभूतान्तरात्मा – the inner Self of all beings; कर्माध्यक्षः – one who presides over all actions; सर्वभूताधिवासः – the indweller of all beings; साक्षी – witness; चेता – pure Consciousness; केवलः – one alone (without a second); निर्गुणः – without any attributes; च – and

11. The one God remains hidden in all beings. He is all-pervasive and the inner Self of all beings. He is the one who presides over all actions and is the indweller of all beings. He is the witness, pure Consciousness, one alone (without a second) and without any attributes.

One God (eko devaḥ): It is worth noting that time and again we are reminded that there is only One God. The word 'ekaḥ' also means 'one that goes everywhere' (eti sarvatra gacchati iti ekaḥ). One is present in all numbers, 0 = 1 - 1, 2 = 1 + 1 and so on. All counting begins with one. It is the substratum of all numbers like God who is the common substratum of the world.

Hidden in all beings (sarvabhūteṣu gūḍhaḥ): Someone asked a saint as to why God keeps Himself hidden. The saint jokingly replied, "Because everyone goes to Him with a demand list, 'I want this!' 'I want that!'" He appears hidden only because we are looking outside and not within. Where does He live within us?

All-pervading God is the inner Self (sarvavyāpi sarvabhūtāntarātmā): God lives as the very Self in all of us. How far is God from us? He is neither near nor far. He is our own Self. God is all-pervading and can be seen everywhere, but strangely it is only when we see Him as our own Self that we are able to recognise Him as the Self of all. What does He do within us?

The inner Self presides over all actions (karmādhyakṣa sarvabhūtādhivāsaḥ): He presides over all our actions and connects us with the result of our actions. He is the Awareness in the light of which all actions take place. He illumines all and knows all. He dwells not only in human beings, but all beings and also in the inert matter. As what does He dwell in everything?

God – the witnessing Consciousness (sākṣī cetā): He is the witnessing Consciousness within us. Sākṣī means 'one who illumines itself and illumines all others without any aid.'[1] Also a witness must be impartial. God is that self-evident Consciousness who illumines all thoughts impartially and needs nothing – external light or internal thoughts – to illumine Himself or others. He enlivens all – the body, senses

[1] svayaṁ vibhāti-atha-anyāni bhāsayet sādhanaṁ vinā – *Dṛg Dṛśya Viveka* 5

and mind – with life, vitality and knowledge, by His mere presence. Lord Śrī Kṛṣṇa says, 'I am life in all living beings.'[1]
God – the attributeless One (kevalo nirguṇaḥ): God is one without a second, free from any differences, undivided, indivisible, partless and complete. He is without attributes as He is unconditioned by time, space or objects which have qualities and properties.

One may ask, "Are not knowledge, love, peace and joy, God's inherent qualities?" They are not God's attributes but are His very nature. For example – a peaceful mind is the quality of the mind, but the absence of all agitation is the peace which is the nature of the Self. Finitude is sorrow. Infinitude which is the nature of the Truth is all Bliss.

The phrase 'sākṣī cetā kevalo nirguṇaśca' is famous and often quoted to indicate the nature of Truth.

[1] jīvanaṁ sarvabhūteṣu – *Gītā* 7.9, bhūtānām asmi cetanā – *Gītā* 10.22

The more we know about ourselves, our origin and purpose of life, the less we get involved with the non-essentials and the greater is the joy in life. This mantra urges us to be truly happy.

**एको वशी निष्क्रियाणां बहूनाम् एकं बीजं बहुधा यः करोति।
तमात्मस्थं येऽनुपश्यन्ति धीराः तेषां सुखं शाश्वतं नेतरेषाम्॥ १२॥**

eko vaśī niṣkriyāṇāṁ bahūnām ekaṁ bījaṁ bahudhā yaḥ karoti, tam-ātmasthaṁ ye'nupaśyanti dhīrāḥ teṣāṁ sukhaṁ śāśvataṁ netareṣām. (12)

एकः – one; वशी – who controls all; निष्क्रियाणाम् – actionless; बहूनाम् – of the many; एकम् – one; बीजम् – seed; बहुधा – multiples; यः – one who; करोति – does; तम् – Him; आत्मस्थम् – seated in themselves; ये – those; अनुपश्यन्ति – see continually; धीराः – wise; तेषाम् – for those; सुखम् – happiness; शाश्वतम् – permanent; न – not; इतरेषाम् – for others

12. Only those wise people who are able to see continually the one Lord – who controls all and who multiplies the one seed of the many that are actionless – seated in themselves, attain happiness that is permanent, not others.

The wake-up call: At the time of dissolution, the innumerable living beings (jīvas) along with their vāsanās (latent tendencies), go into a dormant state, along with all the realms of experience and the elements. This unmanifest condition is called 'sāmya avasthā' as the qualities of sattva, rajas and tamas are balanced. When the time is right and ripe and the total vāsanās are ready to manifest from that primordial seed by the will of God, the elements, the realms of experiences and the living beings come into being. It is said, God wills – 'Let Me become many' and then the world and beings are created and He entered into all the beings – enlivening them.'[1] The individuals who are dormant during dissolution in turn start responding to this wake-up call of God expressed as the ripening of the vāsanās. They start their journeys again by assuming different bodies in different worlds with little respite in between. Then again at the time of dissolution they merge back into the primordial state for a long rest.

The true awakening: Some rare few wise individuals sit back and review this endless journey and turn within to find permanence and true meaning in this changing world and their fleeting life.[2] They approach a Guru, learn from him and thereafter they too realise the immortal Truth (upadeśam anu paśyati). Another meaning of 'anu' is continuous. Those wise men are thereafter able to see God in their heart continuously and enjoy everlasting Bliss. This is true awakening.

True happiness: 'True happiness is that which puts an end to all sorrow permanently.'[3] Most individuals alternate between happy and unhappy moments or times. Many spend time 'preparing' to become happy. Many toil through the year

---

[1] so'kāmayata, bahusyāṁ prajāyeyeti ... tat sṛṣṭvā tadevānuprāviśat – *Taittirīya Upaniṣad* 2.6

[2] kaścid-dhīraḥ pratyag-ātmānam-aikṣat-āvṛttacakṣuḥ-amṛtatvam-icchan – *Kaṭhopaniṣad* 2.1.1

[3] duḥkhāntaṁ ca nigacchati – *Gītā* 18.36

for a vacation in the Caribbean. After all the time, money and effort expended only in preparing, the actual vacation gives but a few moments of joy interspersed with the usual unhappy and negative thoughts. So thereafter they 'pretend' to be happy! We think that by getting 'x, y, z' we will be happy, but after getting it, the joy fades and we start looking for 'a, b, c'. A child promises his parents that he will not ask for another toy if they buy him this one toy he wants. But the very next day, that toy is discarded and a new one catches his fancy. This is the state of all individuals, irrespective of their age. Rarely does a wise person come to know the Lord seated in His heart and he then enjoys everlasting Bliss.

We are always looking out for 'forever relationships'. With whom should we forge such a relationship?

नित्यो नित्यानां चेतनश्चेतनानाम् एको बहूनां यो विदधाति कामान्।
तत्कारणं साङ्ख्ययोगाधिगम्यं ज्ञात्वा देवं मुच्यते सर्वपाशैः ॥ १३ ॥

nityo nityānāṁ cetanaś-cetanānām eko bahūnāṁ yo vidadhāti kāmān, tatkāraṇaṁ sāṅkhyayogādhigamyaṁ jñātvā devaṁ mucyate sarvapāśaiḥ (13)

नित्यः – eternal; नित्यानाम् – of all eternals; चेतनः – sentiency; चेतनानाम् – of all sentients; एकः – single-handed; बहूनाम् – of all; यः – who; विदधाति – fulfills; कामान् – desires; तत्कारणम् – cause of this (world); साङ्ख्ययोग-अधिगम्यम् – who can be known through Sāṅkhya Yoga; ज्ञात्वा – by knowing; देवम् – God; मुच्यते – liberated; सर्वपाशैः – from all bondages

13. One is liberated from all bondages by knowing God, who is the eternal of all that is eternal, who is the sentience of all that is sentient, who fulfils all desires of all people single-handed, who is the cause of this world and can be known through Sāṅkhya Yoga.

God is forever (nityo nityānām): To an ant that lives for a few days, human life seems endless. For us who are meant to live a hundred years, the deities and Lord Brahmā seem to live forever. Also thousands of generations have seen the same sun, moon, stars and galaxies which seem eternal. The body perishes but the five elements from which it is made live on always. The body is discarded and burnt, but the individual (jīva) who owns and disowns it will go on doing so forever. The world too manifests and goes back to an unmanifest condition, so it is always there, in either state. There seem to be many eternal factors in this world. With what should we form a forever relationship? Everything is born in time or conditioned by time and is therefore ever changing even though appears to exist forever (pravāha nitya). Like the anvil on which metal is given different shapes, God/Truth is the one changeless eternal substratum (kūṭastha nitya) for all the changes, modifications and manifestations seen in everything. Only a relationship with the truly changeless will not change and last forever.

God is life (cetanaś-cetanānām): God is the one Consciousness enlivening the body, senses and mind. He manifests as life in all beings.[1] We do not live because of oxygen or food. If that were the case none would die in the present times and live forever on artificial respirator and saline. 'Man does not live due to inhalation or exhalation, but some other factor on which both depend.'[2]

God is the wish-fulfiller: Some people can fulfill some desires of a person and some can fulfill some desires of many people. Some may also achieve a superhuman task of fulfilling all the desires of one person, but none can fulfill all the desires of everyone! Only God can do so.

The deities when duly propitiated fulfill certain desires as do others. Lord Śrī Kṛṣṇa says, 'They do so only with My

[1] jīvanaṁ sarvabhūteṣu – *Gītā* 7.9

[2] na prāṇena na-apānena martyo jīvati kaścana,
itareṇa tu jīvanti yasmin-etau-upāśritau. – *Kaṭhopaniṣad* 2.2.5

power.'[1] We should therefore not take pride that we fulfill the wishes of others. We are mere instruments for His divine will. He alone is the true cause (tatkāraṇam). The scriptures on devotion compare God to the heavenly wish-fulfilling tree (kalpa-vṛkṣa), the heavenly wish-fulfilling cow (kāmadhenu) and the wish-fulfilling crystal (cintāmaṇi) all put together.

Realisation through Sāṅkhya Yoga: This can be understood in two ways. The Truth can be realised through the Path of Knowledge (Sāṅkhya Yoga). Sāṅkhya also means discrimination between the Self and the not-Self. First we must initiate such an enquiry and know what is the Self and not-Self which to the ignorant appears as one. Thereafter we must absorb the mind in the Self and realise the Truth/Self. That is called Yoga.

[1] mayaiva vihitān-hi-tān – *Gītā* 7.22

The next mantra is most famous and chanted whilst showing the vesper lights – 'ārati', during ritualistic worship.

न तत्र सूर्यो भाति न चन्द्रतारकं नेमा विद्युतो भान्ति कुतोऽयमग्निः।
तमेव भान्तमनुभाति सर्वं तस्य भासा सर्वमिदं विभाति ॥ १४ ॥

na tatra sūryo bhāti na candra-tārakaṁ nemā vidyuto bhānti kuto'yam-agniḥ,
tameva bhāntam-anubhāti sarvaṁ tasya bhāsā sarvam-idaṁ vibhāti (14)

न – not; तत्र – there; सूर्यः – the sun; भाति – shine; न – not; चन्द्रतारकम् – the moon and the stars; न – not; इमाः – these; विद्युतः – (flashes of) lightning; भान्ति – shine; कुतः – how can; अयम् – this; अग्निः – fire; तम् एव – He Himself; भान्तम् – shining; अनुभाति – shines after it; सर्वम् – all; तस्य – His; भासा – by light; सर्वम् – all; इदम् – these; विभाति – shine

14. The sun does not shine there, nor does the moon, nor the stars. The lightning does not shine there, much less this fire. When He shines, everything shines after Him. By His light alone do all these shine.

This mantra is also there in the *Kaṭhopaniṣad (2.2.15)* and the *Muṇḍakopaniṣad (2.2.10).*

None can illumine God/Truth: The five natural sources of light in this world are the sun, moon, stars, lightening and fire. The moon reflects the light of the sun and every star is also a sun. The sun evaporates the waters of the sea which form clouds which clash and generate lightening. The earth as a planet was once a part of the sun and through ages of changes created fuel in terms of natural oil or wood which lights up the fire. Man-made sources of light like the electricity too ultimately depend on the sun. Hence the sun is the chief source of all light. None of these natural or man-made sources of light can illumine God. The effect cannot illumine the cause. The grandchild cannot have seen the marriage of his natural grandparents! Also the 'known' cannot know the knower or the seen cannot know the Seer. The sun, moon etc. are seen by the eyes and known to the mind. God is the Consciousness that illumines them and therefore cannot be known to them.

The sun is the presiding deity of the eyes (representing all sense organs of perception); the moon of the mind (representing mind, intellect, memory and I-sense) and fire is the presiding deity of speech (representing all the sense organs of action). It means that God/Truth illumines the senses and the mind, but they in turn cannot illumine God/ Truth. Neither can the eyes see the Self nor the mind conceive of Him nor the speech describe Him.

The significance of the āratī: As we wave the light of the āratī before the Lord, we say 'When the sun, moon, stars or lightening which are such great illuminators cannot illumine God, then how can this little light that I show illumine God?'

In South Indian temples the sanctum sanctorum is usually dark. Only with the light of the āratī the form of the Lord is seen. God is always there in our own heart even when not seen due to the darkness of ignorance. The light of the lamp represents the knowledge-thought (akhaṇḍākāra vṛtti) 'I am infinite' which dispels the ignorance that 'I am the body' or 'I am finite'. Once the darkness is dispelled the self shining God/Truth is realised as one's own Self. The thought 'I am the infinite Truth/Self' cannot illumine the Truth, but it serves the purpose of removing the ignorance that I am finite. The Self is self shining and does not need any natural light, sense organ or thought to illumine it. It is the light in which we see our dream, the light that illumines the absence of all thoughts in the deep sleep and the thoughts of knowledge and ignorance of objects and the Self. In fact all exist and function only in the light of God/Truth.

After the āratī we put our hands over the light of the lamp and then touch our eyes and head. As we do this we pray, 'May I gain such divine knowledge.' It can also mean, 'This light which has revealed His divine form, may it purify and divinise my vision and thoughts.'

‘There is no other way to liberation’ asserts the Ṛṣi again after due reflection and his personal Realisation.

एको हंसो भुवनस्यास्य मध्ये स एवाग्निः सलिले सन्निविष्टः।
तमेव विदित्वा अतिमृत्युमेति नान्यः पन्था विद्यतेऽयनाय॥ १५॥

eko haṁso bhuvanasyāsya madhye sa evāgniḥ salile sanniviṣṭaḥ,
tam-eva viditvā atimṛtyum-eti nānyaḥ panthā vidyate'yanāya. (15)

एकः – one; हंसः – supreme Self; भुवनस्य – of the universe; अस्य – of this; मध्ये – in the midst; सः – He; एव – only; अग्निः – fire; सलिले – in the waters; सन्निविष्टः – fully established; तम् – Him; एव – alone; विदित्वा – by knowing; मृत्युम् – death; अति एति – goes beyond; न – no; अन्यः – other; पन्था – path; विद्यते – there is; अयनाय – for liberation

15. There is one supreme Self in the midst of this universe. He alone is the fire that exists in the water. Only by knowing Him death can be overcome; there is no other way for liberation.

God as fire in water (agniḥ salile sanniviṣṭaḥ): This is an unusual phrase. The fire in the forest is called ‘dāvānala’ and the fire or the molten lava that emerges from the depths of the ocean is called vaḍavānala. The fire element and water have a special relationship. Usually the subtler cannot be destroyed by the grosser, but fire which is the subtler element is doused with water. Space accommodates fire and air spreads it further, but water alone can put it off.

The cause is always present in the effect, the subtler in the grosser. Fire is subtler and the cause of water and so is always present in water. Similarly God, the cause of all, the subtlest of all is present in all the effects, His manifestations – gross and subtle elements and world. It also means God is present in the primordial waters as fire – the one who takes forward or leads (agre nayati) the creation of the world. Śaṅkarācārya gives another beautiful meaning. When the seeker's mind becomes pure like water through spiritual practices, the fire of knowledge kindled by the teachings of the Guru, burns away the ignorance and the Lord shines within as the Self.

There is no other way to Realisation (nānyaḥ panthā vidyate'yanāya): This statement has come earlier (3.8). The cause of bondage – sorrow, finitudes, stress and its other expressions – is ignorance of our infinite nature.

A king was to enter a cave which was pitch dark. His servants went in advance to remove the darkness. They swept, dusted, washed, beat up and finally cursed the darkness, but it did not go. The wise minister brought a light which dispelled the darkness instantly. The darkness of ignorance can only be removed by the light of knowledge of our true Self.

Some say, 'Only my God saves' or 'My religion liberates' or 'My method of breathing works'. People have got liberated before those Gods, religious and breathing techniques came into existence. You need not believe only in a particular ideology or practise a particular spiritual practice or worship a particular deity. Those may help in the preparation of the mind if done rightly. But Realisation comes only through Self-knowledge irrespective of our faith, caste, creed or religious practices.

Some more elaboration on God's nature is given in the mantra.

स विश्वकृद् विश्वविदात्मयोनिः ज्ञः कालकारो गुणी सर्वविद्यः ।
प्रधानक्षेत्रज्ञपतिर्गुणेशः संसारमोक्षस्थितिबन्धहेतुः ॥ १६ ॥

sa viśvakṛd viśvavid-ātmayoniḥ jñaḥ kālakāro guṇī sarvavidyaḥ,
pradhāna-kṣetrajña-patir-guṇeśaḥ saṁsāra-mokṣa-sthiti-bandha hetuḥ. (16)

सः – He; विश्वकृत् – creator of the universe; विश्वविद् – knower of the universe; आत्मयोनिः – self-existing; ज्ञः – omniscient; कालकारः – creator of time; गुणी – virtuous; सर्वविद् यः – who is all knowledge; प्रधान-क्षेत्रज्ञ-पतिः – the lord of matter and spirit; गुणेशः – the controller of all the guṇas; संसार-मोक्ष-स्थिति-बन्ध-हेतुः – cause of transmigration, liberation, existence and bondage

16. That Truth (Paramātmā) who is the creator of this entire universe, the knower of the whole universe, the source of Himself, omniscient, the creator of time, the repository of all virtues and all knowledge, the lord of all matter and spirit, the controller of all the guṇas (sattva, rajas and tamas), is the cause of saṁsāra, liberation, existence and bondage.

He creates all and knows all (sa viśvakṛt viśvavid): It means being all He knows all.

He is self-created and knows all (ātmayonir-jñaḥ): It means that His knowledge too is causeless and is His inherent nature. He is pure Consciousness.

He is the creator of time, endowed with all virtues and knows all (kālakāro-guṇī sarvavidyaḥ): It means He alone creates all the knowledges and virtues and also is their illuminator and knower.[1]

God is the lord of the matter and the spirit and the controller of the three qualities (pradhāna-kṣetrajña-patir-guṇeśa): He controls sattva, rajas and tamas which manifest in the matter and spirit. He alone controls all bodies (pradhāna) and the individuals (kṣetrajña) that weilds the bodies through the three qualities which He controls.

Guṇeśa also means the lord of all virtues. Beauty, memory or vitality fade with age. Adverse circumstances or power may corrupt an honest man, but God's virtues are timeless, always in full-measure and totally in His control.

He is the cause of liberation, continuation and bondage (saṁsāra-mokṣa-sthiti-bandha-hetuḥ): Since He is the very cause of worldly existence; He is naturally the cause of bondage, its continuation and its end as well. His avidyā māyā – ignorance characterised by rajo guṇa and tamo guṇa, binds and His vidyā māyā characterised by sattva guṇa, liberates. Saint Tulasīdāsa therefore says that the one who has tied us in this saṁsāra, He alone takes responsibility of liberating us.[2] The father wears a mask to surprise the child. The child gets frightened and runs away to his mother weeping. The father removes the mask and the child goes running to embrace him. The same father became the cause of sorrow as well as joy. Similarly not knowing God is the cause of bondage, knowing Him liberates.

[1] Vedāntakṛt-vedavideva cāham – *Gītā* 15.15

[2] joi bāndhyo soi chhore

When we understand the nature of God/Truth all our worries and fears end. Why? Because –

स तन्मयो ह्यमृत ईशसंस्थो ज्ञः सर्वगो भुवनस्यास्य गोप्ता।
य ईशेऽस्य जगतो नित्यमेव नान्यो हेतुर्विद्यत ईशनाय ॥ १७ ॥

sa tanmayo hyamṛta īśasaṁstho jñaḥ sarvago bhuvanasyāsya goptā,
ya īśe'sya jagato nityam-eva nānyo hetur-vidyata īśanāya. (17)

सः – He; तन्मयः – of that nature; हि – indeed; अमृतः – immortal; ईशसंस्थः – who is existing as the Lord; ज्ञः – omniscient; सर्वगः – all-pervading; भुवनस्य – of the world; अस्य – of this; गोप्ता – the protector; यः – who; ईशे – rules; अस्य – of this; जगतः – of the world; नित्यम् – always; एव – indeed; न – no; अन्यः – other; हेतुः – agent; विद्यते – there is; ईशनाय – for ruling

17. Indeed, He is the (essential) nature of the whole world. He is immortal and the ruler (of the whole world). He is omniscient, all-pervading and the protector of this world. He rules over this world eternally; there is none other who can rule over Him.

The all-capable Controller: When I know that the car is in the hands of a very experienced, safe and alert driver, I sit back and enjoy the ride and sleep when I want to, without care or worry. The world is complex and endless. A million factors interplay simultaneously to make it what it is. No one except the omnipotent, omnipresent and omniscient Lord is capable of creating, sustaining, dissolving and controlling it.

No finite entity can ever control or protect it. Knowing that there is a totally committed (tanmaya), immortal (amṛta), omniscient (jñaḥ), omnipotent (īśasaṁstha), omnipresent (sarvagaḥ), protector of the world (bhuvanasya goptā), who is always in command (nityam eva īśe asya jagataḥ), we should give up all worry and care in His hands and live happily. Ādi Śaṅkarācārya chides the worried man, 'Is there not a God who is looking after everyone?'[1]

One sufi saint said that countless kings have come and gone and governments have changed, but the rule and power of my Lord can never change. He rules unchallenged and can never be displaced. History shows instances of people who thought they could rule over the entire earth like Napoleon and Hitler or all the three worlds like Rāvaṇa and Hiraṇyakaśipu, but they have become the dust of the same earth they claimed to conquer. Mother Earth laughs at their foolishness. Born from dust they go back to dust. The rule, control and protection of the Lord alone are eternal.

[1] vātula kiṁ tava nāsti niyantā – *Bhaja Govindam* 13

Having realised that God alone can liberate us from bondage the seeker now seeks refuge in Him.

यो ब्रह्माणं विदधाति पूर्वं यो वै वेदांश्च प्रहिणोति तस्मै ।
तं ह देवमात्मबुद्धिप्रकाशं मुमुक्षुर्वै शरणमहं प्रपद्ये ॥ १८ ॥

yo brahmāṇaṁ vidadhāti pūrvaṁ yo vai vedāṁśca prahiṇoti tasmai, taṁ ha devam-ātma-buddhi-prakāśaṁ mumukṣurvai śaraṇam-ahaṁ prapadye. (18)

यः – who; ब्रह्माणम् – the creator; विदधाति – creates; पूर्वम् – in the beginning (of creation); यः – who; वै – indeed; वेदान् – the Vedas; च – and; प्रहिणोति – reveals; तस्मै – to Him; तम् ह – in that very; देवम् – God; आत्मबुद्धि-प्रकाशम् – who illumines the intellect; मुमुक्षुः – seeker of liberation; वै – indeed; शरणम् – refuge; अहम् – I; प्रपद्ये – seek

18. The Lord who manifested the Creator in the beginning, who gave Him the Vedas, who illumines my intellect – in Him do I, who seek (ultimate) liberation, take refuge.

God – the first Guru (vedāṁśca prahiṇoti): The seeker has clearly understood that God alone liberates (6.16) and also that knowledge alone liberates (6.15). Now he connects the two.

God/Truth in His absolute nature is pure Existence-Consciousness-Bliss with no time, space, mind or instruments to teach the knowledge. However He manifests as the Total Mind – Hiraṇyagarbha – Lord Brahmā, the creator of the world. He also bestows Lord Brahmā with all knowledge to create and sustain the world, especially the knowledge of the Vedas, its essence being Self-knowledge. Lord Brahmā thereafter taught this knowledge to sincere seekers and thus started the exalted lineage of Self-knowledge. The *Muṇḍakopaniṣad* traces its origin to Lord Brahmā who gave Self-knowledge to His great son Atharva.[1] Self knowledge as revealed in *Kaivalyopaniṣad* was given by Lord Brahmā to his well qualified disciple Āśvalāyana.[2]

This thought is picturised beautifully with Lord Viṣṇu sleeping on the thousand-headed serpent in the milky ocean (God in His absolute nature). A lotus emerges from His navel and Lord Brahmā with four heads facing four directions is seen sitting with the Vedas in His hands. Thus every disciple can trace his knowledge lineage to God.

God the illuminator of Self-knowledge (ātma-buddhi-prakāśam): God not only enlightened Lord Brahmā with Self-knowledge, but all Gurus and disciples who realise, teach and seek this knowledge are also enlightened by Him alone.

The seeker resolves to meditate, withdraws his mind from the world of objects and directs it within toward God/ Self. With sincere practice he finally realises, 'I am the infinite

---

[1] brahmā devānāṁ prathamaḥ sambabhūva viśvasya kartā bhuvanasya goptā, sa brahmavidyāṁ sarvavidyā-pratiṣṭhām-atharvāya jyeṣṭha-putrāya prāha.
– *Muṇḍakopaniṣad* 1.1.1

[2] atha-āśvalāyano bhagavantaṁ parameṣṭhinam-upasametya-uvāca
– *Kaivalyopaniṣad* 1.1,
tasmai sa hovāca pitāmahaśca – *Kaivalyopaniṣad* 1.2

Self'. This knowledge that liberates and all his previous efforts happen in the Awareness of God/Truth.

In India wherever the flow of the river turns towards its source, the place is considered holy and a dip in the river in that place purifying. The flow of thoughts when turned God-wards are indeed purifying. Whenever we feel happy, we attribute it to an external source like good music or food, but actually the peace and joy experienced is because the thoughts have for that brief moment turned inwards. God/ Truth is the illuminator of all our thoughts and He alone graces our enlightenment.

The true seeker's surrender (mumukṣurvai śaraṇam ahaṁ prapadye): It is very rare to find a true seeker and very difficult to truly surrender.

Mumukṣu is one who desires to liberate himself from the cycle of birth and death, all joys and sorrows of worldly existence, all finitude – here and now. Some may claim to seek liberation but do not wish to give up their worldly possessions, petty attachments, favourite TV serial or the morning hot cup of coffee. Aṣṭāvakra Mahārāja says, 'It is strange that on the one hand man desires liberation and yet is scared of giving up anything.'[1] 'It is only by the grace of God that one has the desire for the non-dual Truth.'[2]

One who sees the limitations of all worldly pleasures and possession and wants to free himself of all finitude

1 āścaryaṁ mokṣakāmasya mokṣādeva vibhīṣikā

2 īśvarānugrahād-eva puṁsām-advaita vāsanā

becomes a true mumukṣu. Like Naciketā nothing can tempt such a sincere seeker from his goal of Self-realisation.

Surrender comes when we feel helpless and understand our limitations. 'I am limited in my abilities and efforts. You are all-capable and compassionate. I surrender to You, I seek refuge in You. Guide me and help me to go beyond māyā.'

Surrender to the Lord with attributes means to give up one's personal will and wish and live according to God's will. What does it mean to surrender to the attributeless God/Truth?

निष्कलं निष्क्रियं शान्तं निरवद्यं निरञ्जनम्।
अमृतस्य परं सेतुं दग्धेन्धनमिवानलम्॥ १९॥

niṣkalaṁ niṣkriyaṁ śāntaṁ niravadyaṁ nirañjanam,
amṛtasya paraṁ setuṁ dagdhendhanam-ivānalam. (19)

निष्कलम् – partless; निष्क्रियम् – actionless; शान्तम् – peaceful (peace itself); निरवद्यम् – blemishless; निरञ्जनम् – taintless; अमृतस्य – to immortality; परम् – supreme; सेतुम् – bridge; दग्धेन्धनम् – which has burnt its fuel; इव – like; अनलम् – fire

19. (I seek refuge in that Truth) which is partless, actionless, peaceful, blemishless, taintless, the supreme bridge to immortality and like a fire which has burnt its fuel.

Surrender to the nameless, formless and attributeless God/Truth is to give up the 'I' notion or ego that separates us from God/Truth and become one with Him. It is to become of His nature which is –

Actionless, peaceful and pure (niṣkriyaṁ śāntaṁ nirañjanam): Actions are performed by the body and the mind becomes agitated by desires or peaceful when they are fulfilled. Ignorance in the unmanifest state (good or bad vāsanās) express as desires in the mind and actions through the body. God/Truth is beyond the gross body therefore actionless, the subtle body therefore all peace and the causal body therefore free from the stain of ignorance and vāsanās.

Partless and blameless (niṣkalaṁ niravadyam): That which has a name, form and qualities is subject to phases, growth, division, imperfection or blemishes. A diamond is multifaceted, the moon has phases and a person can have a split personality or moods. God/Truth is nameless, formless and attributesless and therefore partless and free of all phases or aspects. People may curse Him or accuse Him of many things, but He remains blameless and blemishless.

Like smokeless fire (dagdha-indhanam iva analam): Fire in the fire place is always surrounded by smoke, the smell of burning fuel, the sound of crackling that comes due to moisture and the flickering of the flames due to the air. God/Truth is that light of Consciousness free of any extraneous factors or their qualities. He is self shining and in His own glory.

The bridge to immortality (amṛtasya paraṁ setum): Self-knowledge is the bridge to realise God/Truth who is immortal. It is the means to dispel our ignorance and free us from the fear of change and death.

I therefore surrender my ego and finitude and remain as the immortal Truth.

The human mind always seeks an alternative. Even when convinced that knowledge alone liberates, one disciple still asks the Guru for an alternative. The Guru says –

यदा चर्मवदाकाशं वेष्टयिष्यन्ति मानवाः ।
तदा देवमविज्ञाय दुःखस्यान्तो भविष्यति ॥ २० ॥

yadā carmavad-ākāśaṁ veṣṭayiṣyanti mānavāḥ,
tadā devam-avijñāya duḥkhasyānto bhaviṣyati. (20)

यदा – when; चर्मवत् – like leather or carpet; आकाशम् – space; वेष्टयिष्यन्ति – will roll up; मानवाः – people; तदा – then; देवम् – God; अविज्ञाय – without knowing; दुःखस्य – of sorrow; अन्तः – end; भविष्यति – there will be

20. When people will roll up space like leather or carpet, then there will be an end to sorrow without knowing or realising God.

This mantra is quite popular amongst sannyāsins and those who expound Vedānta. It is an interesting way of saying –

There is no other way. "Can I put an end to my sorrow and limitations by any way, other than God-realisation?" asks the disciple. The Guru in turn asks, "Can you roll up the sky like a carpet?" "But Guruji, that is impossible. No one can do so" said the disciple. "That is precisely what I am trying to tell you" said the Guru. God-realisation is the only way to end sorrow. The other alternative is to remain in sorrow and finitude.

Saint Tulasīdāsa says, "O my mind, why are you wandering hither and thither and struggling so much to end sorrow. Worldly afflictions do not end even through greatest of efforts. Do you not understand that you can never be happy by turning away from Lord Śrī Rāma? Great Sages like Śukadeva too have declared this same Truth. You cannot get butter by churning a pot of water."[1]

The saints go one step further and say that the impossible may also become possible – we may get butter from water, but we will never be happy without knowing God. This is not a fanatic statement.

If sorrow was caused by lack of money, power, pleasures or comforts, those who are wealthy, powerful, indulgent and comfortable should all be happy. But we see that they too are searching for happiness. We should therefore surrender to God and the Guru who give us knowledge and fill our hearts with devotion which puts an end to sorrow.

[1] kāhe ko phirata mana karata bahu jatana, miṭe nā dukha vimukha vimukha raghukula vīra,
kīje jo koṭi upāi trividha pāpa na jāi, mile na mathata vārī vāri ghṛta binu cīra.

The next mantra explains how Śvetāśvatara Ṛṣi the Seer of this Upaniṣad, himself attained God-realisation.

तपःप्रभावाद् देवप्रसादाच्च ब्रह्म ह श्वेताश्वतरोऽथ विद्वान्।
अत्याश्रमिभ्यः परमं पवित्रं प्रोवाच सम्यगृषिसङ्घजुष्टम्॥ २१॥

tapaḥprabhāvād devaprasādācca brahma ha śvetāśvataro'tha vidvān,
atyāśramibhyaḥ paramaṁ pavitraṁ provāca samyag-
ṛṣisaṅghajuṣṭam. (21)

तपःप्रभावात् – through the power of penance; देव-प्रसादात् – by the grace of God; च – and; ब्रह्म – Truth/Reality; ह – it is well known; श्वेताश्वतरः – Sage Śvetaśvatara (one who had perfect mastery over his senses); अथ – thereafter; विद्वान् – one who has realised (the Truth); अत्याश्रमिभ्यः – to those who have gone beyond all the stages of life (āśramas); परमम् – supreme; पवित्रम् – holy; प्रोवाच – taught; सम्यक् – very well; ऋषिसङ्घ-जुष्टम् – in which the groups of great sages revel

21. As it is well known, Śvetāśvatara (one who has perfect mastery over his senses), having realised the Truth through the power of penance and the grace of God, thereafter fully taught to those monks who have gone beyond all the stages of life (āśramas) the supreme and the holy Truth in which the great sages revel.

Śvetāśvatara vidvān: This great Sage Śvetāśvatara, who had mastery over his senses (ref. Introduction), was well versed in the scriptures (vidvān) and had realised the Truth (brahma ha vidvān). How did he do so?

By the power of penance (tapaḥ prabhāvāt): Penance has many meanings. He practised concentration of the senses and the mind. The performance of one's duties uncompromisingly according to one's stage in life is also called tapas (sva āśrama vihita karma). This is a good way to focus the senses and the mind. For example, for a student, study and serving the teacher was his enjoined duty. Sage Śvetāśvatara practised physical, verbal and mental austerity (tapas) and mastered his senses and mind. He then employed them in reflection and meditation on the Truth.

By the grace of God (deva-prasādāt): Our own efforts are finite and at times faltering. Years of worship of God (samyak-ārādhita-parameśvarasya) invokes the Grace of God which strengthens our efforts and fulfills them with direct Realisation of the knowledge meditated upon. Thereafter what did he do?

He taught this knowledge to fit students (atyāśramibhyaḥ provāca): This speaks of the glory of the Guru, the knowledge and the students of Self-knowledge. The Guru was a Realised Master revered by his students (samyak-ṛṣi-saṅgha-juṣṭam). The knowledge taught is supremely sacred (paramaṁ pavitram) and revered and meditated upon by great sages (samyak-ṛṣi-saṅgha-juṣṭam). Lord Śrī Kṛṣṇa says that 'there is no greater purifier than Self-knowledge' (*Gītā 9.2*) as it not only washes away our sins, but also puts an end to the sinner – the I-sense which would otherwise sin again. A thief was once kept in a prison for ten days more than his sentence. The warden apologised for the error. The thief said, "Never mind, you may adjust these ten days when I come the next time!" Self-knowledge puts an end to any chance of sinning again. The knowledge is taught well (samyak-provāca) by the great Master to students who were extraordinary. They had gone beyond all āśramas (atītya āśrama) and belonged to the most revered state of paramahaṁsa (ati-pūjanīya āśrama).

When a Guru initiates the disciple into the holy order of a sannyāsi, he tells the disciple that now you have no more worldly duties to perform. You are free from all worldly do's and don'ts and even I cannot give you any more commands. This is the glory of sannyāsa. However the disciple says, 'I may not have any worldly obligations or duties, but I shall always do whatever you say!' That is the beautiful relationship that they enjoy.

In order to gain true knowledge everyone has to become an atyāśrami – not belong to any āśrama or stage of life. If one has the pride or identification with being a householder or a sannyāsin then how will he understand the Truth which is beyond all attributes of the body or mind? Sage Śvetāśvatara was surrounded by great disciples to whom he taught Self-knowledge. This indicates the glory of the lineage of the teacher and the taught (Guru-śiṣya-paramparā). Knowledge gained through this tradition of teacher and taught blesses the student.

The next mantra gives clear instructions on who should or should not be given this knowledge.

वेदान्ते परमं गुह्यं पुराकल्पे प्रचोदितम्।
नाऽप्रशान्ताय दातव्यं नापुत्रायाशिष्याय वा पुनः ॥ २२ ॥

vedānte paramaṁ guhyaṁ purākalpe pracoditam,
nā'praśāntāya dātavyaṁ nāputrāyāśiṣyāya vā punaḥ. (22)

वेदान्ते – in the Upaniṣad; परमम् – supreme; गुह्यम् – secret; पुराकल्पे – in the earlier cycle of creation; प्रचोदितम् – was taught; न – not; अप्रशान्ताय – to one who is not peaceful (with impure mind or no self-control); दातव्यम् – should be given; न – not; अपुत्राय – to one who is not a son; अशिष्याय – to one who is not the disciple; वा – or; पुनः – again

22. The supremely mystical knowledge in the Upaniṣads was taught in the previous cycle of creation. It is not to be given to one who has no self-control; nor to one who is not a son, or again, to one who is not a disciple.

vedānte paramaṁ guhyam: Self-knowledge is called Vedānta or Upaniṣad. It may be in the form of spoken or written words – as knowledge taught by the Guru or as texts. This knowledge is deep and cannot be known through perception or rationalisation. It can be known only when it is taught by a great Master. Even when it is taught and we are not prepared, then nothing happens.

purākalpe pracoditam: This knowledge has been taught even in earlier cycles of creation. It is very ancient. It is impossible to date its beginning in human years and centuries. How fortunate are we that we are able to directly study this ancient knowledge which is so relevant to our life even now. But are we fit to be taught?

na dātavyam: It is said that this great knowledge should not be given to an unqualified person as the knowledge will not benefit him but may also harm him. For example, one who is lazy will find an excuse for not doing any work saying that the Self is niṣkriya – actionless! This knowledge in the wrong hands could also be misused and confuse others.

It takes years of study before a person is qualified to operate on a patient. Nuclear weapons in the hands of terrorists could destroy the world. So first we must qualify for this knowledge through spiritual practices, service to others, performance of duties and so on. Then who should not be given this knowledge?

apraśāntāya: One who does not refrain from bad conduct or sinful ways, one whose mind is full of likes, dislikes, attachments, desires, one who has no control over the senses and mind – and because of the above he is restless and agitated always. Such a person should not be given this knowledge.[1]

na aputrāya aśiṣyāya: This knowledge should not be given to one who is not your son or disciple. It means one who

[1] nāvirato duścaritāt nāśānto nāsamāhitaḥ,
nāśāntamānaso vāpi prajñānenainam-āpnuyāt. – *Kaṭhopaniṣad* 1.2.24

has no love and reverence towards the Guru. If the student has no reverence towards the Guru, he will have no value for the scriptures or the knowledge. A disciple is one who approaches the Guru and has a deep thirst for learning and also great love for the knowledge. Such a person will be blessed by the knowledge taught by the teacher.

The last mantra of this great Upaniṣad gives 'the' sure way of gaining God-realisation.

यस्य देवे परा भक्तिः यथा देवे तथा गुरौ ।
तस्यैते कथिता ह्यर्थाः प्रकाशन्ते महात्मनः ॥ २३ ॥
प्रकाशन्ते महात्मन इति ।

yasya deve parā bhaktiḥ yathā deve tathā gurau,
tasyaite kathitā hyarthāḥ prakāśante mahātmanaḥ. (23)
prakāśante mahātmana iti.

यस्य – who has; **देवे** – in God; **परा** – supreme; **भक्तिः** – devotion; **यथा** – as; **देवे** – for God; **तथा** – as much; **गुरौ** – in the Guru; **तस्य** – for Him; **एते** – these; **कथिताः** – which have been spoken; **हि** – indeed; **अर्थाः** – the meaning (of the Upaniṣads); **प्रकाशन्ते** – shine or become revealed; **महात्मनः** – to the great person; **इति** – thus

23. He who has the same supreme devotion for the Guru as for God, indeed to the great person the spoken meanings of the Upaniṣads become revealed.

Supreme devotion for God (yasya deve parā bhakti): Śaṅkarācārya clearly states that amongst all the qualifications needed for liberation, devotion alone is the most important.[1] Love unites us with the beloved. Love for God unites us with God. I can be known through devotion[2], says Lord Śrī Kṛṣṇa.

[1] mokṣa-kāraṇa-sāmagryāṁ bhaktireva garīyasī – *Vivekacūḍāmaṇi* 31
[2] bhaktyā mām abhijānāti – *Gītā* 18.55

Supreme devotion for Guru as for God (yathā deve tathā gurau): A true disciple understands that God, Guru and the Self are one Truth in three forms (īśvaro gururātmeti mūrtibhedavibhāgine). Therefore we should have the same devotion for Guru as we have for God. The scriptures say that the position of the Guru is higher than God as it is he who reveals God to the student. If his devotion and faith in the Guru is strong, even when his faith in God or scriptures or in himself falters, the Guru will re-establish his faith and lead him onwards. The Guru indeed plays a vital role in the spiritual journey of the student.

The Guru reveals the knowledge – 'You are the infinite Truth' to the disciple and the disciple tries to realise, 'I am infinite'. But it is strange that he considers his Guru as a person, a finite being and even finds faults in him! Such a student can never understand the true import of Self-knowledge. However, to one who has supreme love and reverence for the Guru, when the knowledge is taught, the meaning of the words, their true and deep import is realised at once. They do not have to study many books to understand and realise. Rāmāyaṇa tells us the beautiful story of Śabari who had great faith and devotion in her Guru, Mātaṅga Ṛṣi. The Guru asked her to chant the name 'Rāma, Rāma', all the time. She asked whose name it was. The Guru said that you need not understand who it is. The meaning of Rāma will come walking towards you in time. For years she did as she was told. Sure enough, Lord Śrī Rāma Himself came to her hermitage and blessed her with Self-knowledge and she was liberated. Śaṅkarācārya says that when you unconditionally surrender at the feet of your Guru, you are liberated ere long from saṁsāra.[1]

A person asked Swami Rāmadāsa how long it takes a disciple to get liberated after meeting his Guru. He said, "How long does it take the river to meet the ocean?" Such a meeting between the Guru and disciple is true meeting. A meeting of minds and the passing of knowledge happens only when there is deep reverence for the Guru. It is indeed inspiring to hear and read about the Guru Bhakti of great saints like Jñāneśvara Mahārāja, Tukārām, Kabīrdāsa and our own Śrī Gurudev.

The last phrase 'prakāśante mahātmanaḥ' is repeated twice to express our reverence towards the great Guru who reveals Self-knowledge and the great disciple who realises It. It also indicates the end of the text.

We too pray to God and Param Pūjya Śrī Gurudev to bless us with such devotion which reveals the knowledge of our true nature and bestows liberation. May all be blessed with devotion and knowledge.

Om tat sat

[1] gurucaraṇāmbuja-nirbhara-bhaktaḥ saṁsārād-acirād-bhava muktaḥ
– *Bhaja Govindam* 31